MW01532333

# Introduction

Skudera's Ultimate Guide to New Jersey is the first ever combination travel guide and multimedia CD-ROM produced in the United States. Being a lifelong resident, I am extremely proud that New Jersey is the first state to be part of a new series of exciting travel guides. The Garden State is filled with many beautiful parks, contains miles and miles of relaxing beaches, and features a rich history that is just waiting to be explored.

The guidebook starts by listing tours of several unique towns and villages of New Jersey. Its fourteen chapters cover many topics including amusement parks, campgrounds, gardens, lighthouses, and museums. Each write-up includes hours, location, admission prices, and contact information.

Where the guidebook ends, the accompanying multimedia CD-ROM only begins! Now your only option isn't just to read about a particular place, you actually see it before you go! The easy to install and navigate multimedia CD companion puts you in control of the action. With a click of the mouse you can tour Atlantic City, climb to the top of the Barnegat Lighthouse, or locate your favorite outdoor activity. You can enter a page number from the book into the software to instantly locate and extend your travel research. You also have the option to print a specific point of interest, including maps and contact information, so you don't have to take the entire book with you on your excursions. The CD features over 3,500 beautiful color photographs and over 1,000 points of interest throughout the state. I personally took all the photographs while carefully documenting and researching every place that I explored!

This guide would not be complete without my talented staff of writers, editors, and software testers. A lot of hard work and dedication went into this product making it truly the Ultimate Guide to New Jersey.

I hope you enjoy Skudera's Ultimate Guide to New Jersey and I look forward to hearing about your travels!

*Michael Skudera*

# Facts and Official Symbols

**Admission to Statehood:** Dec. 18, 1787

**Capital:** Trenton, Mercer County

**Counties:** 21

**Governor:** James McGreevey

**Highest Elevation:** 1,803 feet

**Nickname:** The Garden State

**Official Website:** www.state.nj.us

**Population:** 8,115,011

**Total Area:** 7,419 square miles

**State Animal:** The state animal is the horse. Governor Brendan Byrne signed the bill into law on August 14th, 1977 while attending a horse show at Sussex County.

**State Bird:** Measuring four and one half inches in length and having a tail no more than two inches long, the Eastern Goldfinch became the state bird in 1935.

**State Flag:** By legislative action the state flag of New Jersey was approved on March 26th, 1896. The law provides that it "shall be of buff color, having in the center thereof the arms of the state properly emblazoned thereon." The official colors for use on the state flag were established in 1965 as "buff" and "Jersey blue".

**State Flower:** In a resolution passed by both the state legislature, the common meadow violet, Viola Sororia, became New Jersey's state flower on April 2nd of 1971.

**State Insect:** In 1974, the state legislature enacted bill A-671 and Governor Brendan T. Byrne signed it into law making the honeybee the state insect. It was encouraged by a group of children from Sunnybrea School in Hamilton Township who came to the state house with a presentation that included a song and a poem.

**State Motto:** The state motto of "Liberty and Prosperity" was informally adopted in 1821 as the best of several suggested mottos. Finally in 1928 it was adopted along with a new design of the state seal.

**State Postage Stamp:** On September 22nd, 1956, a three-cent stamp was issued to commemorate Nassau Hall's 200th anniversary. This building was the first structure, which Princeton University erected. V.S. McCloskey Jr. created the design of the stamp from a 1764 Dawkins engraving of the building. A total of 122,100,100 stamps were printed.

**State Tree:** Authorized by a joint resolution of the state legislature and signed into law by Governor Alfred E. Driscoll in 1959, the Northern red oak became the official tree of New Jersey. The Northern red oak has leaves that are anywhere between five and nine inches long and turn red in autumn. Acorns from the tree have either a shallow or deep cup and are usually no more than an inch in length.

# Famous Firsts

**1642:** Hoboken, located in Hudson County, becomes the site of the *first brewery* in the United States.

**1811:** The town of Hoboken in Hudson County establishes the *first ferry service* in the United States. It operated between Hoboken and Manhattan.

**1831:** In Bordentown, Burlington County, John Stevens builds the *first steam locomotive in America* that pulls a train on a track.

**1846:** *First organized baseball game* under modern rules played in Hoboken, Hudson County.

**1870:** Atlantic City builds the *first boardwalk* in the world.

**1879:** Thomas A. Edison invents the *first incandescent lamp*.

**1896:** Trenton becomes the site of the *first professional basketball game* ever played.

**1899:** Thomas A. Edison develops the *first motion picture* at his laboratory in West Orange, Essex County.

**1933:** A ten-acre lot in Camden County transforms into the worlds *first drive-in movie theater*.

**1940:** *First solid body electric guitar* is invented by Les Paul of Mahwah, Bergen County.

# Skudera's Ultimate Guide to New Jersey

## *First Edition*

### The first ever combination travel guide and CD-ROM of New Jersey

*Over 1,000 points of interest*

*Over 3,500 color photographs*

# Skudera's Ultimate Guide to New Jersey

Author: Michael Skudera
Senior Editor: John M. Kertland V
Additional Editing: Joan Skudera and Jean Vogrin
Photographer: Michael Skudera
Production Assistant: Nadia Skudera
Contributor: Marie Steets
Software Design and Programming: Michael Skudera
Software Testing: Charles H. Collins, Jr. and Daniel Romanov
Marketing: Net Profit$

## Copyright

Copyright 2002 Skudera Creations Corporation

Published by Skudera Creations Corporation

First Edition, First Printing

ISBN: 0-9713978-0-5

Printed in the United States of America

All rights reserved. No part of this book or CD-ROM may be reproduced or transmitted in any form or by any means, electronic or mechanical, including photocopying, recording, or by any information storage and retrieval system, without written permission from the publisher.

## Special Sales

Both this guidebook and multimedia CD-ROM are available at special discounts for bulk purchases and for sales promotions. Special editions including personalized covers and corporate imprints can be created in large quantities for special needs. For more information please write to Special Sales, Skudera Creations Corporation, P.O. Box 940, Eatontown, New Jersey 07724 or visit our website at www.skudera.com.

## An Additional Note

Every effort was made to make both this book and the accompanying multimedia CD-ROM guide as accurate as possible in regard to prices, hours and other details listed. Information was verified at press time however, changes occur frequently and Skudera Creations cannot accept responsibility for facts that become outdated or for errors or omissions. It is recommended that you confirm all relevant information before planning your trip.

# Contents

# Town Tours

*Morristown*

# Atlantic City

**Atlantic City Visitor Welcome Center:** (Atlantic City Expressway) A stop here will provide visitors with information about the area's activities, shops, and attractions. Same day reservations for casinos, hotels, and other activities may also be made. The center has an ATM machine and a souvenir shop. *Phone:* 609-449-7107. *Hours:* Daily from 9 A.M. to 5 P.M., Memorial Day through Labor Day, hours are extended on Fridays, Saturdays and Sundays from 9 A.M. to 8 P.M.

**Absecon Lighthouse:** (Corner of Rhode Island and Pacific Avenue) Built in 1856, this famous lighthouse stands 169 feet in height and has recently been fully restored. Visitors may climb the 228 steps to the top for amazing views of the area. *Phone:* 609-449-1360. *Hours:* Memorial Day through Labor Day, Thursdays to Mondays 11 A.M. to 4 P.M., open daily during July and August. *Admission Fee:* $4 per person.

**Atlantic City Convention Center:** (1 Ocean Way) This modern Convention Center features more than 500,000 square feet of exhibition space, 45 meeting rooms, and a 1,400 space indoor parking garage, making it the premiere venue for concerts, extravaganzas, and special events. *Phone:* 609-449-2000.

**Atlantic City Helicopter:** Offers a 20-mile helicopter ride over Atlantic City and its scenic coastline. *Phone:* 888-868-7359. *Hours:* Saturdays and Sundays (subject to weather conditions) from 4 P.M. to 9 P.M. *Admission Fee:* $49 per person.

*Atlantic City*

**Blue Waters Adventures:** (New Jersey Avenue and the Bay) This company operates a party boat that charters fishing, diving, and pleasure cruises. *Phone:* 609-926-5353.

**Boardwalk:** The world famous Atlantic City Boardwalk was built in 1870 and is the world's oldest boardwalk. At over four and a half miles in length, and studded with the sites and sounds unique to the Jersey shore, this is the must-see attraction for everyone.

**Boardwalk Hall:** (2301 Boardwalk) Previously known as Convention Hall, Boardwalk Hall was built in 1929 and is today a national landmark. In its heyday, the hall hosted all of Atlantic City's shows and events and is still the home of the world's largest pipe organ. Even now, the building plays host to special events such as the annual Miss America Pageant. *Phone:* 609-348-7000.

**Central Pier:** (St. James Place and Tennessee Avenue) Among the numerous piers that jut out from the boardwalk, the Central Pier is kept bright and noisy by the games, arcades, and the racecar speedway built on its wooden planks.

**Chicken Bone Beach:** (Boardwalk near Convention Hall) Until the 1950s, with the end of segregation, African Americans were allowed only on this section of the Atlantic City beach. At that time, it was a favorite vacation spot for many famous celebrities including Joe Louis, Sammy Davis Jr., "Moms" Mabley, and baseball greats Jackie Robinson and Larry Doby. As many as 5,000 people a day would visit this beach, which received its colorful nickname from affectionate locals because of the remnants of pan-fried chicken lunches left scattered on the sands.

**Garden Pier:** (South New Jersey Ave and Boardwalk) The Fine Arts capitol of the boardwalk includes among its structures:

> **Atlantic City Arts Center:** Paintings, sculptures, and photographs are featured in the museum's three galleries. There are also monthly exhibits of unique artwork by national and regional artists. *Phone:* 609-347-5837. *Hours:* Daily from 10 A.M. to 4 P.M. *Admission Fee:* Free.

> **Atlantic City Historical Museum:** This museum is committed to preserving the rich history of Atlantic City. *Phone:* 609-347-5839. *Hours:* Daily from 10 A.M. to 4 P.M. *Admission Fee:* Free.

**FACT:** *In 1976, gambling was legalized in Atlantic City. Two years later, on May 26th, 1978, Resorts International became the first casino to open.*

**Gardener's Basin:** (800 North New Hampshire Avenue) Among the sites of the Basin are several attractions exclusive to Atlantic City:

> **Atlantic City Cruises:** Enjoy a leisurely cruise along the coastal waters of Atlantic City. *Phone:* 609-347-7600.
>
> **Bayside Basin Antiques:** Features collectables in fine art, pottery, and oriental rugs. *Phone:* 609-373-7143. *Hours:* By appointment only.
>
> **Flying Cloud:** Located on the waterfront, this seafood restaurant features live music every Wednesday night from Memorial Day through Labor Day. *Phone:* 609-345-8222. *Hours:* Mondays to Fridays from 11 A.M. to 9 P.M., and weekends from 11 A.M. to 10 P.M.
>
> **Ocean Life Center:** This marine education center's star attraction is a 750-gallon aquarium that displays many varieties of local marine life in their natural habitat. The center also has informative ocean exhibits, which serve to astound and enlighten. *Phone:* 609-348-2880. *Hours:* Daily from 10 A.M. to 5 P.M. *Admission Fee:* $7 adults, $5 seniors, and $4 children.

**Hard Rock Café:** (Trump Taj Mahal, 1000 Boardwalk at Virginia Avenue) This trendy, celebrity-inspired restaurant features an All-American menu served in a rock and roll atmosphere. *Phone:* 609-441-0007.

**Ocean One:** (1 Atlantic Ocean, at Boardwalk and Arkansas Avenue) Built on the site of the famous Million Dollar Pier, Ocean One contains over 100 specialty shops, four restaurants, and an international food court overlooking the ocean. At the Boardwalk Visitor's Center (open daily from 11 A.M. to 7 P.M.) visitors may make same day hotel reservations, learn about special events and local activities, and purchase souvenirs. *Phone:* 609-347-8086. *Hours:* Mondays to Fridays from 10 A.M. to 7 P.M., Saturdays from 10 A.M. to 8 P.M., and Sundays from 11 A.M. to 7 P.M.

**Official All-Star Café:** (Trump Taj Mahal on the Boardwalk) Superstar athletes from every sport sponsor this family restaurant, which features sports memorabilia displays, and serves classic burgers and sandwiches. *Phone:* 609-347-8326. *Hours:* Sundays to Thursdays from 11 A.M. to midnight, bar open until 1 A.M.; Fridays and Saturdays from 12 P.M. to 1 A.M., bar open until 2 A.M.

**Planet Hollywood:** (Caesars Palace, 2100 Pacific Avenue) Movie stars and celebrity glitz and glamour dominate this restaurant, which serves trendy Californian cuisine with a Hollywood inspired flare. *Phone:* 609-347-7827. *Hours:* Daily from 11 A.M. to 2 A.M.

**Ripley's Believe It or Not Museum:** (New York Avenue and Boardwalk) This strange but fascinating museum includes a wax display of the world's tallest man and a model of the Sydney Harbor Bridge made from matchsticks. No trip to Atlantic City is complete without a visit to this collection of the weird, the bizarre, and the unbelievable. *Phone:* 609-347-2001. *Hours:* May through August, daily from 10 A.M. to 10 P.M.; September through April, Mondays to Fridays from 11 A.M. to 5 P.M., and weekends from 10 A.M. to 8 P.M. *Admission Fee:* $8.95 adults, $7.95 student, and $6.95 seniors and children.

**Rolling Chair:** (On the Boardwalk) The Rolling Chair is a push-powered, wheeled chair that was introduced by local hardware dealer William Hayday. At first, the units were rented to physically challenged people, but by 1887, the chairs were available to everyone for rent. Still in use today, you may sit and relax while the pusher takes you to your favorite attractions along the boardwalk. *Phone:* 609-347-7148.

**Sandcastle Stadium:** (545 North Albany Avenue) Visit New Jersey Minor League Baseball at its finest. This new 5,900-seat stadium is home to the Atlantic City Surf of the independent Atlantic League. The season begins in May and ends in September. *Phone:* 609-344-7873.

**Sea Skate Pavilion:** (Kennedy Plaza, Mississippi Avenue, and Boardwalk) This NHL sized ice skating rink offers a panoramic view of the Atlantic Ocean in addition to traditional ice skating activities. *Phone:* 609-347-2414 *Hours:* October through March, Mondays to Wednesdays from 1:15 P.M. to 3:15 P.M., Thursdays from 1:15 P.M. to 5 P.M., Fridays from 11:15 P.M. to 3:15 P.M. and 6:45 P.M. to 9:45 P.M., and weekends from 1:30 P.M. to 4:30 P.M. *Admission Fee:* $5 per person.

**Steel Pier:** (1000 Boardwalk at Virginia Ave) The world famous Steel Pier features 24 rides, a food court, and a custom made, double-decker carousel with hand-painted scenes from the Atlantic City's past. *Phone:* 609-345-4893. *Admission Fee:* Free.

**Tivoli Pier:** (Brighton Avenue and Boardwalk) In good weather or bad this indoor amusement park is great for the entire family. *Phone:* 609-340-4444.

**Warner Brothers Studio Store:** (2225 Boardwalk) Bugs, Daffy, and all of the Warner Brother's characters both new and old make this huge store a happy place for adults and children to shop. Browse through an assortment of clothing, toys, and household items all emblazoned with your favorite cartoon characters. *Phone:* 609-344-1440.

# *Travel*

**Atlantic City International Airport:** (Off Atlantic City Expressway, Exit 9, Egg Harbor Township) From the airport, it is a 20-minute ride to the center of Atlantic City. *Phone:* 609-645-7895.

**Jitney Service:** Once in town, Jitney mini-buses are available 24 hours a day. They make stops at all of your favorite casinos on Pacific Avenue and the Marina. *Phone:* 609-344-8642. *Fare:* $1.50 per person.

**Limousine Service:** There are a number of car services available, including: Ace Luxury Car Service: 609-412-5068; Atlantic Limousine: 609-348-2683; Enchantment Limousine: 800-448-5460; and Silver Spoon Transportation: 609-703-5008.

**Municipal Bus Terminal:** (Michigan and Atlantic Avenue) New Jersey Transit: 800-582-5946; Greyhound: 800-231-2222; Academy Bus Lines: 800-992-0451; Grayline of New York: 800-669-0051.

**Railroad Station:** (Ocean Way) Adjoining the Convention Center, this station runs direct from Philadelphia's 30th Street Station. Free shuttle service is offered to all Atlantic City casinos. *Phone:* 1-800-772-2222.

**Taxi Service:** Like most cities, taxis are available at designated pick-up/drop-off locations and randomly throughout the city. For more prompt service call one of the following directly: Atlantic City Airport Taxi: 609-383-1457; Egg Harbor Atlantic City Taxi Alliance: 609-457-0624; or Silver Spoon Transportation: 609-703-5008.

# *Lodging*

**Atlantic City-Boardwalk Days Inn:** (Boardwalk and Morris Avenue) *Phone:* 800-544-8313. *Rooms:* 105. *Price Range:* $40-$175.

**Atlantic City Hilton:** (Boston and Pacific Avenue) *Phone:* 800-257-8677. *Rooms:* 850. *Price Range:* $99-$225.

**Comfort Inn-Boardwalk:** (154 South Kentucky Avenue) *Phone:* 609-348-4000. *Rooms:* 80. *Price Range:* $80-$107.

**Comfort Inn-North:** (539 East Absecon Boulevard, Absecon) *Phone:* 609-641-7272. *Rooms:* 205. *Price Range:* $75-$150.

**Econo Lodge Boardwalk:** (117 South Kentucky Avenue) *Phone:* 800-323-6410. *Rooms:* 51. *Price Range:* $89-$116.

**Fairfield Inn by Marriott:** (405 East Absecon Boulevard, Absecon) *Phone:* 609-646-5000. *Rooms:* 200. *Price Range:* $69-$159.

**Flagship Resort:** (60 North Main Street) *Phone:* 800-647-7890. *Rooms:* 300. *Price Range:* $90-$145.

**Hampton Inn:** (240 East White Horse Pike, Absecon) *Phone:* 609-652-2500. *Rooms:* 129. *Price Range:* $89-$129.

**Hampton Inn-West:** (7079 Black Horse Pike, West Atlantic City) *Phone:* 609-484-1900. *Rooms:* 143. *Price Range:* $66-$159.

**Holiday Inn-Boardwalk:** (Boardwalk and Chelsea Avenue) *Phone:* 609-348-2200. *Rooms:* 216. *Price Range:* $79-$189.

**Howard Johnson Hotel:** (Boardwalk and Chelsea Avenue) *Phone:* 800-695-4685. *Rooms:* 121. *Price Range:* $53-$179.

**Super 8-Absecon:** (229 East Route 30, Absecon) *Phone:* 609-652-2477. *Rooms:* 58. *Price Range:* $50-$175.

## *Casinos*

**Bally's Park Place:** (Park Place and Boardwalk) *Phone:* 609-340-2000.

**Caesars:** (Arkansas and Pacific Avenue) *Phone:* 609-343-2400.

**Claridge:** (Indiana Avenue and Boardwalk) *Phone:* 609-340-3400.

**Harrah's:** (777 Harrah's Avenue) *Phone:* 609-441-5000.

**Hilton:** (Boston Avenue and Boardwalk) *Phone:* 609-347-7111.

**Resorts:** (1133 Boardwalk) *Phone:* 609-344-6000.

**Sands:** (Indiana Avenue and Brighton Park) *Phone:* 609-441-4000.

**Showboat:** (810 Boardwalk and Delaware Avenue) *Phone:* 609-343-4000.

**Tropicana:** (Brighton Avenue and Boardwalk) *Phone:* 609-340-4000.

**Trump Marina:** (Huron Ave. and Brigantine Boulevard) *Phone:* 609-441-2000.

**Trump Plaza:** (Mississippi Avenue and Boardwalk) *Phone:* 609-441-6000.

**Trump Taj Mahal:** (Boardwalk and Virginia Avenue) *Phone:* 609-449-1000.

# Bridgeton

**Tourist Information Center:** (50 East Broad Street) Once a passenger station for the Pennsylvania-Reading-Seashore Railroad, this building is now home to the Bridgeton-Cumberland Tourist Association. *Phone:* 800-319-3379. *Hours:* Year round, Mondays to Fridays from 9 A.M. to 4 P.M. and also on weekends from April to October from 10 A.M. to 4 P.M.

**Bridgeton Fire House:** (Orange Street) Erected in 1898, this is one of the oldest continuously working firehouses in New Jersey. Inside, past and present meet as the fire engine of today sits side by side with an 1877 Silsby steam fire engine.

**Bridgeton Library:** (150 East Commerce Street) Built in 1816, this structure, once used as a bank, maintains a vital link with the past through its books and displays. Over 20,000 artifacts related to the Lenni-Lenape Indian Tribe, originally located throughout the area, are on display in the Woodruff Indian Museum located in the basement of the building. *Phone:* 856-451-2620. *Hours:* Library open Mondays through Thursdays from 9 A.M. to 9 P.M., Fridays from 9 A.M. to 5 P.M., Saturdays 10 A.M. to 4 P.M., museum open Mondays through Fridays from 1 P.M. to 4 P.M. and Saturdays from 10 A.M. to 1 P.M. *Admission Fee:* Free.

**Cohanzick Zoo:** (Bridgeton City Park) This is the first zoo ever established in New Jersey. It is home to over 200 birds and animals from around the world. *Phone:* 800-319-3379. *Hours:* Daily during spring and summer months from 10 A.M. to 6 P.M. Daily during the fall and winter months from 9 A.M. to 4 P.M. *Admission Fee:* Free.

**Crooked-End House:** (249 & 251 East Commerce Street) In 1792, Joseph Fauver, a local carpenter, lawyer, and Corporal in the Salem County Militia, built this quaint country manor to be his homestead. It owes its nickname to a unique architectural flaw that left the east gable-end of the house crooked.

**Cumberland County Courthouse:** (West Broad and Fayette Street) Built on the site of the first county courthouse, this stone and mortar courthouse replaced the original wooden structure built in 1752. Construction for the present courthouse was finished in 1761. Among its many features is an exhibit on the Liberty Bell, which rang on July 7, 1776 for the city's formal reading of the Declaration of Independence. *Phone:* 856-451-8000. *Hours:* Mondays through Fridays from 8:30 A.M. to 4:30 P.M.

**Cumberland Nail and Iron Company Museum:** (1 Mayor Aitken Drive) This building, constructed in 1815, was once the main office of the Cumberland Nail and Iron Company. It now serves as a museum exhibiting many artifacts from the nail industry and from the American Revolution. The museum also hosts special events and displays throughout the year. *Phone:* 856-455-4100. *Hours:* April through December, Tuesdays to Fridays from 10:30 A.M. to 3:30 P.M., and on weekends from 11 A.M. to 4 P.M. *Admission Fee:* Free.

**Dame Howell School:** (Mayor Aitken Drive in Bridgeton City Park) The tiny, wooden Dame Howell School building was originally on Pine Street, but during a period of urban renewal the structure was moved from this location to a more pleasant spot in the park. This type of one-room private school was usually run by an educated woman, with the given title of "Dame," who taught young children the fundamentals in reading, spelling, and religion. *Phone:* 856-455-3230. *Hours:* Open by appointment only.

**David Sheppard House:** (31 West Commerce Street) Built in 1791, this house was originally the residence of local, well-to-do businessman David

---

**FACT:** *Bridgeton is New Jersey's largest historic district with over 2,000 Colonial, Federal, and Victorian style buildings. Bridgeton dates back to 1686 when Richard Hancock constructed a sawmill and workmen's houses.*

Sheppard. In 1860, it was converted into a boarding school for girls, and in 1918, it became a nursing home known as Ivy Hall.

**Doctor Francis Gilbert Brewster House:** (6 Atlantic Street). In 1810, Dr. Francis Gilbert Brewster, understanding the town's needs and opportunities, opened the first drug store. Across the street from the store, he had this handsome residence built. It is maintained today in honor of his memory.

**Doctor William Elmer House:** (26 Franklin Drive) Built in 1834, this manor was home to Dr. William Elmer, who rose to prominence as the leading physician in Bridgeton.

**Ebenezer Miller-Andrew Hunter School:** (92 West Broad Street) This red brick house, built in 1759, was originally home to Ebenezer Miller, a wealthy landowner. During the 1780s, Reverend Andrew Hunter had the building converted for use as a school. Reverend Hunter had gained notoriety as a member of a group of local patriots who were inspired by the "Boston Tea Party," and burned crates of tea to protest English taxes.

**First Presbyterian Church:** (Broad Street and Lawrence Street) During the mid–1700s, plans were made for building this church but the outbreak of the Revolutionary War delayed its completion until 1792. The cemetery is the final resting place of many local war veterans including General Ebenezer Elmer, General James Giles, and members of the Potter family.

**George Burgin Storehouse:** (25 West Broad Street) This sandstone structure is one of the few surviving warehouses from the eighteenth century. George Burgin, a businessman and early sheriff, had the storehouse built in 1799 in order to store goods brought in by ship via the Cohansey River.

**General James Giles House:** (143 West Broad Street) This house is a fine example of early Georgian architecture and was built in 1791 by General James Giles, who served in the Continental Army throughout the Revolutionary War. After the war, General Giles practiced law and moved his family to Bridgeton in 1788.

**Hall of Fame Museum:** (Burt Avenue Recreation Center) This museum features memorabilia from famous professional athletes, with a special emphasis on those who were New Jersey natives. *Phone:* 856-451-7300. *Hours:* Tuesdays through Saturdays from 10 A.M. to 3 P.M. (closed from 12 P.M. to 1 P.M.) *Admission Fee:* Free.

**Henry Hann Tavern:** (59 West Broad Street) Established in 1782 by Henry Hann, this old tavern has been extensively remodeled and rebuilt. However a portion of the original structure still remains, located at the east end of the building. The tavern served those on their way to the courthouse and travelers passing along the Kings Highway. It continues to serve the public today as a restaurant called the Hillcrest Tavern.

**Ireland's Mill:** (1 Beebe Run Road) Erected in 1856, this mill was part of the Cumberland Nail and Iron Company and employed a large percentage of the local population. It primarily produced staves for nail kegs.

**Lott-Chamberlain House:** (99 West Commerce Street) Built in 1861, Richard Lott, who operated of a gristmill once located in present day Bridgeton City Park, was the original owner of this residence. Author George Chamberlain, who wrote several novels including *The Taken Child* and *Not All the King's Horses,* later lived and worked in the house. The building has since been converted into apartments.

**Nailmaster's House:** (31 Franklin Drive) This spacious home was reserved for the owner of the Cumberland Nail and Iron Company's private use. It was built in 1850.

**New Sweden Farmstead:** (Bridgeton City Park) A reconstruction of a seventeenth century Swedish-style farmstead, this antique village contains replica log cabins and gives a glimpse of farm life in the 1600s. *Phone:* 856-455-9785. *Hours:* May through September, Saturdays from 11 A.M. to 5 P.M. and Sundays from 12 P.M. to 5 P.M. *Admission Fee:* $3 adults, $2.50 seniors, and $1.50 children.

**Potter's Tavern:** (49-51 West Broad Street) Built in 1767, this tavern, owned by Matthew Potter, was a popular meeting place during the Revolutionary War. It was here, in 1775, that patriots published a manuscript called *The Plain Dealer.* It was dedicated to the cause of liberty and became New Jersey's first regular newspaper. The tavern has been fully restored to its 1776 appearance. *Phone:* 856-453-2180. *Hours:* April through October, Weekends from 1 P.M. to 5 P.M. *Admission Fee:* $1 per person.

**Riverfront:** (Downtown area, Broad Street and Commerce Street) Situated

*Riverfront*

along the bank of the Cohansey River, the riverfront is a picturesque venue playing host to live entertainment and special events. *Admission Fee:* Free.

**Seeley-McGee House:** (274 East Commerce Street) This historic house was originally built in 1799 by Samuel Seeley. In 1815, new owner Robert McGee enlarged the structure and altered the internal layout.

**Seven Gables:** (25 Lake Street) A beautiful example of historic architectural design, this building, constructed in 1781, has served as a residence, a private school, and a maternity hospital.

**William Nixon House:** (81 West Commerce Street) Completed in 1853, this was home to William G. Nixon, who later became the president of the Cumberland National Bank.

**William S. Dubois House:** (69 North East Avenue) A popular representation of mid-nineteenth century charm and construction, this house was completed for the Dubois family in 1862 and was home to Jeremiah Dubois, a former mayor of Bridgeton.

# Burlington City

**Alcazar:** (460 High Street) Alcazar is the oldest building in the city. The original part of this structure was built in the 1680s and first occupied by Thomas Olive. In 1739, Richard Smith Jr., an international trader, purchased the building to be used as his residence. Though the facade retains its historic look, the interior has been completely renovated and is now used for private offices.

**Bard-How House:** (453 High Street) Built in 1743, this was the home of Bennet and Sarah Bard. In 1758, this building was purchased by Samuel How, Sr., who was a representative at the Provincial Congress of New Jersey.

**Biddle-Pugh House:** (130 West Broad Street) Completed in 1799, this was the residence of Delia Biddle-Pugh, an active member of the community who was instrumental in preserving the early historical heritage of the city.

**Birch-Bloomfield Mansion:** (415 High Street) This mansion was once the home of Joseph Bloomfield, who served as a Captain during the Revolutionary War and governor of New Jersey. Its construction was completed in 1750. After Governor Bloomfield, James Birch and his family occupied the house. The building has been extensively renovated and is presently used for private offices.

**Blue Anchor Inn:** (High Street and Broad Street) The original Blue Anchor Inn was built in 1750 by James Smith, Jr. It was here on July 2,

1776, that the Third Provincial Congress of New Jersey gathered to adopt a new State Constitution. During the Revolutionary War, many famous visitors stayed here including General George Washington, General Baron von Steuben, and British General Wilhem von Knyphausen. The present tavern was built in 1856 and was the Republican headquarters during Lincoln's presidential campaign.

**Boudinot-Bradford House:** (207-209 West Broad Street) Built in 1803, this was the home of Elias Boudinot, who served as president of the Continental Congress for a time. The house was originally located on 10 acres of land, but has since been reduced to its present size.

**Burlington County Historical Society:** (457 High Street) This building is the birthplace of James Fenimore Cooper, one of the first, great American authors. Among his better-known works are *The Last of the Mohegans* and *The Deerslayer.* In addition to maintaining its offices, the historical society conducts tours of this house and many others in the city of Burlington. *Phone:* 609-386-4773. *Hours:* Mondays through Thursdays from 1 P.M to 4 P.M., Sunday 2 P.M to 4 P.M. *Admission Fee:* $5 per person.

**Burlington Meeting House:** (340 High Street) The original meeting house was built in 1683. During the early part of the Revolutionary War, it was used to quarter soldiers and store supplies for the Continental Army. Local Quakers constructed the present building in 1783. *Phone:* 609-386-4828. *Hours:* Open by appointment. *Admission Fee:* Free.

**Camden and Amboy Railroad:** (Broad Street) Built in 1834, this was the first railroad ever constructed in New Jersey. The John Bull, one of the original steam locomotives used in the United States once ran along these

*Blue Anchor Inn with Camden & Amboy railroad in foreground*

lines. Passengers on the rail line were always welcome at the Blue Anchor Tavern, which had a room serving as a passenger station.

**Carriage House:** (Union Street across from the Library Company) This brick building was part of an estate once owned by the prominent Woolman family. The house has been restored and is currently maintained by the City of Burlington Historical Society. It is a featured stop on the their tour.

**Collins-Jones House:** (Broad Street and York Street) Built in the 1780s, this was the home of local newspaper publisher Isaac Collins. After several generations, the Collins-Jones family donated this house to the Burlington County Historical Society.

**Doctor John Howard Pugh House:** (214 High Street) In 1768, this house, as it stands today, came into existence when two smaller houses, originally built between 1709 and 1716, were combined. Doctor Pugh had arrived in Burlington in 1854 and moved into this house in 1857. He lived here until his death in 1905.

**Endeavor Fire Company #1:** (19 East Union Street) Burlington City's first permanent fire company began operating in 1795, and is considered to be one of the oldest in the United States. This historic structure serves as a visual reminder of the proud service our fire fighters have provided throughout the times.

**Friends Schoolhouse:** (York Street and Penn Street) The materials used for construction of this schoolhouse were recycled from the original Friends Meetinghouse when the latter was torn down. Today the school is a museum featuring a collection of antique furniture and rare textbooks. *Phone:* 609-386-3993. *Hours:* Open by appointment.

**Hoskins House:** (202 High Street) This 1797 house was built by John Hoskins, Jr., a construction contractor and one of the founders of Burlington's early fire companies. The house has undergone extensive restoration and is now owned by the City of Burlington Historical Society. *Phone:* 609-386-3993. *Hours:* Open by appointment.

**James Lawrence House:** (459 High Street) This house is the birthplace of Captain James Lawrence, a hero of the War of 1812. It was he that uttered the immortal phrase "Don't give up the ship!" This was his final order to his crew after being fatally wounded during a fierce naval battle. It is to honor the Captain's memory that the town flies a flag on the riverfront promenade. This house is featured on the Burlington Historical Society's tour of the city.

**Library Company:** (23 West Union Street) Operating continuously since 1758, this is the second oldest public library in the state and the seventh oldest in the nation. It is also the first library to print a catalogue of books for reference use. A nearby house served as the library's first home. It was not until 1789 that a building was specifically built to house the library. Governor Joseph Bloomfield donated the land for this building from his private holdings. This was the first building in New Jersey to be purposely built as a library. The structure that stands today was built in 1864, and contains the original 1758 catalog and several rare books that were published in the 1500s.

**Lyceum Hall:** (432 High Street) This 1839 building was used as a public hall for lectures and cultural programs. In 1851, it became the seat of the municipal government.

**Nathaniel Coleman House:** (320 High Street) This house was built in 1720 by Richard Smith Jr. In 1792, a silversmith, by the name of Nathaniel Coleman, purchased the house. Located at the rear of the building is a two-story workshop, where Nathaniel and his brother Samuel spent many long hours. To this day many of their works are on display in museums and private collections.

**Old St. Mary's Church:** (West Broad Street and Wood Street) Built in 1703, this is the oldest established Episcopal Church in New Jersey. The church cemetery is the peaceful resting place of many prominent citizens including Governor Joseph Bloomfield and Elias Boudinot, former president of the Continental Congress. *Phone:* 609-386-0902.

**Revell House:** (213 Wood Street) Originally located by the waterfront, this 1685 house is the oldest structure in Burlington County. In the late 1700s, it was expanded and a second floor was added. Legend says that in 1723, while Benjamin Franklin was passing by this house on his way to Philadelphia, he was humbled by an act of kindness when an elderly lady offered him some gingerbread for his journey. The legend has grown into a tradition of sorts as the maintenance of the house is funded by an annual sale of baked gingerbread.

**Ship Shield Marker:** (On the riverbank) A large boulder near the riverbank marks the spot where the first vessel arrived in Burlington in December of 1678. The estate of William Franklin, the last Royal Governor of New Jersey, once occupied the land behind this marker. Today, the Veterans of Foreign Wars building occupies the spot.

**Shippen House:** (Talbot Street at the Delaware River) This 1756 house was used as a summer residence for Judge Edward Shippen and his family. In 1778, with the Revolution under way, a young loyalist named Peggy Shippen, Edward's 17-year-old daughter, met and fell in love with the American General Benedict Arnold. He had recently been appointed, against his wishes, Military Governor of Philadelphia after being wounded

**FACT:** *The Jersey Devil, a supposed mythical creature, has haunted the Pine Barrens since the 1700s. During January of 1909, Burlington City residents reportedly found the creature's footprints in the snow.*

in the battle of Ticonderoga. For Arnold, this new love was the only joy he could take from the position. The couple married two years later. Many historians agree that it was Peggy's staunch support for the English crown that was the catalyst for Arnold's subsequent treason.

**Smith House:** (315 High Street) Built in 1692 for Dr. Richard Smith, this is one of the oldest buildings in the city. Today, an art gallery occupies the first floor of the house and is open to the public. *Phone:* 609-386-2525. Hours: Daily 10 A.M to 5 P.M.

**Ulysses S. Grant House:** (309 Wood Street) During the last years of the Civil War, General Ulysses S. Grant became increasingly concerned for the safety of his wife and children. To ease his fear, and after a personal visit where he concluded the amenities to be suitable, he moved the family to this house. In April of 1865, Grant declined an invitation to attend a play with President Lincoln, so he could return home to visit with his family. On his way home from Washington, he received word that the President had been mortally wounded while watching the performance.

# Morristown

**Historic Morris Visitor's Center:** (6 Court Street) This visitor's center welcomes all guests to historic Morristown and provides detailed information about the local area, as well as maps and listings of local activities. *Phone:* 973-631-5151. *Hours:* Mondays to Fridays from 10 A.M. to 4 P.M. *Admission Fee:* Free.

**Acorn Hall:** (68 Morris Avenue) Named for one of the oldest and largest red oaks in the state, Acorn Hall is a Victorian-style mansion built in 1853. The house is a wonderful example of the fine care and craftsmanship of the era and is furnished with many antique pieces. Located behind the mansion is a beautiful garden. *Phone:* 973-267-3465. *Hours:* Thursdays from 11 A.M. to 3 P.M. and Sundays from 1:30 P.M. to 4 P.M. *Admission:* $3 adults and $0.50 children.

**Admiral Rogers House:** (40 Macculloch Avenue) This 1852 house was built for Christopher Rodgers and his wife. Christopher, an Admiral in the navy, served in the Mexican Wars, and was later appointed Superintendent of the United States Naval Academy.

**Burnham Park:** (Washington Street) This park features a picnic area, walking trails, a pond, and the largest statue of Thomas Paine in the United States. The statue was dedicated to his memory on July 4, 1950. Paine was the author of, among other works, *The American Crisis*. This pamphlet was read aloud to General Washington's army in 1776 just before they crossed the Delaware River on their way to Trenton.

**Doctor Lewis Condict House:** (51 South Street) Doctor Condict had this house built in 1797. An upstanding member of the community, he was a physician, patriot, and public official. Doctor Condict was also an innovator in the field of medicine, as he first introduced a new British vaccine against smallpox to the people of the community. The Women's Club of Morristown now owns this building.

**First Presbyterian Church:** (57 Park Place) Established in 1733, this is one of Morristown's oldest congregations. Though unsubstantiated, the congregation boasts with pride that General George Washington attended services here. During the Revolutionary War, the church served as a hospital, providing aid and comfort to the wounded. The present structure, the third on this site, was completed in 1894. The gravestones in the cemetery next to the church reveal the names of many Revolutionary War soldiers. *Phone:* 973-538-1776.

**Fort Nonsense:** (Western Avenue) Overlooking Morristown, this fort was built in May of 1777. Over the years people started to refer to the structure as Fort "Nonsense" because they thought that it was constructed only to keep the soldiers busy, serving no other military purpose. *Phone:* 973-543-4030. *Hours:* Daily from 9 A.M. to Sunset. *Admission Fee:* Free.

**Forsterfields Historical Farm:** (73 Kahdena Road) This working farm is complete with live animals and workers who dress in period costumes. The main feature of this farmstead is the family mansion, a beautiful example of nineteenth century Gothic Revival architecture. *Phone:* 973-326-7645. *Hours:* April through October, Wednesdays to Saturdays from 10 A.M. to 5 P.M. and Sundays from 12 P.M. to 5 P.M. Tours of the mansion are held Thursdays to Sundays from 1 P.M. to 4 P.M. *Admission Fee:* $4 adults, $3 seniors, and $2 children.

**General Porter House:** (1 Farragut Place) This house was built in the 1880s for General Fitz Porter, a veteran of the battle of Bull Run.

**Historic Speedwell:** (333 Speedwell Avenue) This farmstead originally belonged to the Vail family who also owned an ironworks factory across the street during the nineteenth century. The farmstead has been restored and is complete with many historic buildings. It was on the second floor of the factory building where Samuel Morse and Alfred Vail developed the telegraph in 1838. *Phone:* 973-540-0211. *Hours:* May through October, Thursdays to Fridays from 12 P.M. to 4 P.M. and weekends from 1 P.M. to 5 P.M. *Admission Fee:* $5 adults, $4 seniors, and $3 children.

**FACT:** *Morristown was named in honor of Lewis Morris, the first Royal Governor of the province of New Jersey.*

**Independent Hose Company:** (15 Market Street) Organized in 1834, the Independent Hose Company became Morristown's first fire department. One person who volunteered for the fire department was a popular political cartoonist and resident of Morristown, Thomas Nast. The structure was rebuilt in the 1870s.

**Kedge:** (49 Macculloch Avenue) Built between the 1870s and 1880s, this was the home of Henry Miller, the grandson of George Macculloch. Miller served as a lieutenant commander in the United States Navy. The name "Kedge" comes from a maritime term that means "a small anchor."

**Macculloch Hall:** (45 Macculloch Avenue) This mansion was completed in 1819 for George Perrot Macculloch who many consider the "Father of the Morris Canal." Five generations of his family would call this place their home. Today, the mansion and its gardens are open to the public. Inside is a collection of eighteenth and nineteenth century English and American art featuring works by well-known political cartoonist Thomas Nast. *Phone:* 973-538-2404. *Hours:* Sundays, Wednesdays, and Thursdays from 1 P.M. to 4 P.M. *Admission Fee:* $3 per person.

**Morris County Courthouse:** (Washington Street) This courthouse was completed in 1827. An interesting feature is found above the front entrance of the building, a wooden statue of Justice who, unlike most statues of her kind, is not blindfolded.

**Morris Museum:** (6 Normandy Heights Road) The Morris museum contains an impressive rock and mineral collection, changing art exhibits and an entire room dedicated to the North American Indian. The museum also includes a mock nineteenth century schoolhouse and features a theater with a seating capacity for 300 people. *Phone:* 973-971-3700. *Hours:* Tuesdays through Wednesdays from 10 A.M. to 5 P.M., Thursdays from 10 A.M. to 8 P.M., Fridays and Saturdays from 10 A.M. to 5 P.M., and Sundays from 1 P.M. to 5 P.M. *Admission:* $6 adults, $4 seniors, free for children. No admission is charged on Thursdays from 1 P.M. to 8 P.M.

**Morristown National Historic Park:** (Jockey Hollow Road) During the winter of 1779-80, General George Washington and his troops built a city of log cabins on this spot, to house the soldiers for the winter encampment. Today visitors may tour these reconstructed soldiers huts, an eighteenth century farm, and the Ford Mansion, which served as Washington's headquarters throughout the encampment. *Phone:* 973-543-4030. *Hours:* Daily from 9 A.M. to 5 P.M. *Admission Fee:* $4 per person.

**Park of Artillery:** (Mendham Avenue) While Washington's infantry soldiers settled into their winter encampment in what is now Morristown National Park, General Henry Knox and his artillerymen camped at this location during the winter of 1779-80.

**Pitney House:** (43 Maple Street) Completed in 1864, this was the home of Henry C. Pitney, a distinguished lawyer and a pillar of the community.

**Sansay House:** (17 DeHart Street) This house was built in 1807 for Monsieur Louis Sansay, a French dance instructor. Among his many famous visitors was Revolutionary War hero, Marquis de Lafayette, for whom Monsieur Sansay held a lavish banquet.

**Schuyler-Hamilton House:** (5 Olyphant Place) While the Continental Army was camping at Jockey Hollow for the winter, this house was lent to General Washington's personal physician, Dr. John Cochran. One day Elizabeth Schuyler, the sister of Dr. Cochran's wife, paid a visit to the house. During her stay, she met Colonel Alexander Hamilton. They started to date and later got married in Albany, New York. *Phone:* 973-267-4039. *Hours:* Sundays and Tuesdays from 2 P.M. to 5 P.M. *Admission Fee:* $1.50 adults and $0.10 Children.

**St. Peter's Episcopal Church:** (South Street at Miller Road) Before the church was constructed, services had to be held in George Macculloch's home. Many of Morristown's well-known residents are buried in the cemetery next to the church, including George Macculloch and members of the Ford, Miller Ogden, Wood, Vail, and Foote families. *Phone:* 973-538-0555.

**Thomas Nast House:** (50 Macculloch Avenue) Thomas Nast was a famous political cartoonist who created the popular images of Santa Claus, the Republican Elephant, the Democratic Party Donkey, and Uncle Sam. He moved to Morristown in 1866 and purchased this mansion. Among his friends and frequent visitors, were Mark Twain and Ulysses S. Grant.

**Town Green:** (Park Place) In the 1700s, this was a pasture for animals. During the Revolutionary War it was used as a training facility for the local militia. In 1755, the original Morristown Courthouse, which was little more

*Town Green*

than a log cabin, was built here. In 1871, a Civil War monument, entitled "Soldiers at Rest," was erected on the green. It honors those who lost their lives in the war.

**Vail Mansion:** (110 South Street) This handsome mansion was completed in 1918 for Theodore Vail, then president of AT&T. The first floor was dedicated to the display of his collection of art and family inventions. Sadly, he died just after the completion of the house. In 1922 the town purchased the building and renovated it for use as municipal offices.

# Paterson

**Great Falls Visitor's Center:** (65 McBride Avenue) Visitors will find a plethora of information about local activities and detailed maps of the surrounding area. *Phone:* 973-279-9587. *Hours:* Mondays to Fridays from 9 A.M. to 4 P.M. and Saturdays from 12 P.M. to 4 P.M.

**Argus Mill:** (Mill Street) Originally built in 1878 for use as a silk mill, where people from the surrounding area were employed, the building now serves the community as a public school.

**Barbour's Row:** (Slater Street) The Barbour Flax Spinning Company built this row of tenement houses in the 1880s to house its many workers and their families. At that time, the company employed over 1,500 workers and owned several mills. This area has developed a rich cultural identity due to the large numbers of immigrant workers from Ireland who were housed in these buildings.

**City Hall:** (Colt Street) The City of Paterson was once considered to be a sister city to Lyon, France, when both were centers of the thriving silk production industry. Paterson City Hall was erected in 1836 and is an architectural copy of the city hall building in Lyon.

**Colt Gun Factory:** (Near corner of Mill and Van Houten Streets) Constructed in 1836, this building was a four-story structure with a bell tower. It was built on the site of an old nail mill and is the place where John Ryle first manufactured silk and Samuel Colt developed the "gun that won the West." Fire has since destroyed most of this factory.

**Cooke Locomotive Administration Building and Cooke Mill:** (Market Street) These two buildings plus the building directly across from them on Market Street, located near the southeast corner of Jersey Street, were part of Danforth Cooke and Company. During the nineteenth century, this stretch of land was the heart of the locomotive manufacturing industry in the city, as nearly 12,000 locomotives were built in Paterson.

**Dublin Spring Monument:** (Olive Street and Mill Street) This monument,

*City Hall*

cast in 1931 by noted sculptor Gaetano Federici, was dedicated to the memory of Irish families that worked in the mills and lived in the Paterson area. The spring was a frequent gathering place for these families.

**Essex Mill:** (Mill Street) Built in 1807 to produce paper, this factory expanded in 1872 and added cotton and silk to its production capabilities. It is now a home to many artisans.

**Federici Park:** (Van Houten Street) Gaetano Federici was a gifted sculptor who lived in the city of Paterson. Many of his statues are on display including the one of Lou Costello, a noted comedian who was born in Paterson, which adorns this park.

**First Presbyterian Church:** (Main Street) Built on the site of the original First Church, which had burned down in 1850, this church is a monument to the dedication of the congregation and their architectural craftsmanship.

**Former Post Office:** (Hamilton Street) Built in 1899, this building is an exact duplicate of Guild Hall, located in Holland and built in the twelfth century. The former Post Office now serves as part of the Passaic County Court complex.

**Franklin Mill:** (McBride Avenue and Mill Street) Built in 1860 and

**FACT:** *In 1898, Paterson resident, John Philip Holland, invented the first practical submarine.*

expanded in 1915, this mill originally produced yarn silk and was later converted to make fire engines and machinery.

**Great Falls:** (McBride Avenue) The Great Falls (77 feet high and 280 feet wide) is the second largest waterfall in the Eastern United States. Alexander Hamilton first visited the Great Falls in 1778 and was very impressed with not only the picturesque beauty but by the immense power of the rushing water. When he became the country's first Secretary of the Treasury, he sent a report to Congress informing them that the United States must develop into a manufacturing nation if they truly wanted to be free of all dependence on Britain. At the time, water powered mills were the heart of the manufacturing process. Remembering his visit to the Great Falls, Hamilton used his influence in selecting Paterson to become the first planned industrial city in the nation.

**Haines Overlook Park:** (McBride Avenue) From this park, visitors can witness firsthand the beauty and power of the Great Falls. A statue of Alexander Hamilton, who was instrumental in the founding of this city, stands next to the hydroelectric station located on the park grounds. Built in 1922, the hydroelectric station consists of four giant turbines, which convert the power of the rushing water into electricity. The turbines can produce over 33 million kilowatts of electricity per year.

**Ivanhoe Wheelhouse:** (Spruce Street) The Ivanhoe Wheelhouse is one of only ten buildings that remain from the once vast amount of mills and factory buildings that comprised the Ivanhoe Paper Company. The wheelhouse once housed an 87-inch Boyden water turbine that was used to power the paper mill. The building is now home to a gift shop.

**Lambert Castle Museum:** (3 Valley Road) Built in 1892, this castle was home to Catholina Lambert, the owner of one of the largest mills in the city of Paterson. Today it is a museum devoted to artwork and exhibits of historical importance. The building also serves as the headquarters of the Passaic County Historical Society. *Phone:* 973-247-0085. *Hours:* Wednesdays through Sundays from 1 P.M. to 4 P.M. *Admission Fee:* $3 adults, $2 seniors, and $1.50 children.

**Old School #2:** (Mill Street and Passaic Street) The second public school built in Paterson, work was completed in 1871, and it could accommodate up to 650 students. By 1927, a little over 50 years later, the population of school age children had grown so dramatically that more schools were built.

**Passaic County Courthouse:** (71 Hamilton Street) Erected in 1903, the courthouse is an inspired example of the neo-renaissance-style architecture that was so popular during that era.

**Paterson Museum:** (2 Market Street) Constructed in 1871, this building was originally used as a factory for the Rodger's Locomotive Erecting Shop. In 1982, the building underwent an extensive restoration and remodeling program and was converted into a museum. Inside the building is an impressive mineral collection, displays of contemporary works of art, and exhibits of textile manufacturing in Paterson. Many of Colt's firearms are on display. The museum also has over a quarter-million photographs of the city. *Phone:* 973-881-3874. *Hours:* Tuesdays through Fridays from 10 A.M. to 5 P.M. and weekends from 12:30 P.M. to 4:30 P.M. *Admission Fee:* Free.

**Phoenix Mill:** (Van Houten Street) Built in 1815, this one time silk mill played a giant role in the city's textile manufacturing history. It is now used as a gathering place and venue for the many artisans who reside in the city.

**Question Mark Bar:** (Cianci Street and Van Houten Street) This tavern was established in 1890 and originally known as Nag's Head. It was a popular meeting place, especially during the famous silk strike of 1913.

**St. John's Cathedral:** (Main Street) Finished in 1870, this Roman Catholic cathedral is a sight to behold. The facade is rich in detail and ornamentation, while the interior is a splendor of stained glass, dark wood, and marble.

**Thompson and Ryle Houses:** (Mill Street) These two houses were built in the 1830s. The smaller building belonged to John Ryle, who is known throughout the city as the "Father of the Silk Industry." As the first person to successfully manufacture silk, he helped bring about a revolution in the textile industry and growth and prosperity to the city.

**Union Works:** (Spruce Street and Market Street) Construction for this building was completed in 1890. It was used to manufacture locomotive parts. In 1916, the building underwent a conversion to silk manufacturing. Today it is used as a school.

**Upper Raceway and Park:** Construction for this one and a half mile raceway system started in 1792 and lasted until 1838. As a system of canals and tubes, the raceway brought in the necessary water to power the mills and factories of Paterson.

**Waverly Mill:** (Near corner of Mill and Van Houten Streets) The original mill built on this site in 1855 primarily manufactured cotton. Construction

**FACT:** *In 1947, Larry Doby became the first African-American to play in the American League. A year later, in 1948, Doby led the Cleveland Indians to a World Series victory over the Boston Red Sox. When he returned to his hometown of Paterson, a parade was thrown in his honor. Doby, a seven time all-star outfielder, later became the manager of the Chicago White Sox. On July 6th, 1988, he was inducted into the Cooperstown Hall of Fame.*

of the present building was completed in 1857, and with the new mill came the production of a new material, silk. The Waverly Mill stands adjacent to another historic mill, the Colt Gun Mill. Both buildings suffered severe damage in a fire in 1984.

# Princeton

**Tours of Princeton:** This two-mile, guided, walking tour of the town begins with an introduction given in front of the Historical Society of Princeton. *Phone:* 609-921-6748. *Hours:* Sundays starting at 2 P.M. *Admission Fee:* $6 adults, $4 seniors, and $3 children.

**Alexander Street:** Alexander Street, originally known as Canal Street, was once a busy commercial thoroughfare that included a railroad station, hotels, and industries of all kinds. It also served as a link between the city of Princeton and the Delaware and Raritan Canals.

**Autumn Hill Reservation:** (Herrontown Road) This 78-acre park is great for wildlife viewing and hiking along its many wooded trails. Before the land was protected and commissioned as parkland, local farmers tilled the soil and led their animals to pasture here. The farmers living in this area were called "Herringtown" farmers, because they would go to the shore and bring back herring for use as fertilizer. There are still a number of old stone fences that mark the fields and pastures of the old farms. *Phone:* 609-921-7077. *Hours:* Daily, sunrise to sunset. *Admission Fee:* Free.

**Battle Monument:** (Mercer and Nassau Streets) This monument was dedicated in 1922 to commemorate the Battle of Princeton, which took place on January 3, 1777. It features the seals of the original 13 states and a large sculpture of General Washington leading his troops into battle.

**Beatty House:** (Vandeventer and Park Place) Built in the 1780s, this house was originally located opposite the building that now houses the Historical Society of Princeton located on Nassau Street. It was moved to its present site in 1875. One of the more notable visitors to the house was the Marquis de Lafayette, who spent the night here on July 15, 1825, during his tour of the United States.

**Drumthwacket:** (354 Stockton Street) Charles Olden, whose family was one of the original settlers in the Princeton area, built this beautifully designed mansion in 1835. Today it is the official residence for the governor of New Jersey. *Phone:* 609-683-0057. *Hours:* Wednesdays from 12 P.M. to 2 P.M. *Admission Fee:* Free.

**Einstein House:** (112 Mercer Street) Albert Einstein lived in this house from 1933 until his death in 1955. Famous for his Theory of Relativity and other works to enhance man's understanding of Physics, he was one of the most well known men in the early twentieth century. He also received an honorary degree from Princeton University. At Einstein's request the house has never been turned into a museum or public shrine. Today it is owned by the Institute for Advanced Study and used as a private residence.

**Grover Cleveland House:** (15 Hodge Road) Built in 1854, this house became a landmark when President Grover Cleveland and his wife moved here after his second presidential term ended in 1897.

**Herrontown Woods Arboretum:** (Snowden Lane) This 142-acre arboretum has many trails and is a favorite site for wildlife watching. Internationally known mathematician, Oswald Veblen, donated it to the county in 1957. Professor Veblen was a distinguished faculty member at Princeton University. *Phone:* 609-989-6530. *Hours:* Daily, sunrise to sunset. *Admission Fee:* Free.

**Historical Society of Princeton:** (158 Nassau Street) Built in 1766, this was the home of Job Stockton, a wealthy tanner and descendant of the prominent Stockton family. In 1774, the house was leased to Dr. Absalom Bainbridge. His son William was born here and would later become a naval-hero in the War of 1812. Today the building is a museum featuring exhibits and displays related to the Princeton area. *Phone:* 609-921-6748. *Hours:* Tuesdays through Sundays from 12 P.M. to 4 P.M. and weekends only in January and February from 12 P.M. to 4 P.M. *Admission Fee:* Free.

**Lake Carnegie:** (Faculty Road) Completed in 1906, this 3½ mile lake was financed by Andrew Carnegie to provide a rowing course for the university crew team. This is also one of the Olympic training centers for the United States Crew Team. *Phone:* 609-258-3000.

*Boathouse on Lake Carnegie*

**Marquand Park:** (Lovers Lane) Noted for its scenic beauty, this 17-acre park is a peaceful place with serene trails. It is a great place to have a picnic and to observe the wildlife. *Phone:* 609-497-7634. *Hours:* Daily, sunrise to sunset. *Admission Fee:* Free.

**Mountain Lakes Nature Preserve:** (Mountain Avenue) This 74-acre wooded park was once part of a farm. It is a peaceful place, pleasant for family gatherings and nature walks. The main house on the property was built in the 1950s and was the home of the Menenez Family. Today, the Friends of Princeton Open Space maintains their offices here. *Phone:* 609-924-8720. *Hours:* Daily, sunrise to sunset. *Admission Fee:* Free.

**Morven:** (55 Stockton Street) This was the home of Richard Stockton III, a prominent citizen and signer of the Declaration of Independence. He lived here with his wife Annis, a published poet. The original section of the house dates back to 1750s, while much of the present building was added during the 1790s. New Jersey Governor Walter Edge and his wife donated this house to the State to be used as either the governor's mansion or a museum. It was the governor's residence until 1982, when the official residence was moved to nearby Drumthwacket. *Phone:* 609-683-4495. *Hours:* Wednesdays from 11 A.M. to 4 P.M. *Admission Fee:* Free.

**Princeton Battlefield State Park:** (500 Mercer Street) This park commemorates the Revolutionary War battle fought here on January 3, 1777. During the peak of the fighting, General Mercer was struck by a bullet and wounded. He was treated in the Thomas Clark House but died several days later. The county, to which Princeton belongs, was named in his honor *Phone:* 609-921-0074. *Hours:* Park is open daily from sunrise to sunset. Clark House is open Wednesdays through Saturdays from 10 A.M. to 12 P.M. and 1 P.M. to 4 P.M. and Sundays from 1 P.M. to 4 P.M. *Admission:* Free.

**Princeton Cemetery:** This cemetery was established in 1757 and is now owned by the Nassau Presbyterian Church. Many famous people have been buried there, including President Grover Cleveland, John Witherspoon, a signer of the Declaration of Independence, and Aaron Burr Jr., the vice-president of the United States. Aaron Burr Jr. is infamous for having participated in the duel in which he killed Alexander Hamilton and for attempting to raid a federal armory and use the stolen weapons to seize land out west.

**Stonybrook Meeting House:** (470 Quaker Road) Constructed in 1760, this meetinghouse served as a gathering place for the local Quakers. It still serves as a meeting place for local groups today.

**Woodrow Wilson Houses:** (72 Library Place, 82 Library Place, and 25 Cleveland Lane) While Woodrow Wilson was living in Princeton, he resided in three different homes. After graduating from Princeton University, Wilson led a life of self-sacrifice and dedication to the American public. Among his most notable accomplishments are becoming Princeton University's president in 1902 and President of the United States in 1913.

# *Princeton University*

**Tours of Princeton University:** This tour focuses on sites that best display the features of the university's history, student life, and academics. It begins at the Welcome Desk of the First Campus Center on Washington Road, and lasts about an hour. *Phone:* 609-258-1766. *Hours:* Tours are available Mondays through Saturdays at 10 A.M., 11 A.M., 1:30 P.M., and 3:30 P.M. and Sundays at 1:30 P.M. and 3:30 P.M. *Admission Fee:* Free.

**1879 Hall:** (Washington Road) This hall wasn't built in 1879, but rather, it was named in honor of the graduating class whose donations made its construction possible. The building was completed in 1904 and the hall now serves as offices and classrooms for the philosophy and religion departments.

**Alexander Hall:** (Mercer Street) Constructed in 1817, this building originally housed the Princeton Theological Seminary. The Reverend Dr. Archibald Alexander was the Seminary's first professor. After the Reverend's passing, the building began to be referred to informally as Alexander Hall.

**Art Museum:** (McCormack Hall) This art museum features many prominent collections of African, Asian, American, and European art. *Phone:* 609-258-3788 *Hours:* Tuesdays to Saturdays from 10 A.M. to 5 P.M. and Sundays from 1 P.M. to 5 P.M. *Admission Fee:* Free.

**Blair Hall:** (University Place) This building is part of the Rockefeller and Mathey College at Princeton University. John Insley Blair donated it to the university in 1897. The stunning gothic architecture always leaves a lasting impression on its visitors.

**Brown Hall:** (Elm Drive) Constructed in 1891, this hall is reserved for use by the university's junior and senior classes as dormitories.

**Cannon Green:** (Nassau Street) Cannon Green is located behind Nassau Hall. In the center of the green is a large cannon that saw action in both the American Revolution and the War of 1812. Every year, as a tradition, the senior class paints their graduation year on the cannon. In the middle of the nineteenth century, Cannon Green was a popular place for intramural football games.

**Dillon Gym:** (Elm Drive) The university's first gym was no more than a wooden shed. It had to be purposely destroyed by fire in 1865 after a drifter spent the night in it and infected the building with smallpox. A new gymnasium was built in 1903 and was considered at the time to be the largest in the United States. However, in 1944, it too was destroyed by fire, though this time by accident. Construction for the current gym, Dillon Gym, was made possible through the generosity of Herbert Lowell Dillon.

**Dod Hall:** (Elm Drive) Built in the 1880s, this is another dormitory for upper classmen.

**East Pyne and Chancellor Green:** (Elm Drive) Chancellor Green was built in 1873 and housed the university's ever-growing library. When this facility became inadequate for the enormous collection of books, the Pyne Library was built. Construction for this library was made possible by a donation from Moses Taylor Pyne in 1897. Chancellor Green was then used as a reference room for the new library. However, the university's book collection needed still more space. Today, the collection is located at the Firestone Library. Pyne Library, now known as East Pyne, is used for the offices and classrooms of the language department, and Chancellor Green now serves as a campus social center.

**Firestone Library:** (Washington Road) Built in 1948, this library was named after the Firestone family who made a generous contribution towards its construction. The library contains six levels, housing a major portion of the university's book, manuscript, and microfilm collections. The vast collection consists of more than 10 million printed works and manuscripts. Every month the library receives, on average, another 6,000 volumes. *Phone:* 609-258-3184. *Hours:* Mondays to Saturdays from 9 A.M. to 5 P.M. and Sundays from 2 P.M. to 5 P.M. *Admission Fee:* Free.

**Holder Hall and Tower:** (University Place) Holder Hall is part of Rockefeller College, which is one of five residential colleges serving first and second year students at the university. Rockefeller College was named after famed industrialist John D. Rockefeller, a member of Princeton's graduating class of 1929.

**Joseph Henry House:** (Nassau Street) This 1838 building was moved three times before its present and final location was decided on. In 1832, Joseph

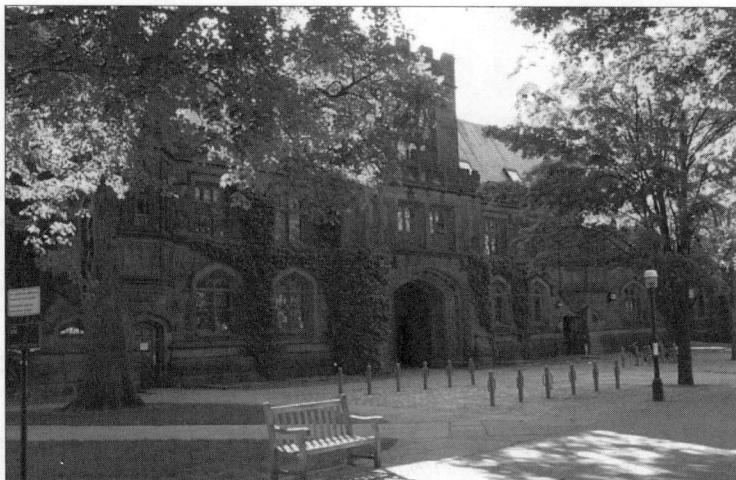

*East Pyne*

Henry came to Princeton to teach at the University. He was notable for having built a large electromagnet that could lift 3,500 pounds. In 1846, Henry left Princeton to become the first director of the Smithsonian Institution in Washington D.C.

**Maclean House:** (Nassau Street) This building is named after its founder, John Maclean. Once called the "Dean's House", this 1756 building was the home of the presidents of the university. Aaron Burr Sr., the first president of the university, was also the house's first resident. Famous visitors to the house included George Washington and Andrew Jackson. The Alumni Association now occupies the building. The Prospect House, located on Washington Road, is the current residence of the University's Presidents.

**McCosh Hall and Courtyard:** (Washington Road) Built in 1907, this building was named after James McCosh, the university's eleventh president. At the time, it was the largest building on campus. The courtyard contains the Mather Sun Dial, a replica of the Turnbull Sun Dial at Oxford's Corpus Christi College. It was a gift from Sir William Mather, the president of Victoria University in Manchester England. The sundial was to symbolize the connection between Oxford and Princeton, and Great Britain and America. It has a 20-foot column that is topped by a pelican, the symbol of Corpus Christi.

**Murray-Dodge:** (Off Elm Road) Built in 1879 and expanded in 1900, the Murray-Dodge building was the university's first student center. Today it contains a theater and is used for offices.

**Museum of Natural History:** (Guyot Hall, Washington Road) This museum contains many exhibits on the Paleolithic Era and has a large collection of fossils. *Phone:* 609-258-5807. *Hours:* Mondays to Fridays from 9 A.M. to 5 P.M. *Admission Fee:* Free.

**Nassau Hall:** (Nassau Street) Completed in 1756, Nassau Hall was named for King William III, Prince of Orange and Nassau. The hall served as the first capitol building of New Jersey and was also the first building used by the college. It now houses administration offices. *Phone:* 609-258-3603.

**Nassau Presbyterian Church:** (Nassau Street) The first church built on this site was completed in 1751. However, the church burned down in 1813. It was subsequently rebuilt only to burn down again in 1835. The present

**FACT:** *In November of 1869, the colleges of Princeton and Rutgers played the first ever intercollegiate football game. Princeton lost the match, however it would take Rutgers 69 years to beat Princeton in football again.*

church was built in 1836. The adjacent cemetery contains the graves of many famous people including the 22nd and 24th President of the United States, Grover Cleveland.

**Palmer Hall and Jones Hall:** (Washington Road) Built in 1908, Palmer Hall housed the offices of the physics department. It was named after Stephen S. Palmer, a University Trustee. Recently renovated, it now serves as the student center. Standing beside Palmer Hall is Jones Hall. It was built in 1876 and named after its donor and benefactor, Thomas D. Jones. Room 209 once served as the office of Albert Einstein, who taught at the university.

**Prospect House:** (Washington Road) Built in 1851, this house was donated to the university. Beginning in 1878, it became the residence for the school's president. Woodrow Wilson lived in this house while he was the University's President from 1902 to 1910.

**Robertson Hall and Fountain:** (Washington Road and Prospect Avenue) One of the few modern buildings on campus, Robertson Hall was completed in 1966 and was dedicated by President Lyndon Johnson. The main floor of the building contains the school's library. It is decorated with many unique and abstract sculptures. In front of Robertson Hall is a reflecting pool, which contains the *Fountain of Freedom*. The fountain symbolizes Woodrow Wilson's vision for lasting world peace. Weighing in at six tons, the fountain is one of the largest and heaviest cast bronze sculptures in the United States.

**School of Architecture:** (Off Elm Drive) The School of Architecture was founded in 1919. The school is a leading institution for the scholarly pursuit and practical application of advanced ideas.

**Stanhope Hall:** (Off Washington Road) Built in 1803, this building was named in honor of the university's seventh president, Samuel Stanhope. Originally it was home to the university's library and its literary societies. Today, Stanhope Hall serves as the center for the Office of Communications and the Department of Public Safety.

**Tiger Mall:** (Off Elm Drive) The plaza between Whig and Clio Halls is adorned with two bronze tigers. The tigers were sculpted in 1969 to commemorate the arrival of women at Princeton. One of the tigers is male, and the other is female.

**University Chapel:** (Washington Road) Completed in 1928, this church tends to the spiritual needs of the students and faculty. It can accommodate up to 1,800 people.

**West College:** (Off University Place) West College and its twin, East College, were built in 1836. Together they were Princeton University's first dormitories. The East College building was razed in 1896 to make room for the construction of Pyne Library. Today West College houses the University administration offices.

# Trenton

**Trenton Visitors Center:** This building was originally constructed in 1793, to serve as the first lodge for Trenton's Masonic order. Their gatherings were held on the second floor. Today, it is a place where visitors meet and gather detailed information about the city, its history, and the many interesting things to do. Located on the second floor is the original lodge meeting room. *Phone:* 609-777-1770. *Hours:* Daily, 10 A.M. to 4 P.M.

**Alexander Douglass House:** (Front and Montgomery Streets) Alexander Douglass held the position of Quarter Master to the Continental Army during the Revolution. After the Second Battle of Trenton, General Washington used this house to hold meetings with his officers to devise plans for advancing into Princeton. This house has moved four times before settling at its present location. It is now owned by the City of Trenton and used to host special events. *Phone:* 609-394-1965. *Hours:* Open by appointment. *Admission Fee:* Free.

**Cadwalader Park:** (Barracks Street at West Front Street) This park was named after Dr. Thomas Cadwalader, who vaccinated the population of Trenton against Smallpox in the late 1740s. On the park grounds is an art museum that includes exhibits from Trenton's once thriving ceramics industry. *Phone:* 609-989-3632. *Hours:* Park is open daily, sunrise to sunset. Museum is open Tuesdays to Saturdays from 11 A.M. to 3 P.M. and Sundays from 2 P.M. to 4 P.M. *Admission Fee:* Free.

**First Presbyterian Church:** (114 East State Street) This church was constructed in 1820. Its cemetery contains the graves of 150 Hessian mercenaries, who died during the First Battle of Trenton, including their commander, Colonel Johann Rall. This is also the resting place of the Reverend John Rosbrugh, who was the first American chaplain to die in the service of his country.

**Friends Meetinghouse:** (East Hanover and Montgomery Streets) The original structure of this Quaker meetinghouse was built in 1739 and has since been expanded. Buried in the adjoining graveyard are Revolutionary War heroes such as General Philemon Dickinson and George Clymer, a signer of the Declaration of Independence.

**Mercer County Waterfront Park:** (1 Thunder Road) This recently constructed stadium is the home field for the Trenton Thunder, a minor league baseball team. They are the AA affiliate for the Boston Red Sox. The season starts in April and ends in August. Throughout the year, when not in conflict with a Thunder home game, the stadium features open air concerts and shows. *Phone:* 609-394-8326.

**Old Barracks of Trenton:** (Barrack Street) Constructed in 1758, this building is the only barracks remaining of the five originally built in the state.

Soldiers were quartered here in both the French and Indian War and the American Revolution. Presently, the barracks are used for different exhibits and programs. *Phone:* 609-396-1776. *Hours:* Daily, 10 A.M. to 5 P.M. *Admission Fee:* $6 adults and free for seniors.

**Old Eagle Tavern:** (431 South Broad Street) This historic building was used as a hotel and a tavern during the Revolutionary War.

**Old Trenton City Hall:** (State Street and Broad Street) It was in 1837 that Trenton's first city hall was built. Part of the ground floor was rented out for stores and the second story was used for town meetings and gatherings. The building was remodeled in 1882 and, thereafter, used solely for municipal purposes.

**Sovereign Bank Arena:** (550 South Board Street) This 10,000-seat facility is home to the Trenton Titans, a minor league hockey team playing in the East Coast Hockey League. During the Titans road trips and off-season, the arena is used for music concerts and consumer trade shows. *Phone:* 609-656-3200.

**St. Michael's Episcopal Church:** (140 North Warren Street) Constructed in 1747, this is one of the oldest houses of worship in Mercer County. During the Revolutionary War its congregation's loyalties were so evenly split between independence and English rule, that the church was forced to cancel services. The church's cemetery contains the grave of David Brearley, a signer of the Constitution.

**Stacy Park:** (West State Street) Stacy Park was named after Mahlon Stacy who arrived in America onboard the ship *The Shield* from England. She

*Stacy Park with the State Capital Dome in the background*

had a mill built at the juncture of the Assanpink Creek and the Delaware River. It was in 1680 that she is credited with founding the village that would grow into the city of Trenton. The park was created in 1916 to serve as a backdrop for the State House and other nearby buildings.

**State Archives:** (225 West State Street) This is the official repository for all state government records of historical value, dating back as far as the colonial period. It has the largest holdings of original documents on microfilm in New Jersey. *Phone:* 609-292-6260. *Hours:* Tuesdays to Fridays from 8:30 A.M. to 4:30 P.M. *Admission Fee:* Free.

**State House:** (West State Street) This is the nation's second oldest state capitol building that has been in continuous use. Guided tours are conducted through the building, explaining its history, art, and architecture. The State House also offers information about the legislative process and the elected officials who make the laws in the state. Tours last about an hour. *Phone:* 609-633-2709. *Hours:* Mondays to Fridays from 10 A.M. to 3 P.M. and Saturdays from 12 P.M. to 3 P.M. *Admission Fee:* Free.

**State House Annex:** (West State Street) In 1929, construction for the State House Annex began. This was a major addition to the capitol complex. It is connected to the State House by an underground tunnel. An impressive feature of the annex is a 10-foot by 15-foot skylight, assembled in 1995 and composed of over 1,500 pieces of glass. This beautiful work of art features many scenes from New Jersey's history.

**State Library:** (185 West State Street) The library contains over half a million books with extensive holdings in law, political science, genealogy, and state history. *Phone:* 609-292-6220. *Hours:* Mondays to Fridays from 8:30 A.M. to 5 P.M. and Saturdays from 9 A.M. to 5 P.M. Closed Saturdays in August. *Admission Fee:* Free.

**State Museum:** (205 West State Street) The New Jersey State Museum contains an impressive collection of fine art, cultural history displays, and natural history exhibits. The museum also includes a 150-seat planetarium with state-of-the-art sound and lighting equipment and a 400-seat auditorium that showcases dance, music, and children's programs. *Phone:* 609-292-6308. *Hours:* Tuesdays to Saturdays from 9 A.M. to 4:45 P.M. and Sundays from 12 P.M. to 5 P.M. *Admission Fee:* Free.

---

**FACT:** *Norman H. Schwarzkopf was born in Trenton in 1934. He graduated from West Point in 1956 and served two tours of duty in the Vietnam War. In 1991, Schwarzkopf commanded the successful allied invasion of Iraq in the Persian Gulf War. Schwarzkopf retired a year later as a four-star general.*

**State Police Museum:** (State Police Headquarters, River Road) Visitors touring the exhibits will learn a great deal of information about the role of the State Police in New Jersey and gain a keen insight into the criminal investigation process. *Phone:* 609-882-2000 Ext. 6400. *Hours: Admission Fee:* Free.

**Trenton Battle Monument:** (Warren Street and Broad Street) Standing 150 feet in height, this granite column marks the spot of the Continental Army's artillery placement during the First Battle of Trenton, which took place on December 26, 1776. Two bronze statues representing the New York and Massachusetts regiments, whose soldiers manned the cannons, flank the entrance of the monument. An elevator takes visitors to the top of the monument where they can see impressive views of the surrounding area. *Phone:* 609-737-0623. *Hours:* Saturdays from 10 A.M. to 12 P.M. and Sundays from 1 P.M. to 4 P.M. *Admission Fee:* Free.

**Trenton City Hall:** (309 East State Street) This complex is the location of the city's administration offices. Everyday, the functions of the government take place throughout these hallowed halls.

**War Memorial Theater:** (Memorial Drive) Completed in 1932, the memorial was built to commemorate the lives of the soldiers who fought in World War I, those who died and those who survived forever changed. It features live theater, music, and dance. *Phone:* 609-984-8484.

**William Trent House:** (15 Market Street) Before this city was named Trenton, people called it "The Falls of the Delaware." Then, in 1719, William Trent came to the area and established this homestead. He was a man of great wealth, whose contributions ensured the success of the growing community. In response, people began to refer to the area as Trent's Town. Through the years, the name was shortened to Trenton. Visitors may tour the inside of his house, which is the oldest building still standing in the city. *Phone:* 609-989-3027. *Hours:* Daily, 12:30 P.M. to 4 P.M. *Admission Fee:* Free.

# Villages

*Allaire Village*

# Allaire Village

James P. Allaire was born on July 12, 1785 in New York. He was a descendent of Pierre Allaire, a knight in the service of King Louis XI at LaRochelle, France in 1465. During his childhood, James did not receive a great deal of formal education. To make up for this, later in his life, he had college professors tutor him in various subjects. By 1799, James had started his technical training as an apprentice in the brass industry. A few years later he met Robert Fulton and the two began a close friendship. James joined Fulton's company and started working in the marine engineering and construction field. While working for Fulton's company, James completed the brass work on the *Clermont,* the first successful steamship in history, and the *Demologus,* the first steam frigate ever built.

When Fulton died in 1815, Allaire was named executor of his estate. He formed a partnership with Charles Stoudinger, who had been Fulton's foreman. Together, they took over the steam engine factory and dry dock at Paulus Hook. It was considered the most advanced of its kind in the United States. While at this plant, Allaire developed the first compound engine ever applied to marine use.

In 1822, James P. Allaire purchased a factory called the Monmouth Furnace. He changed the name to Howell Works because most of the original 5,000 acres were in Howell Township. He purchased this facility to obtain his own supply of pig iron for his marine engine plant located in New York. Allaire immediately made extensive improvements to the property. He rebuilt and enlarged the furnace, which would afterwards be considered one of the largest in the United States. By 1839 the village grew to over 70 brick buildings. The iron works became almost entirely self-sufficient, having raw materials and farmland nearby. Allaire's Village peaked by the end of the 1830s, employing nearly 500 workers.

By the early 1840s, Pennsylvania had begun monopolizing the production of iron. They had a more efficient process and made the Howell Iron Works and other New Jersey iron works obsolete.

---

*Location:* Allaire State Park, Route 547, Farmingdale, Monmouth County. *Phone:* Main Office: 732-919-3500. Park Office: 732-938-2371. Village Information: 732-938-2253. *Hours:* Grounds are open daily from sunrise to sunset. Buildings are open Memorial Day to Labor Day, Wednesdays to Sundays from 10 A.M. to 4 P.M. and weekends after Labor Day through November from 10 A.M. to 4 P.M. *Admission Fee:* $3 per car from Memorial Day through Labor Day.

**Bakery:** Built in 1835, this building provided baked goods for the village employees. Still in use, visitors may purchase cookies, pastries, breads, and muffins. Also on display are antique baking implements. *Hours:* March though December 16, weekends from 10 A.M. through 4 P.M.

**Big House and Dormitory:** During the 1830s, the Big House was the residence of the superintendent of the iron works and his family. The dormitory wing was added on at a later date and was used to house non-married workers. Today only its foundation remains. After the works closed down, Mr. Allaire lived here in retirement with his family.

**Blacksmith Shop:** Built in 1836, the smithy utilized four forges to fabricate various household items and tools. It was completely rebuilt in the 1960s and restored to its original condition. Blacksmith demonstrations are conducted here.

**Blast Furnace:** This once huge complex has given way to time and neglect. Today, only the blast furnace remains. The complex originally contained a bridge house for charging the furnace, a wheelhouse, casting shed, and several smaller cupola furnaces. At the time, the furnace was considered one of the largest in the United States.

**Carpenter Shop:** Built in 1835, this shop produced the wood patterns necessary for making cast-iron products.

**Carriage House and Gardener's Cottage:** These buildings were completed in 1833. The Carriage House provided an enclosure in which to keep the company's carriages. Today, it has been converted into a museum displaying antique wagons, carriages, and sleighs. The Gardner's Cottage, located at the rear of the Carriage House was the residence of the village gardener and his family.

**Charcoal Depot Site:** This was the site of a three-story structure built in 1832. It was here that coal loads were stored until the coal was needed to fuel the furnaces. Today, only the foundation remains.

**Enameling Furnace:** Finished in 1834, this structure housed the furnaces used for firing the enamel that was coated onto the cookware. Today, it is a museum displaying special exhibitions.

**Episcopal Church:** Construction for this church was completed in 1836. The church had a dual purpose, serving the spiritual needs of the congregation on the Sabbath and serving as a school for the children during the week.

**Foreman's House:** This small, two-story, brick structure was built in 1827 and was the residence of the foreman of the iron furnace.

**General Store:** Built in 1835, this is the largest structure still standing in the village. It once supplied the village with necessities like meat, dairy, and grains among other important items. This general store was fashioned like a department store, with a post office, drug store, furniture gallery, and food market inside. People from all over would shop at this "state of the art" general store. Today, it contains a historical interpretive center and a gift shop that sells reproductions of antique pieces. *Phone:* 732-938-3311.

**Horse and Mule Barn:** The original date of construction is not known, and the original structures have been destroyed. This building has since been rebuilt and stands on the original foundation. It was used, as the name implies, to house the company's horses and mules.

**Manager's House:** During the 1850s this building housed the superintendent of the iron works along with his family.

**Visitor's Center:** Originally built in 1833, these buildings housed the village workers and their families. In 1985, they were renovated and are now used as the village Visitors' Center and museum. *Phone:* 732-938-6707. *Hours:* Weekends year round from 10 A.M. to 4 P.M. and daily from Memorial Day through Labor Day from 10 A.M. to 4 P.M.

# Batsto Village

In 1766, Charles Reed, a wealthy and influential merchant, acquired 60,000 acres of land and built a furnace at Batsto Lake. The area was an ideal location for a blast furnace, having water and wood close by. The dense cedar swamps and streams feeding the rivers were rich in raw limonite, the bog ore from which iron is extracted. Woodcutters were employed to gather fuel for the furnace and long, narrow, Durham boats filled with the collected bog ore were pulled along the streams to deliver the ore to the furnaces.

John Cox became the next owner of the facility in 1770. During the Revolutionary War he rose to prominence and was appointed Assistant Quartermaster General of the Continental Army. His iron works produced invaluable materials for the American effort.

In 1784, William Richards took over ownership of the works. He had the facilities renovated and improved. This stimulated the industry and the village subsequently flourished. The Richards family had created a huge empire through ownership of many of the iron works in New Jersey. However, the discovery of coal in Pennsylvania sounded the death knell for New Jersey furnaces, which depended on vast tracts of timber for fuel.

Joseph Wharton, a speculator from Philadelphia, purchased the land in 1847. He had an idea to dam the rivers and streams throughout the Pine Barrens and create a vast water storage reservoir. He wanted to export the water to the city of Philadelphia, which at the time had limited resources and bad drinking water. Ultimately, the State of New Jersey learned about this plan and passed a bill prohibiting the export of water. It was through Wharton's many land purchases in the Pine Barrens that he unintentionally preserved a treasure that might otherwise have been lost.

*Location:* Wharton State Forest, Route 542, Hammonton, Burlington County. *Phone:* 609-561-3262. *Hours:* Grounds are open daily from sunrise to sunset. Visitors Center is open daily from 9 A.M. to 4:30 P.M. Interpretive Programs are available September through May, Wednesdays through Sundays and Memorial Day through Labor Day daily. *Admission Fee:* $3 per car Labor Day through Memorial Day. Mansion tours are $2 adults, $1 children.

**Batsto-Pleasant Mills Church:** Built in 1808, villagers would attend service at this Methodist Church. Today it still serves the spiritual needs of the Pleasant Mills community. Several members of the Richards family are buried here.

**Blacksmith and Wheelwright Shop:** The blacksmith shop made and repaired the iron working tools, farming tools, and other hardware. The wheelwright shop had specialized equipment to make and repair carriage wheels. These two shops were a necessary part of village life because of the constant need to repair horse-drawn vehicles and other vital equipment.

**Bog Ore Exhibit:** This is the raw material from which iron was extracted by the furnace. It was usually found along the stream and swamp beds and transported by ore boats.

**Carriage House:** This building stored the village carriages.

**Corn Crib:** This building was used to store and shell corn. It was powered by a belt and shaft system on the second story, which received its energy from the nearby gristmill.

**General Store and Post Office:** Village employees would buy grains, hardware, clothing, and other items in this store. On the second floor is a post office that was established in 1852 and is still in operation today. Because of the historical significance of the area, no zip code is required for mail being delivered to the village.

**Gristmill:** Built in 1828, this mill was originally powered by a waterwheel. In 1882, the waterwheel was replaced with a more efficient water turbine. The gristmill produced gains that were sold at local markets and in the village general store.

**Horse Stable and Threshing Barn:** Dating back to 1830, this multi-stall stable housed the riding and carriage horses. Inside the Threshing Barn, a machine was used to separate grain from straw and chaff.

**Ice and Milk Houses:** The icehouse was used to store ice, which had been cut from Batsto Lake during the winter months. It was stacked in layers and covered with sawdust. With the right conditions, the ice would last most of the year. In the adjacent building, milk and other dairy products were stored using a similar technique and a lot of ice.

**Mansion:** Originally built in 1766, this was the ironmaster's home. When Joseph Wharton purchased the village he enlarged the mansion to better suit his needs.

**Mule Barn:** This barn held eight stalls and housed both horses and mules.

**Ore Boat:** This modified Durham boat was excavated from the bottom of Batsto Lake in 1957. It was once used to transport raw bog iron ore to the village's furnace in the early nineteenth century.

**Range Barn:** Cattle were kept in this barn. The attached underground silo was used to store the fodder for the animals.

**Sawmill:** John Fort built the original sawmill in 1761. When Joseph Wharton bought the operation, he had the sawmill completely re-built. Work was completed in 1882 and visitors will see this version of the mill while touring.

**Site of Glass Works:** Constructed in 1846, this complex consisted of seven buildings and produced window glass and glass for street lamps. None of the buildings remain today.

**Stone-House Barn:** This small barn housed the horses that were primarily used for the Ironmaster's carriage.

**Village Houses:** These buildings were used to house the employees of the iron works. Each unit was big enough for a family, containing three rooms downstairs and two rooms upstairs.

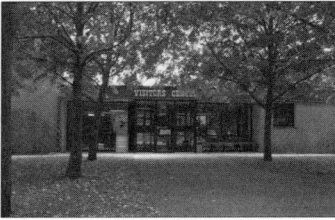

**Visitors Center:** Located at the entrance to the village, this building contains an information desk, souvenir shop, and a research center.

**Woodhouse:** This was the main storage area for wood used in the mansion's stoves. Today, there are displays of various agricultural items for visitors to view and learn about.

# Double Trouble Village

The cranberry, which is a native North American fruit, received its name from Pilgrims, who thought the pinkish-white flowers resembled the head and neck of a crane as they opened and twisted back. The name "Crane berry" was later contracted to cranberry.

In the wild, cranberries grow in marshlands, swamps, bogs, and along streams. Generally wherever water is likely to cover them and thus protect them from both frost and insects. When farmers began to cultivate these berries, they grew them in bogs on damp peat sites. Only a few areas in the world can support the growth of cranberries and the New Jersey Pine Barrens is considered one of the best.

The production of cranberries near what is present day Double Trouble State Park began in the 1850s. In 1863, a cranberry craze was sweeping through Ocean County. Swampland was cleared and cranberry operations were established at an impressive rate. Speculators snatched up as much available land as possible and started intense bidding wars over the swampland. This caused an artificial inflation in swampland real estate value and prices for the berry soared. During this time, New Jersey was first in the United States in overall production of the fruit. However, the high times ended with the panic of 1873, as overproduction of the berry caused a glut on the market and crop values plummeted. With the drop in market prices, farms could not pay off their debt and many were forced to close. Cultivation was left to just a few financially healthy groups.

In 1904, Edward Crabbe purchased the remaining industries at Double Trouble, a sawmill and a lumber business. He continued in the lumber business until most of the bogs were cleared of forest. Then in 1909, he switched to cranberry production and formed the Double Trouble Company, which soon became the leading producer of cranberries in the state.

Legend holds that Thomas Potter gave the village its name when he coined the phrase "double trouble." He had a milling operation in the area and was said to utter the phrase in exasperation after spring rains twice washed out his dam.

Cranberries were first harvested by workers hand picking the fruit. This

*Location:* Double Trouble State Park, Double Trouble Road, Berkeley Township, Ocean County. Phone: 732-341-6662. *Hours:* Information Center: During the summer, Wednesdays to Sundays from 8 A.M. to 4:30 P.M. September through November, weekends from 8 A.M. to 4:30 P.M. *Admission Fee:* Free.

technique was called dry harvesting and was very labor intensive. With the lack of preservation techniques, cranberries harvested in this manner could only be sold as fresh fruit. Soon a new method, called wet harvesting, replaced the outmoded dry technique. The introduction of wet harvesting brought with it new ways of utilizing and preserving the cranberries, including the making of cranberry juice. The natural flooding of the bogs during the fall became a major    boon to industry wide methods of harvesting the fruit for the processed food market.

When the berries arrived at the screening house from the bog, they underwent an intense manual screening process to separate the good berries from the bad ones and debris. This process improved in 1880, with the invention of separating machines that utilized the inherent bounciness of the berries, good berries would actually bounce. The machines first sorted the berries by a bounce board and then by size on a grate or screen. Lathrop Hayden and H.R. Baily both patented and improved bounce-type separators. Most of these features were not new but combining them into one machine was.

Cranberry operations continued at Double Trouble until the 1960s, when the land and facilities were sold to the State of New Jersey. Today, some of the bogs are still leased to private growers and the annual fall flooding and harvesting still continues as both a business and a festival complete with sampling and hands-on attractions. New Jersey now ranks third behind Massachusetts and Wisconsin in overall cranberry output.

**Bunk House:** Built in 1900, this building provided housing for the single workers who were employed during the seasonal cranberry harvest.

**Burke House:** Built in 1900, this building served as the residence of the Burke family. In later years, it housed the company foremen, who were in charge of cranberry operations.

**Cranberry Sorting and Packing House:** This building was constructed in stages from 1911 through 1925. It was used to sort and pack cranberries that were picked from the nearby fields. Inside, on display, are cranberry separators, one designed by Baily and three by Hayden. Each machine is a system of conveyor belts designed to help with the manual sorting of cranberries. The building was restored in 1996 and tours are offered at various times.

**Cook House:** This was the kitchen and eating hall for the permanent village employees and seasonal pickers.

**Foreman's House:** This structure was once used as a laboratory for investigations into improving cranberry and blueberry production.

**General Store:** Built in 1900, this one and a half story, wooden structure was the source of hardware, grain, dairy, and other products for the village.

**Pickers' Cottages:** These cottages provided housing for seasonal pickers and their families. Each cottage could accommodate two families.

**Sawmill:** Completed in 1909, this sawmill was first powered by a steam engine using the waters from the creek. By 1920, the mill was converted to a more modern power source and a gasoline engine was used to power the mill. The building was recently restored and tours are offered at various times.

# Speedwell Village

During the American Revolution, a sawmill operation and an iron forge were located on the banks of, what is today, Speedwell Lake. In 1788, Jacob Arnold and Thomas Kinney purchased the site and began to make improvements to the mill and forge. They also built a slitting mill that was designed to roll iron into thin sheets, which could be cut in strips for hinges, nails, and barrel hoops.

In 1807, Stephan Vail, Dr. William Campfield, and Isaac Cannfield purchased half an interest in the slitting mill and began to build the Speedwell Iron Works. By 1815, Stephan Vail had bought out his partners to become the sole owner. As the business prospered, Vail expanded the works and purchased an adjacent farm, making Speedwell an industrial and agricultural complex. Soon, his younger son George became a full partner and together, they improved their skills through experience, reading trade journals, and discussing projects with expert craftsmen.

On September 2, 1837, Stephan's son Alfred went to visit his alma mater, the University of New York. While there, he accidentally walked in on a demonstration by the inventor, Samuel Morse. He was showing off his electro-magnetic telegraph, which transmitted messages coded as a series of dots and dashes over wire. Alfred was impressed with the idea and pressured his father and brother to become Morse's benefactors and provide him with a workshop, tools, and money to perfect the telegraph. A workshop was set up on the second floor of an old mill at Speedwell, where Alfred Vail and Samuel Morse perfected the design of the telegraph. Alfred contributed immensely on the design and is credited with inventing the dot

*Location:* 333 Speedwell Avenue, Morristown, Morris County. *Phone:* 973-540-0211. *Hours:* May through October, Thursdays and Sundays from 1 P.M. to 5 P.M. *Admission Fee:* $5 adults, $4 seniors, and $3 children.

and dash alphabet. Today, the second story of this mill features an exhibit on the telegraph.

During the 1850s, Speedwell was at its peak of success, employing almost 50 people, including blacksmiths, machinists, carpenters, millers, and clerks. However, by 1873, with the decline of the iron industry in New Jersey and the lowering of the rivers water level, which resulted in a loss of waterpower for the mills, the works were forced to close.

The buildings began to slowly decay from neglect and the elements of nature. A fire in 1908 destroyed everything except two portions of the original iron works walls. Their remains can still be seen at the foot of the falls on Speedwell Lake, located directly across the street from the village. The restoration of the Vail family homestead started in 1967, when local citizens banded together to preserve what was left of this piece of history.

**Ford Cottage:** Gabriel Ford Jr., the grandson of Colonel Jacob Ford Sr., once lived in this house. Before arriving at Speedwell it stood near the Ford Mansion, which is now part of Morristown National Park.

**Granary:** In 1830, when Stephen Vail purchased the farmstead, the granary was one of the outer most buildings. It was built above the ground, on stone pillars, with a storage space at ground level for farm machinery. A unique feature of the granary is the top portion, which was used to store corn. Corncribs usually have slatted sides to allow for ventilation. Here, the clapboard sides are louvered outward to allow air to circulate and still provide protection from the weather.

**Gwip House:** This building originally stood on Spring Street, in Morristown and was purchased by John Gwip in 1755. The house was relocated to Speedwell when an urban renewal project threatened to destroy it.

**Moses Estay House:** This house is a fine example of nineteenth century, American-Georgian architecture. It once stood on the corner of Spring Street and Water Street, directly opposite the Gwip house. Captain Moses Estay, a veteran of the Revolutionary War, built this house in 1786, after a fire destroyed his earlier home on the same site. Estay was a chair maker by trade and had a shop located in back of his residence. His daughter Hanna married David Burnet who would later become the first president of the Republic of Texas.

**New Carriage House:** This building was finished in 1849 and used to store the Vail family's carriages.

**Old Carriage House:** Built in the early 1800s, this building was once used by Stephen Vail to house his horses and carriages. Later on it was converted into a garage. The upper level of this building features a display of a large collection of wooded patterns that were essential to the process of making finished iron products. Many of these patterns were found in the attic of the factory.

**Telegraph Factory:** This building was refitted for weaving and general homestead usage in 1829. On the second floor of this factory building, Alfred Vail and Samuel Morse first publicly demonstrated the electromagnetic telegraph.

**Vail Homestead:** Even though this home resembled nothing more than a decorated farmhouse, Stephan Vail referred to it as his "mansion." He was a very wealthy individual and could have afforded a real mansion, but his tastes were too simple for him to have been comfortable in such an extravagant style. However, Stephen did enjoy the many modern conveniences that were offered at the time as exampled by his having central heating and plumbing installed in his house.

# Waterloo Village

A 1743 survey conducted by John Lawrence, recorded an Indian settlement located at what would become the present site of Waterloo Village. In 1760, William Allen and Joseph Turner purchased 500 acres of land along the Musconetcong River where the village now stands. They started construction on several buildings, including an iron works factory adjacent to their nearby furnace. The iron works, called Andover Forge, consisted of a four-fire, two-hammer forge, mills, and workers' houses. Pig iron from their nearby furnace was transformed under enormous water-driven hammers into bar iron for the manufacture of finished goods. The site produced some of the finest iron in the colonies and much of it was shipped to England.

During the Revolutionary War, the Continental Army confiscated the iron works from its loyalist owners. Andover Forge then became a major supplier of munitions for the American war effort.

With the completion of the Morris Canal in 1831, the village of Waterloo was transformed from a small, industrial village to a growing, prosperous town. It became an important lock and incline plane stop along the canal. The Smith family was responsible for building most of the structures. By 1901, however, with the increased competition of the railroad, the canals

*Location:* 525 Waterloo Road, Stanhope, Sussex County. Phone: 973-347-0900. *Hours:* Mid April through mid November, Wednesday through Friday 10 A.M. to 4 P.M., Saturday and Sunday 11 A.M. to 5 P.M. Admission Fee: $9 adults, $8 seniors, and $7 children.

were no longer vital the nation's transportation network. The Morris Canal was later dismantled and Waterloo Village began to decline.

Today, visitors may tour this restored canal-port town, complete with its beautiful landscape and architecture. A museum devoted to the Morris Canal offers insight about the day-to-day lives of the canal workers and the company's rise and fall.

**Apothecary and Herb-Drying Room:** Once a horse barn, this structure now houses an apothecary shop and herb drying room.

**Blacksmith Shop:** During the village's iron days, the blacksmith made and repaired tools and hardware. When the Morris Canal was operational, the shop was used to produce shoes for the canal mules.

**Broom Shop:** Inside this building is an exhibit on the history of brooms as well as a demonstration on how they were made.

**Canal House:** Built sometime during the 1700s, during the "iron days" of the village, this structure housed the employees of the forge and factory.

**Canal Museum:** Once the residence for the village schoolteacher, this building is now the Museum of the Canal Society of New Jersey.

**Church:** This Methodist Church was constructed in 1859 and is still in use today. It has become a popular site for weddings.

**Foundation Office:** Originally constructed as a hunting lodge, this building is now used as the main offices of the Waterloo Foundation.

**Gristmill:** Built during the 1700s, the gristmill was used to grind corn and other grains.

**Gunsmith and Sign Shop:** Once a carriage barn, this building now houses a sign making shop and a working gunsmith.

**Homestead:** Originally built as a horse barn in the 1700s, this building was converted into the residence of Peter Smith during the 1830s.

**Ironmaster's House:** Constructed during the 1700s, this was once the home of ironmaster Samuel T. Smith, who later was elected State Senator and served from 1873 to 1876. Today, the Canal Society of New Jersey uses this building as a museum. *Phone:* 973-722-9556.

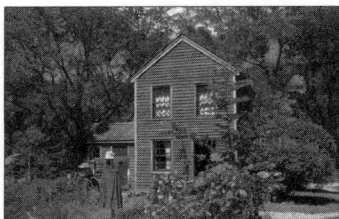

**Jake's House:** Built around 1847, this house now serves as a seamstress shop specializing in the manufacture of period clothing and other traditional crafts.

**Lenape Indian Village:** This re-created seventeenth century Native American village shows how the local Indians of New Jersey lived and worked. There are numerous huts and buildings as well as information posted throughout the village.

**Library:** Once the former laundry of the Ironmasters house, this building now houses administration offices.

**Miller House:** Built around 1760, this house was once owned by the gristmill operator.

**Nathan Smith House:** Built around 1860, this was once the home of Nathan Augustus Smith, patriarch of the family that helped spur the growth of the village. It is now used as a parish house for the church.

**Peter D. Smith House:** This house was built in 1874 as the private residence of Peter Decker Smith. He was the President of Hackettstown National Bank and also a State Senator from 1889 to 1891.

**Pottery Shed:** This was once used to store wood and ice for the Wellington House. It is now used for exhibits of locally crafted pottery.

**Rutan Cabin:** Built in 1825, this cabin was originally located in upper Sussex County. It is a fine example of a pre-mechanized, low-income farmhouse of the mid 1800s.

**Sawmill:** This is a working recreation of a sawmill and is similar to the ones in service during the early 1880s.

**Simulated Archaeological Site:** This is a re-creation of an actual archeological dig.

**Site of Andover Forge:** In 1763 Andover Forge was constructed on this site. The area was rich in iron ore and had an abundance of trees, which were used to power the forge.

**Smith's General Store:** Constructed in 1831, this general store was on the second story of the building and was owned and managed by the Smith family. It supplied goods to the workers of the Morris Canal. Today, it is a gift shop. On the first floor, below the shop, is the Towpath Tavern, which is open on the weekends for lunch.

**Stagecoach Inn and Tavern:** Built in 1760, this structure was later converted into a tavern by the Smith family and was a very popular place for canal workers.

**Weaving Barn:** Textile artisans now use this building, which was once a horse barn.

**Wellington House:** Built in 1879, this was the residence of Seymour R. Smith, who, like his father, helped the village to grow economically and was the President of the Hackettstown National Bank.

**White Barn:** This is the former carriage house of Samuel T. Smith.

# Unique Places

*Tuckerton Seaport*

**Cold Spring Village:** Cold Spring was established in 1688, taking its name from a fresh water spring that bubbled up through the salt marsh. In the eighteenth century, as the community developed, Cold Spring became a stagecoach stop. Although little remains of the original village, there are 20 historical buildings that have been moved here from various locations re-creating an early American village. *Location:* 720 Route 9, Cape May County. *Phone:* 609-898-2300. *Hours:* Memorial Day through June 24, daily from 10 A.M. to 4:30 P.M. June 25 through Labor Day, Tuesdays through Sundays from 10 A.M. to 4:30 P.M. Labor Day through September 17, weekends from 10 A.M. to 4:30 P.M. *Admission Fee:* $7 adults, $6 seniors, and $5 children.

**Cowtown Rodeo:** The Cowtown Rodeo brings a little bit of western entertainment to New Jersey. Cowboys, clowns, and feisty animals come together to enthrall the audience with wild acts and rodeo events including bareback bronco riding, calf roping, saddle bronco riding, and steer wrestling. *Location:* Route 40, Woodstown, Salem County. *Phone:* 856-769-3200. *Hours:* May through September. *Admission Fee:* $10 adults and $5 children.

**Drumthwacket:** This is the official residence of the Governor of New Jersey. Charles Smith Olden, whose family was among the earliest settlers in Princeton, had it constructed in 1835. The name of the mansion is derived from two Scottish words "drum," meaning hill and "thwacket," meaning woods. Guided tours of the mansion and gardens are offered on Wednesdays, except during the months of January and August. *Location:* 354 Stockton Street, Princeton, Mercer County. *Phone:* 609-924-3044. *Hours:* 12 P.M. to 2 P.M. *Admission Fee:* Free.

**Ellis Island:** From 1892 to 1954, almost 12 million immigrants passed through this processing center in order to enter the United States, many of them fleeing hardships such as poverty, religious persecution, and political unrest. Now, after years of restoration, Ellis Island is an Immigration Museum, which contains many exhibits that depict their struggle. It also features an interactive learning center and more then 30 separate galleries containing photographs and personal memorabilia of those who passed through here. Ferries from Battery Park, New York and Liberty State Park, New Jersey provide the transportation. *Location:* Hudson County. *Access:* Ferry service is available at Castle Clinton, Battery Park, New York located at the corner of State Street and West Side Highway. Ferry service from New Jersey is located at Liberty State Park, Hudson County. Ferry service is available from 8:30 A.M. to 4:30 P.M. with extended hours in the summer. *Phone:* Ellis Island: 212-363-7620, Ferry Service: 212-269-5755. *Admission Fee:* Only for ferry service, $7 adults, $6 seniors, and $3 children.

**Grounds for Sculpture:** Located on the former site of the New Jersey State Fairgrounds, this 22-acre landscaped park includes two 10,000 square foot museums featuring sculptures by well-known and internationally recognized artists. There are numerous benches and chairs scattered throughout the grounds where you can sit and reflect upon its beauty. If you get hungry, you can stop by Rat's, which is located near the main building. Don't judge it by the name as this place serves gourmet French Cuisine. *Location:* 18 Fairgrounds Road, Hamilton, Mercer County. *Phone:* Park Office: 609-586-0616, Restaurant: 609-584-7800. *Hours:* Tuesdays to Sundays from 10 A.M. to 9 P.M. *Admission Fee:* Tuesdays to Thursdays: $4 adults, $3 seniors and students, and children are free. Fridays and Saturdays: $7 adults, $6 seniors and students, and $3 children. Sundays: $10 per person.

**Historic Smithville:** Smithville features over 60 boutiques and specialty shops that are housed in beautiful historic buildings. It also includes a miniature train ride and a boathouse that rents paddleboats. After a full day of shopping you can dine at the Historic Smithville Inn. *Location:* Route 9 and Moss Mill Road, Smithville, Atlantic County. *Phone:* 609-652-7777. *Hours:* Mondays to Saturdays from 10 A.M. to 8 P.M. and Sundays from 10 A.M. to 6 P.M. The Village Greene is open daily, 11 A.M. to 6 P.M. *Admission Fee:* Free.

**Medieval Times:** Experience the adventure and romance of the Middle Ages complete with battling knights, who joust for the honor of the King and the favor of a Lady. The whole experience is housed beneath one large "castle" where food is served and eaten in authentic style, without utensils. When you arrive, you're given a colored piece of paper that informs you where you'll sit and which color knight to cheer for. After the festivities, the knights mingle with the audience. There's also a small nightclub for dancing and mingling set up in the waiting room. *Location:* 149 Polito Avenue, Lyndhurst, Bergen County. *Phone:* 800-828-2945. *Hours:* Wednesdays and Thursdays at 7:30 P.M., Fridays and Saturdays at 8 P.M. and Sundays at 4:30 P.M. *Admission Fee:* $41.95 adults and $31.95 children.

**New Jersey Performing Arts Center:** Located in New Jersey's largest city, this 250,000 square-foot building, which opened in 1997, features New Jersey's greatest talents and some of the world's top performers. The building houses an auditorium, a theater, and a restaurant. One-hour guided tours are also available. *Location:* One Center Street, Newark, Essex County. *Phone:* 888-466-5722. *Hours:* Tours begin Mondays at 10 A.M., 11 A.M., and 12 P.M., Wednesdays at 10 A.M., and Saturdays at 10 A.M. *Admission Fee:* $3 per person.

**New Jersey Renaissance Festival:** For a few weeks each summer, this section of New Jersey transforms into a place of high art and drama, where magic and myth become reality. Knights, nobles, and peasants walk about tending to the day's business, whether it is a duel of swords or a living chess game. There's a town square, a royal castle, and an enchanted forest for all to explore. In addition to the performers and entertainers, there are shows and displays of skill to entertain the crowds. *Location:* Davidson Avenue, Franklin, Somerset County. *Phone:* 732-271-1119. *Hours:* Weekends in late May through early June. *Admission Fee:* $12 adults, $8 seniors, and $6 children.

**Northlandz:** Model train enthusiasts will appreciate this monumental exhibit. It features eight miles of track and over 10,000 rail cars. If model railroading isn't your passion, then you may want to check out the doll museum and its 94-room dollhouse, complete with an indoor swimming pool, ballroom, and a two-story library. The doll museum also features over 200 costumed collectible dolls. There's also a music hall, which features a large pipe organ, a gift shop where you can purchase railroad memorabilia, and a snack bar. *Location:* 495 Route 202 South, Flemington, Hunterdon County. *Phone:* 908-782-4022. *Hours:* Mondays to Fridays from 10:30 A.M. to 4 P.M. and Saturdays and Sundays from 10 A.M. to 6 P.M. *Admission:* $13.75 adults, $12.50 seniors, and $9.75 children.

**PNC Bank Arts Center:** This open-air auditorium was specially designed for live concerts, with a state-of-the-art sound and lighting system and large seating capacity. The season begins late in May and continues through September, and features as many as 50 performances by artists representing every musical style. Special events and exhibits are also scheduled throughout the year. In particular, the complex transforms into a spectacular holiday light show during the month of December featuring over one million lights and over 130 displays. *Location:* Exit 116, Garden State Parkway, Holmdel, Monmouth County. *Phone:* 732-335-0400.

**Statue of Liberty:** The Statue of Liberty stands at the entrance of New York Harbor. A gift to the United States from the people of France, it was dedicated in 1886 and has become a global symbol of freedom. When immigrants arrived in the United States, this tall, majestic statue welcomed them. For many, it symbolized their goal and dreams of freedom and liberty. Visitors may climb the 22 stories to top of the statue for breathtaking views of the New York and New Jersey skylines. A museum, located in the pedestal, contains an exhibit explaining how the statue was conceived, designed, and constructed. *Location:* Hudson County. *Access:* Ferry service is available at Castle Clinton, Battery Park, New York located at the corner of State Street and West Side Highway. Ferry service from New Jersey is located at Liberty State Park, Hudson County. Ferry service is available from 8:30 A.M. to 4:30 P.M. with extended hours in the summer. *Phone:* Liberty Island: 212-363-3200, Ferry Service: 212-269-5755. *Admission Fee:* Only for ferry service, $7 adults, $6 seniors, and $3 children.

**Sterling Hill Mine:** Sterling Hill Mine was named after Lord Sterling, who owned the property from 1761 to 1766. The mine produced zinc primarily, however, over 340 additional minerals have been found, including 80 types of fluorescent minerals. Two of these minerals, zincite and franklinite, are unique to the area and are not found anywhere else. The mining operation at Sterling Hill went out of business in 1986. Shortly thereafter, the Hauck brothers decided to restore the mine and keep it open for tours. The old buildings were converted into an educational museum. Visitors may tour the underground mine shafts and learn about the inherent geological wonders and the day-to-day life of the workers. Keep in mind the inside of the mine is a cool 56 degrees, so it's best to wear something warm. There's also a snack bar and a gift shop that sells sample specimens of the many minerals. *Location:* 30 Plant Street, Ogdensburg, Sussex County. *Phone:* 973-209-7212. *Hours:* April 1 to November 30, daily from 10 A.M. to 4 P.M., tours of the mines are at 1 P.M. and 3 P.M. *Admission Fee:* $9 adults, $8 seniors, and $6 children.

**Tuckerton Seaport:** Just opened in May of 2000, this re-created, authentic, working seaport is an open exhibit of the rich maritime history of the Jersey Shore. The seaport contains 16 buildings, including shops and restaurants and features live demonstrations of the skilled crafts specific to maritime life. Visitors can observe the day-to-day life of the bay area's fishermen, boat captains, lighthouse keepers, and ocean lifesavers. *Location:* 120 West Main Street, Tuckerton, Ocean County. *Phone:* 609-296-1623, 609-296-8868. *Hours:* Daily, 10 A.M. to 5 P.M. Lighthouse tours available on weekends beginning at 11 A.M. Walking tours available on weekends beginning at 2 P.M. *Admission Fee:* $6 adults, $4 seniors, and $3 children.

**Tweeter Center:** This 25,000 seat outdoor amphitheater features numerous concerts throughout the summer months. The complex includes a spacious lawn, a giant video screen, and a state-of-the-art sound system. The amphitheater converts into a fully enclosed, climate-controlled theater during the fall and winter months and hosts a variety of concerts and Broadway theatrical productions. *Location:* 1 Harbor Boulevard, Camden, Camden County. *Phone:* 856-365-1300.

**U.S. Equestrian Team Headquarters:** The U.S. Equestrian Team selects, trains, and finances equestrians of the highest possible standard to represent our county in international competition. Its main offices, actually a remodeled stable built in 1916, have been described as one of the largest and most lavish in the United States. Visitors may tour the Trophy Rooms, which house the many trophies and prizes American's finest equestrians have won. There are special events throughout the year including the Festival of Champions in June. *Location:* Pottersville Road, Gladstone, Morris County. *Phone:* 908-234-1251. *Hours:* Mondays to Fridays from 8:30 A.M. to 4:30 P.M. *Admission Fee:* Free.

**Wheaton Village:** This historic village was once a hub of the glass-making industry and features displays and exhibitions from that era. Visitors can watch skilled artisans hand-blow glass every day at 11 A.M., 1:30 P.M., and 3:30 P.M. You can even try your luck at making glass yourself. The Museum of American Glass features over 6,500 of the finest glass pieces ever made in this country. The village has several shops and restaurants and miniature train rides are available for the children. *Location:* 1501 Glasstown Road, Millville, Cumberland County. *Phone:* 800-825-6800. *Hours:* April through December, daily from 10 A.M. to 5 P.M. Stained glass studio tours begin at 2 P.M. Museum of American glass tours begin at 2:30 P.M. *Admission Fee:* $7 adults, $6 seniors, and $3.50 students.

**Wild West City:** This western heritage theme park features 22 live-action shows including a re-enactment of the Gunfight at the OK Corral. There are also miniature train rides, stagecoach rides, pony rides, and a petting zoo. You can even try to strike it rich by panning for gold! Even if you don't find the mother lode, you may turn up a few sparkling rocks and leave with some lasting memories. Be sure to stop by the Golden Nugget Saloon and enjoy a real Western-style stage show. You can also purchase authentic western clothing at the many shops the park has to offer. *Location:* Route 206 North, Netcong, Sussex County. *Phone:* 973-347-8900. *Hours:* May 1 to June 19, weekends from 10:30 A.M. to 6 P.M. June 20 to Labor Day, daily from 10:30 A.M. to 6 P.M. Labor Day through Columbus Day, weekends from 10:30 A.M. to 6 P.M. *Admission Fee:* $7.50 adults, $6.75 children, and $5.25 seniors.

# Outdoors

*River Bend County Park*

**Birch Grove Park**
Burton Avenue
Northfield
Atlantic County
609-641-3778
Open Summer 9 A.M. to 7 P.M.
Rest of year 9 A.M. to 5 P.M.
Entrance fee charged Memorial
    Day through Labor Day
280 acres

**Activities:** baseball, camping, fishing, hiking, picnicking, a playground, soccer, and volleyball.

This municipal park contains five miles of hiking trails, a two-mile fitness trail, live animals on display, a nature center, ponds that are stocked with trout and a food stand.

**Edwin B. Forsythe Wildlife
    Refuge**
Brigantine Division
Great Creek Road
Oceanville
Atlantic County
609-652-1665
Open sunrise to sunset
Entrance fee charged Memorial
    Day through Labor Day
24,000 acres

**Activities:** boating, crabbing, fishing, hiking, and hunting.

Named in honor of the late New Jersey congressman, this refuge is part of a nationwide system of over 500 wildlife areas. Most of the area is tidal-salt meadow and marsh, interspersed with shallow coves and bays. The refuge provides an important resting and feeding habitat for hundreds of thousands of water birds. Over 200,000 people visit this refuge each year and enjoy the self-guided, eight-mile long, wildlife drive through a variety of upland and wetland habitats. There are also two nature trails, less than a half-mile each, which wind through the forest and marshland. The nature center is open weekdays from 8 A.M. to 4 P.M.

**FACT:** *Mays Landing is named after Captain George May, who in 1756 established a trading post and a shipyard near Babcock Creek.*

**Estell Manor County Park**
109 State Highway 50
Mays Landing
Atlantic County
609-645-5960
Open Mon. through Fri. 8 A.M. to
    4 P.M.
Sat., Sun., holidays, 10 A.M. to
    4 P.M.
No entrance fee
1,672 acres

**Activities:** baseball, biking, boating, camping, canoeing, cross-country ski-ing, fishing, hiking, horseback riding, hunting, picnicking, a playground, soccer, and volleyball.

A glassworks factory, once operated and owned by the Estell family in the nineteenth century, is a great place for visitors to explore. During World War I, the Bethlehem Loading Company based their operations here. However, all that remains today are a few decaying structures and railroad beds that are now part of the 13 miles of trails within the park. The Warren E. Fox Nature Center, which is the headquarters for the county park sys-tem, offers educational and environmental programs, guided tours of the park, and rents various recreation equipment.

**Gaskill County Park**
River Drive
Mays Landing
Atlantic County
609-645-5960
Open sunrise to sunset
No entrance fee
10 acres

**Activities:** boating, canoeing, fishing, picnicking, a playground, and vol-leyball.

Located at the bulkhead of the Great Egg Harbor River, this park was part of a shipyard during the mid 1800s. Gaskill Park is now a beauti-fully landscaped park that is ideal for walking or enjoying a quiet picnic. The gazebo in the park is a popular location for weddings and picture taking.

**Lake Lenape County Park**
Harding Highway
Mays Landing
Atlantic County
609-645-5960
Open sunrise to sunset
No entrance fee
1,900 acres

**Activities:** biking, boating, camping, canoeing, cross-country skiing, fishing, hiking, hunting, picnicking, and a playground.

This is the largest park in Atlantic County and includes a 334-acre lake. It is an excellent location for spotting Bald Eagles during the winter months. Visitors can also enjoy the various recreational activities this park has to offer.

**Penny Pot Park**
Eighth Avenue
Folsom
Atlantic County
609-645-5960
Open sunrise to sunset
No entrance fee
20 acres

**Activities:** canoeing, fishing, hiking, hunting, and picnicking.

This park is a favorite starting point for canoe trips along the Great Egg Harbor River. You can travel to Lake Lenape, taking rest stops at Weymouth County Park and Camp Acagisca. The park system does not rent canoes, but other campgrounds in the local area do.

**FACT:** *The earliest inhabitants of New Jersey were the Lenape Indians. The Lenape, which translates into "Original People", belonged to the Algonquian Tribe. The Lenape were a peaceful people and welcomed others into their homeland. The three main foods that the Lenape consumed were corn, beans, and squash, which were not native to this region but originated in South America. The various campsites and planting fields, which the Lenape used, were linked by an extensive network of trails, many of which went on to become colonial roads and later, modern streets.*

**River Bend County Park**
Betsy Scull Road
Egg Harbor
Atlantic County
609-645-5960
Open sunrise to sunset
No entrance fee
535 acres

**Activities:** canoeing, fishing, and hunting.

River Bend is a beautiful and peaceful place to fish or canoe. Hunting is permitted during the winter months.

**Weymouth County Park**
Intersection of Routes 322 and
    559
Hamilton
Atlantic County
609-645-5960
Open sunrise to sunset
No entrance fee
6 acres

**Activities:** canoeing, fishing, and picnicking.

This small park was once the site of the Weymouth Iron Forge. Production began in 1802 and peaked by the 1850s. In addition to the furnace, there was a gristmill, sawmill, church, owner's mansion, blacksmith shop, and workers' houses. During the War of 1812, Weymouth was a major supplier of ammunition for the U.S. Army. However, its prosperity ceased when the forge could no longer compete with anthracite coal-powered forges in Pennsylvania. After the forge burned down in 1862, two papers mills were built on this site and were in operation until 1897. After many years of neglect and vandalism, this area was donated to the county and became a very popular attraction due to its ruins. This is also an excellent place to enjoy a canoe trip along the Lenape River.

### Campgaw Mountain Reservation
Campgaw Road
Mahwah
Bergen County
201-327-7800
Open sunrise to sunset
No entrance fee
1,351 acres

**Activities:** camping, hiking, picnicking, and skiing.

Campgaw has many trails that wind through the peaceful woods. The park features a ski center (201-327-7804) with a 1,650-foot main slope and a total of eight trails (open Mondays to Fridays from 1 P.M. to 10 P.M., Saturdays from 9 A.M. to 10 P.M., and Sundays from 9 A.M. to 5 P.M.). Snow enthusiasts will enjoy skiing, snowboarding, and snow tubing. The visitor's center has a fireplace, snack bar, and pro shop that offers lessons and rents and sells skiing equipment.

### Dahnert's Lake County Park
Midland Avenue
Garfield
Bergen County
201-478-8242
Open sunrise to sunset
No entrance fee
9.5 acres

**Activities:** basketball, bocce, ice-skating, picnicking, and a playground.

The lake is the main attraction and center of activity in this small park. Ice-skating is popular in the winter months and model boat sailing is a frequent sight during the warmer weather.

**FACT:** *In 1700, a widow named Blandina Bayard received an Indian deed to a large block of land, which included most of present day Mahwah. Friendly with the local Indians and fluent in their language, Bayard opened a trading post and constructed the first house in the area. Today, Mahwah is home to one of the largest Ford Motor Company plants in the United States.*

## Darlington County Park
Darlington Avenue
Mahwah
Bergen County
201-327-3500
Open 10 A.M. to 8 P.M.
Entrance fee during swimming
   season
232 acres

**Activities:** basketball, fishing, handball, picnicking, a playground, swimming, tennis, and volleyball.

Two lakes in this park are designated spots for swimming. Both have sandy beaches and are lifeguard supervised. Changing facilities, a snack bar, and comfort stations are only a short walk from the beach. The season starts in early April and ends on November 1. The beaches are open daily from 10 A.M. to 6 P.M. The third lake is a favorite fishing hole for many.

## Flat Rock Brook Nature Center
443 Van Nostrand Avenue
Englewood
Bergen County
201-567-1265
Open sunrise to sunset
No entrance fee
150 acres

**Activities:** bird watching, hiking, picnicking, and a playground.

Flat Rock Brook was founded in 1973 and was intended to protect open space and provide recreational and educational activities. There are 3.2-miles of trails that stretch through wetlands, ponds, and wildflower meadows. There are many opportunities for bird watching throughout the trails. An 800-foot boardwalk trail with rest areas and interpretive signs is available for those who cannot walk the woodland trails but wish to enjoy the beautiful natural settings. There are picnic tables and playground equipment located on Jones Road. The nature center, open Mondays to Fridays from 9 A.M. to 5 P.M., offers educational programs and promotes an understanding of environmental issues.

**James A. McFaul Wildlife Center**
Crescent Avenue
Wyckoff
Bergen County
201-891-5571
Open sunrise to sunset
No entrance fee
81 acres

**Activities:** bird watching, hiking, and picnicking.

The exhibit building is open Mondays to Fridays from 8 A.M. to 4:45 P.M. and weekends from 1 P.M. to 4:45 P.M. Features include an aquarium and a snake display. An observatory overlooks the pond and offers excellent opportunities for viewing wildlife. Among the many attractions are trails through wooded areas and small swamps, live animals on display, and a variety of gardens outside the main building.

**Lorrimer Sanctuary**
790 Ewing Avenue
Franklin Lakes
Bergen County
201-891-2185
Open Tues. to Fri. 9 A.M. to 5 P.M.
    Saturday 10 P.M. to 5 P.M.
    Sunday 1 P.M. to 5 P.M.
No entrance fee
14 acres

**Activities:** bird watching and hiking.

This sanctuary is named after Ms. Lucine Lorrimer, who donated the land in 1956, to the New Jersey Audubon Society. The society promotes environmental awareness and the conservation of plants and animals. The building for the visitor's center dates back to the 1700s and has interpretive displays, hands-on exhibits, and a gift shop. A large window overlooks a

**FACT:** *Franklin Township, one of the oldest towns in Bergen County, was established in 1771. It was named after the last Royal Governor of New Jersey, William Franklin, the son of Benjamin Franklin.*

bird feeding station and a butterfly garden. There are also self-guided nature trails, programs, and natural study workshops.

## Overpeck County Park
Leonia, Palisades Park, and
Ridgefield Park
Bergen County
201-807-0201
Open sunrise to sunset
No entrance fee
661 acres

**The Henry Hoeble Area,** Fort Lee Road, Leonia.
Activities include a fitness area, tennis courts, and a one and one-quarter mile bicycle/pedestrian path.

**Leonia South Area,** Fort Lee Road, Leonia. (Across from Henry Hoeble Area).
Activities include horseback riding, picnicking, a playground, volleyball, and a wildlife refuge area.

**Palisades Park Area,** Roosevelt Street off Grand Avenue, Palisades Park.
Activities include tennis and picnicking.

**Ridgefield Park Area,** Challenger Road off Emerson Road, Ridgefield Park.
Activities include soccer and softball.

## Ramapo Valley County
##     Reservation
584 Ramapo Valley Road
Mahwah
Bergen County
201-325-3500
Open sunrise to sunset
No entrance fee
2,145 acres

**Activities:** camping, canoeing, cross-country skiing, fishing, and hiking.

Fifteen miles of trails traverse through woodlands and hillsides and offer spectacular views of the area and its wildlife. The Ramapo River is ideal for fishing, canoeing, and camping along its riverbanks. A bridge next to a picturesque waterfall is near the park entrance.

### Richard W. DeKorte Park
2 Dekorte Park Plaza
Lyndhurst
Bergen County
201-460-8300
Open sunrise to sunset
No entrance fee
110 acres

**Activities:** boating, canoeing, fishing, and hiking.

Once a landfill, this area has now returned to its natural wetland habitat thanks to New Jersey Senate Majority Leader, Richard DeKorte, who was very instrumental in the passage of legislation to create this park. Wetlands are very beneficial since they cleanse the water of pollutants and provide food and shelter to many species of wildlife including over 260 types of birds. The visitor's center is open daily from 10 A.M. to 3 P.M. and is glass-enclosed to provide spectacular views of the meadowlands. The visitor's center also features a 288-seat auditorium, a conference room, and a 1,000-gallon brackish creek exhibit stocked with animals native to the area. The environmental center is open Mondays to Fridays from 9 A.M. to 3 P.M. and weekends from 10 A.M. to 3 P.M. It features an informational exhibit about solid waste and associated environmental problems as well as an exhibit about the history of the interaction between people and the meadowlands. The Trash Museum, located inside the center, showcases the thousands of objects that can be found in landfills. The Lyndhurst Nature Reserve, a small 2.5-acre tract, has an outdoor amphitheater that is perfect for bird watching and observing wildlife. There are a number of trails that lead through the meadowlands including the Marsh Discovery Trail, the first barrier-free marsh nature trail in the state.

### Riverside County Park
Lyndhurst and
North Arlington
Bergen County
201-935-7742
Open sunrise to sunset
No entrance fee
110 acres

**The Joseph A. Carucci, Jr. Area,** Riverside Avenue, Lyndhurst.
Activities include bocce, horseshoes, picnicking, concession operated batting cages, a seven-mile bicycle pedestrian path along the river, tennis, and an 18-station fitness trail.

**South Area,** River Road, North Arlington.
Activities include baseball, horseshoes, picnicking, a playground, tennis, and a six-tenths of a mile bicycle/pedestrian path that travels along the river.

**Saddle River County Park**
Ridgefield, Saddle Brook and
Rochelle Park
Bergen County
201-444-8843
Open sunrise to Sunset
No entrance fee
596 acres

**Wild Duck Pond Area,** East Ridgefield Avenue, Ridgefield.
Activities include fishing, horseshoes, ice-skating, picnicking, a playground, and shuffleboard.

**Glen Rock Area,** Alan Avenue, East of Prospect Street.
Activities include fishing, picnicking, a playground, and tennis.

**Dunkerhook Area,** East Ridgefield Avenue, Ridgefield.
Activities include picnicking and tennis.

**Otto C. Pehle Area,** Saddle River Road, Saddle Brook.
Activities include biking, fishing, and horseshoes.

**Rochelle Park Area,** Railroad Avenue, Rochelle Park.
Activities include picnicking, a playground, tennis, and a one-mile trail that follows along the river.

This major park system includes two main trails. The North Trail is a five-mile loop, running along the Saddle River between the towns of Fair Lawn and Ridgewood. It begins at Williams and Union streets in Fairlawn and ends in the vicinity of the Wild Duck Pond in Ridgefield. The South Trail, which is 3 miles, crosses the Otto and Rochelle Park Areas.

**Samuel Nelkin County Park**
Rose Street, off Paterson Ave
Wallington
Bergen County
201-778-6184
Open sunrise to sunset
No entrance fee
23 acres

**Activities:** baseball, fishing, ice-skating, picnicking, a playground, sledding, and tennis.

Ice-skating is popular in the winter months, while model boat sailing is a frequent sight in the warmer weather.

**Tenafly Nature Center**
313 Hudson Avenue
Tenafly
Bergen County
201-568-6093
Grounds open sunrise to sunset
Parking lot open 9 A.M. to 5 P.M.
No entrance fee
52 acres

**Activities:** cross-country skiing, hiking, ice-skating, and picnicking.

The adjoining Lost Brook Preserve adds another 330 acres to this nature center. There are over six miles of trails through peaceful woodland surroundings. This is an ideal spot for bird watching because of its location along the Atlantic Flyway. Hundreds of birds rest here during the spring and fall migrations and over 50 species build permanent nests here. The nature center contains exhibits, programs, a library, and a store.

**Van Saun County Park**
Forest and Continental Avenues
Paramus
Bergen County
201-262-2627
Open 9 A.M. to sunset
No entrance fee
140 acres

**Activities:** fishing, ice-skating, picnicking, a playground, and tennis.

The Continental Army camped in this area from September 4 to September 20, 1780. A spring that runs through the park provided fresh water for the troops. It is said that General Washington drank from this spring while reviewing his troops on September 13, and in remembrance of this, the area has been given the name "Washington Spring Garden." The gardens, as well as all of the other attractions in this park, are open for visitors.

The Bergen County Zoological Park (201-262-3771) is also located here and has 24 species of mammals, 19 species of birds, and 16 species of reptiles. There is also a 1860s-style farmyard, complete with live animals such as pigs, cows, and goats. A replica of an 1866 steam locomotive circles the zoo and is a popular attraction with the children. A stable area located adjacent to the zoo, offers pony rides to the children for a nominal fee.

Van Saun also has an education center (201-262-4082) and a 12-court concession operated tennis center (201-265-1028), which includes a practice wall, locker rooms, and a pro shop with instructors available. The tennis center is open from March 27 to November 7; hours are weekdays from 9 A.M. to sunset and weekends from 8 A.M. to sunset.

**Wood Dale County Park**
Prospect Avenue
Woodcliff Lake
Bergen County
201-391-6707
Open sunrise to sunset
No entrance fee
52 acres

**Activities:** fishing, ice-skating, model-boat sailing, picnicking, a playground, and tennis.

The central attraction to this park is a beautiful pond, where fishing, model-boat sailing, and picnicking are favorite activities.

**Bass River State Forest**
Stage Road
New Gretna
Burlington County
609-296-1114
Open sunrise to sunset
Entrance fee from Memorial Day
    through Labor Day
18,208 acres

**FACT:** *Shorebirds use flyways, timing their arrivals at the best stopping places for feeding. Many of the birds using the Atlantic Flyway start at the southern tip of South America and fly across the Caribbean until they reach the United States. The shorebirds usually make stops in Maryland, Virginia, and Delaware before heading to Canada.*

**Activities:** boating, camping, canoeing, fishing, hiking, horseback riding, hunting, picnicking, a playground, and swimming.

The state began acquiring land for this park in 1905. It was preserved for public recreation, water conservation, and wildlife and timber management. The Absegami Nature Area is rich with many native plants, animals, and birds. A half-mile nature trail begins at the 67-acre Lake Absegami and leads you through woodlands filled with oak, white-cedar and pine trees. A nature center is located in the south camping area and serves as a contact point for nature study.

Swimming is permitted in Lake Absegami and it is lifeguard supervised. Changing facilities, beach supplies, and a snack bar are located nearby. A boathouse, open during the summer, rents paddleboats and rowboats. There are 178 family campsites, six fully enclosed lean-tos, and three large, group campsites available for those who want to enjoy this park for an extended stay. The park also has six cabins, if you prefer, located in a peaceful wooded area beside the lake. Each cabin has a living room, fireplace, bathroom, two bunkrooms, a kitchen and can house up to six people. All sites have modern conveniences located close by.

**Lebanon State Forest**
Route 72
New Lisbon
Burlington County
609-726-1191
Open sunrise to sunset
No entrance fee
32,012 acres

**Activities:** biking, camping, hiking, horseback riding, hunting, and picnicking.

The Pine Barrens is an area rich in natural resources such as sand and wood for charcoal, which are necessary for the glass manufacturing industry. Throughout the years, there have been numerous factories producing glass products, based in the Pine Barrens. This park is named after the most successful of these factories, the Lebanon Glass Works, which was established in 1851 and operated until 1867. The factory's insatiable need for fuel to feed its furnaces led to the radical depletion of the surrounding woodlands. By 1867, after most of the forests were devoured, the factory closed. In 1908, the state purchased a tract of land and began to replant trees and establish forest management practices. Before long, the land was again flourishing with pine, oak, and maple trees.

The 737-acre Cedar Swamp Nature Area contains Atlantic white cedar and is surrounded by pine forests. It supports endangered plant species and many birds. There are several trails in this nature area as well as miles of trails throughout the park that pass near ruins of long forgotten villages and towns.

One of these forgotten villages, Whitesbog Village, was a cranberry and blueberry producing community during the late nineteenth and early twentieth centuries. The village is currently undergoing extensive restoration and is open for exploration. Several of the cranberry bogs are still farmed and harvested each year by private companies. The Whitesbog Preservation Trust (609-893-4646) oversees preservation and restoration of the village.

Pakim Pond, originally a reservoir for a cranberry bog, contains a picnic area and many camping sites. Camping areas are open April through October and include nearby modern facilities and spaces for tents. The three cabins near the south shore of the pond, which can be rented for up to two weeks, include a furnished living room, fireplace, bunk beds for four people, and a kitchen with a refrigerator.

There are many miles of trails, including sections of the Batona Trail, which connects Lebanon State Forest to Bass River State Forest and, at almost 50-miles long, is New Jersey's longest hiking trail. Camping is permitted at Batona Camp, which is located near the Carranza Memorial, the crash site of Captain Emilio Carranza, Mexico's foremost aviator. Carranza's plane crashed while he was returning home from New York. His voyage was to repay a goodwill flight made to Mexico by his friend, Charles Lindberg.

*Carranza Memorial*

**Rancocas Nature Center**
795 Rancocas Road
Mount Holly
Burlington County
609-261-2495
Open Tuesdays through Sundays
    from 9 A.M. to 5 P.M.
No entrance fee
120 acres

**Activities:** fishing and hiking.

The New Jersey Audubon Society operates the Rancocas Nature Center. The center operates out of a farmhouse that dates back to the 1800s and sits on 120 acres of undeveloped land. Natural history exhibits, hands-on displays, and a small museum that interprets the natural history of the Rancocas Valley are located inside the building. The bookshop contains many field guides and naturists tools. In addition, there are numerous programs and workshops for people of all ages. Information regarding the hiking trails that wind through the park and lead to the Rancocas River can also be obtained. This is a great place to enjoy nature and observe many species of wildlife.

**Berlin Park**
Park Drive
Berlin
Camden County
609-795-7275
Open 6 A.M. to 10 P.M.
No entrance fee
152 acres

**Activities:** baseball, basketball, biking, fishing, hiking, an in-line hockey rink, picnicking, a playground, tennis, and volleyball.

There are many activities to enjoy here, including fishing in the Great Egg Harbor River, which cuts through the park. There are over five miles of trails that are suitable for walking or bicycle riding. The Camden County Environmental Studies Center, which is open Mondays through Fridays from 8:30 A.M. to 4:30 P.M., is located on Park Drive at Broad Avenue and includes a reference library and a collection of exhibits on natural history. In addition, several educational and on-site nature programs are offered.

## Challenge Grove
Corner of Caldwell and Brace
    Roads
Cherry Hill
Camden County
609-795-7275
Open 6 A.M. to 12 A.M.
No entrance fee
18 acres

**Activities:** baseball, basketball, biking, boccie, hiking, picnicking, and a playground.

The Cooper River runs through this beautiful park, which is a great place to enjoy a day off. There are paths for walking and biking and a quarter-mile running track and fitness area.

## Cooper River Park
South Park Drive
Cherry Hill
Camden County
609-795-7275
Open 6 A.M. to 12 A.M.
No entrance fee
347 acres

**Activities:** baseball, biking, boating, canoeing, cross-country skiing, fishing, fitness trail, hiking, picnicking, a playground, and volleyball.

This is a linear park that runs parallel with the Cooper River and features several quiet trails and picnic areas. A four mile paved trail is ideal for walking, running, or bicycle ridding.

The Hopkins House (250 South Park Drive, Haddon Township, 856-858-0040) was built in the 1740s by Ebenezer Hopkins, a wealthy and prominent citizen. Today this well preserved Georgian-style building houses the offices and gallery of the Camden County Cultural and Heritage Commission.

Cooper River Park also includes the Cooper River Yacht Club

**FACT:** *Camden County was named after Charles Pratt, the Earl of Camden and an English nobleman who supported the American cause in Parliament.*

(Collingswood, 856-869-9145), Jack Curtis Stadium (North Park Drive, Pennsauken), and The Lobster Trap (North Park Drive, Pennsauken, open daily 11 A.M. to 10 P.M.), a restaurant overlooking the Cooper River. Two unique features of Cooper River Park are the heated driving range (Route 130 South at the Airport Intersection, Pennsauken, 856-486-7737) and Pooch Park (North Park Drive, Pennsauken), a dog park that has separate facilities for large and small dogs to run leash free.

**New Brooklyn Park**
Between New Freedom and
 Brooklyn Roads
Winslow
Camden County
609-795-7275
Open 6 A.M. to 10 P.M.
No entrance fee
759 acres

**Activities:** amphitheater, baseball, basketball, biking, boating, canoeing, fishing, in-line hockey, picnicking, a playground, and volleyball.

The 100-acre New Brooklyn Lake, featured in this park, is a great place for fishing and boating. There are numerous open fields in this park and a variety of activities to enjoy.

**Newton Lake Park**
Cuthbert Boulevard
Haddon
Camden County
609-795-7275
Open 6 A.M. to 10 P.M.
No entrance fee
104 acres

**Activities:** biking, boating, cross-country skiing, fishing, picnicking, a playground, and volleyball.

Several miles of paved trails extend through this park and are ideal for both walking and bicycle riding. The 25-acre Newton Lake is an exceptional spot for fishing. There are piers at Matrimony Avenue, Lees Lane, and Beetleweed Avenue and a boat ramp is available for small, car-top boats. A unique attraction of this park is the miniature golf course.

## Belleplain State Forest
County Route 550
Woodbine
Cape May County
609-861-2404
Open sunrise to sunset
Fee charged only for day use
    area from Memorial Day to
    Labor Day
15,660 acres

**Activities:** boating, camping, cross-country skiing, fishing, hiking, horse-back riding, hunting, picnicking, a playground, and swimming.

Belleplain State Forest was established in 1928, as a reserve for public recreation, wildlife management, and conservation of water supplies. The woodlands contain pine, oak, and southern white cedar trees. The old Meisle Cranberry Bog, which was converted into a 26-acre lake, is the centerpiece for recreational activities. The bog has been renamed Lake Nummy, in honor of the last Lenni Lenape Indian Chief who ruled this area. A one and a half-mile nature trail begins at the picnic area and encircles the lake, thus providing magnificent views of the natural surroundings.

A swimming beach, located on the northern side of Lake Nummy, is lifeguard supervised and contains a bathhouse, a playground, and refreshment stand. It is open from Memorial Day through Labor Day.

A boat rental facility operates during the summer months. A fitness trail with eight stations is located along a mile of gravel running track and a six and a half-mile hiking trail connects Lake Nummy with the 65-acre East Creek Pond. Fishing is permitted in both bodies of water.

There are 188 family campsites located near Lake Nummy, which have picnic tables and fire rings. Many sites can accommodate a camping trailer and modern conveniences are nearby. There are 14 fully enclosed lean-tos, each having one unfurnished room that can accommodate up to six people. Two adjacent group campsites are west of the lake and can accommodate 75 people. A third of all the campsites and lean-tos are open year-round.

The East Creek Lodge, on the southern shore of East Creek Pond, can accommodate groups of up to 24 people and is available for overnight rentals. Lodge amenities include a fireplace, kitchen with refrigerator, bathroom, and central heating. A small boat ramp is located at the lake.

**FACT:** *The United States produces nearly 85% of the world's cranberries. New Jersey ranks third in overall cranberry output with approximately 4,000 acres devoted to its production.*

**Cape May Bird Observatory**
Northwood Center
701 East Lake Drive
Cape May Point
Cape May County
609-884-2736
Open 10 A.M. to 5 P.M.
No entrance fee
0.5 acres

**Activities:** bird watching.

John James Audubon and Alexander Wilson both studied and painted in this house during the 1830s. Both had published numerous books on natural history and on the study of birds. In 1975, Anne Northwood donated the house and a half-acre of land to the New Jersey Audubon Society. This nature center is very close to Cape May's popular birding hotspots and is a great informational resource. A store that sells books, optical equipment, and gifts is located inside the house. In addition, many natural history educational programs are offered. A butterfly garden and bird feeding stations, where many species of birds and wildlife can be viewed, are adjacent to the house.

**Cape May County Park**
Route 9 and Crest Haven Road
Cape May Court House
Cape May County
609-465-5271
Open 9 A.M. to sunset
No entrance fee
184 acres

**Activities:** biking, fishing, hiking, picnicking, and a playground.

Cape May County Park features both a zoo and a recreation area. A beautiful gazebo, located in the middle of a pond, is a favorite site for photographs. There are also several nature trails that traverse through the woods. The zoo, which is open from 10 A.M. to 4:45 P.M., is located on 80 acres of land and contains about 250 species of animals, birds and reptiles. Cape May County Park East is across the street and features tennis and basketball courts and a baseball field.

## Cape May Migratory Bird Refuge

Sunset Boulevard
Lower Township
Cape May County
609-861-0600
Open sunrise to sunset
No entrance Fee
212 acres

**Activities:** bird watching and hiking.

This was once part of a Victorian-era resort town called "South Cape May." The town was destroyed and most of it collapsed underwater during a fierce storm in the early 1950s. Debris from houses washes up on the mile-long beach of this bird refuge even to this day. This site was kept as an open meadow for farming and cattle grazing until 1981, when the Nature Conservancy acquired it for use as a migratory bird refuge. This area is located along the Atlantic Flyway and provides spectacular bird watching opportunities during the spring and fall migration seasons.

## Cape May Point State Park

Lighthouse Avenue
Cape May Point
Cape May County
609-884-2159
Open sunrise to sunset
Entrance fee from Memorial Day
    through Labor Day
190 acres

**Activities:** bird watching, fishing, hiking, picnicking, and swimming.

Located at the southern most point of New Jersey, this state park was once used as a coastal defense base during World War II. The base was deactivated in 1963 and the land was transferred over to the state. The military buildings were renovated and are now used as the park office, visitor's center, and museum. The Environmental Education Center, which displays the cultural heritage of the Cape May region, has an exhibit on "Cape May Diamonds," the smooth, clear, quartz pebbles that are found on nearby beaches. In addition, there's a bird migration display, a shoreline erosion display, and a Native American display. Environmental programs and workshops are also offered.

The park includes 153-acre preserve that features wetlands, forests, and ocean beach habitats, which contain many species of plants and animals. It is used as a resting area for many species of birds, especially during the spring and fall migration seasons. A hawk platform overlooks the area and provides great views. There are many hiking paths including a one and a half-mile nature trail.

Visitors may climb to the top of the 157-foot tall Cape May Lighthouse, to glimpse the spectacular views. The lighthouse, constructed in 1859, is the third such structure built in this area. The first two were lost to beach erosion and have since fallen into the sea. The adjacent oil shed has been converted into a welcome center and gift shop (609-884-5404).

**Corson's Inlet State Park**
Ocean Highway (Route 619)
Ocean City
Cape May County
609-861-2404
Open sunrise to sunset
No entrance fee
861 acres

**Activities:** biking, boating, crabbing, fishing, and hiking.

This is one of the few undisturbed stretches of coastline between Atlantic City and Cape May. Corson's Inlet is a known nesting area for shore birds in the spring and summer. It is also situated along the migration path for dolphins and Monarch Butterflies. Guided walking tours of the beach are offered twice a week from late spring to early fall. Visitors can also enjoy the numerous hiking and nature trails that the park has to offer. There is also access to a boat ramp, which is located near the parking lot.

**FACT:** *On December 15th, 1901, a fierce storm forced the 329-foot, four-masked ship the Sindia, to run aground on the Ocean City beach. The ship, which was owned by the Standard Oil Company, was en route from Kobe, Japan to New York City. Fortunately, its 33-member crew was rescued and much of its cargo was salvaged. Until recently, the Sindia's hull could be seen jutting out of the sand on the 17th street beach. A beach replacement project covered the last remaining visible evidence of the ship.*

## Higbee Beach Wildlife Area
New England Road (Route 641)
Lower Township
Cape May County
609-292-2965
Open sunrise to sunset
No entrance fee
940 acres

**Activities:** bird watching, fishing, and hiking.

"Cape May Diamonds" (see page 85) may be found all along the one and a half-miles of beach. A jetty on the north end is a favorite spot for fishing. Several hundred acres of wooded upland, including two freshwater ponds, a hardwood swamp, and old farm fields provide shelter for migratory birds. This is one of the last remaining coastal dune forests in the area, with dunes that can reach as high as 20 feet is some places. A viewing platform and two miles of nature trails provide great access for observing this natural area. It is a great place for bird watching, especially during the spring and fall migration seasons. The Monarch Butterfly can also be spotted here.

## Nature Center of Cape May
1600 Delaware Avenue
Cape May
Cape May County
609-898-8848
Open Tuesdays to Saturdays
    from 10 A.M. to 3 P.M. and
    Summers, daily from 9 A.M.
    to 4:30 P.M.
No entrance fee
18 acres

**Activities:** bird watching.

Founded in 1992 and adopted by the New Jersey Audubon Society in 1995, this nature center is located along the shores of the Cape May Harbor. The grounds include an herb garden, a butterfly garden, and wildlife meadows, where many species of birds can be found. The nature center features natural history displays, interpretive exhibits, locally collected marine life, and a main classroom that can accommodate up to 70 people. Field trips and workshops are also offered. Do not forget to visit the gift shop, which sells books and other items.

## Wetlands Institute

1075 Stone Harbor Boulevard
Stone Harbor
Cape May County
609-368-1211
Open May 15 to October 15,
    Mondays to Saturdays from
    9:30 A.M. to 4:30 P.M. and
    Sundays from 10 A.M. to 4 P.M.
October 16 to May 14, Tuesdays
    to Saturdays from 9:30 A.M. to
    4:30 P.M.
$5 adults, $3 children
6,000 acres

**Activities:** bird watching, hiking, and picnicking.

The Wetlands Institute, founded in 1969, attracts over 40,000 visitors a year. It promotes an appreciation for the wetlands, the most productive ecosystem in the world. You can climb to the top of the 40-foot observation tower to experience the magnificent 360-degree panoramic view. A hiking trail takes you through the salt marshes and stops at a 125-foot long pier, which extends out over the bay. The world's largest display of laughing gulls is also located here. Guided walks are offered in-season daily at 10 A.M., Noon, and 2 P.M. The Institute also has an aquarium, a children's discovery room containing games and hands-on exhibits, and a museum.

## Bridgeton City Park

Mayor Aiken Drive
Bridgeton
Cumberland County
609-445-3230
Open sunrise to sunset
No entrance fee
1,100 acres

**Activities:** an amphitheatre, boating, fishing, hiking, picnicking, a playground, and swimming.

There are three museums located here. The Nail Mill Museum, once the main office of the Cumberland Nail and Iron Company, displays artifacts from the early Colonial period and the American Revolution. This museum is open April through December, Tuesdays to Fridays from 10 A.M. to 3:30 P.M. and weekends from 11 A.M. to 4 P.M. Admission is free. For further information call 609-455-4100.

The New Sweden Farmstead Museum, which is a replica of a seventeenth century farmstead, features walkthroughs of log cabin homes, a blacksmith shop, storehouses, a barn, a stable, and authentic artifacts from Sweden and the Swedish immigrants who populated the area. This museum is open May through September, Saturdays from 11 A.M. to 5 P.M. and Sundays from Noon to 5 P.M. For further information call 609-455-9785. There is a fee for admission.

The Hall of Fame All Sports Museum, located in the Burt Avenue Recreation Area, features sports memorabilia displays dedicated to the teams and athletes of New Jersey. This museum is open year-round, Tuesdays to Saturdays from 10 A.M. to Noon and again from 1 P.M. to 3 P.M. For further information call 609-451-7300.

Also of interest is The Cohanzick Zoo, the first zoo ever established in New Jersey, which includes an impressive display of animals, birds, and reptiles. The featured attractions, which no one should miss, are the beautiful and rare white Bengal tigers.

Visitors may also swim in Sunset Lake, which is lifeguard supervised, or enjoy a picnic and visit to the amphitheatre, where children's productions and festivals are held.

**Branch Brook Park**
Park Ave and Lake Street
Newark
Essex County
973-857-8530
Open sunrise to sunset
No entrance fee
360 acres

**Activities:** baseball, basketball, hiking, horseshoes, picnicking, a playground, and tennis.

Named for the Branch Brook, which flows through the area, this four-mile long park is the largest in Essex County. It was officially opened in 1895 and holds the distinction of being the first county park to be opened for public use in the United States. This park was once a former army-training center during the Civil War. During World War I and World War II, it was used as a cantonment area for training exercises and contained a landing strip for the post office ensuring the speedy arrival of mail.

A greenhouse, built in 1910, is the horticultural center of the park. Many cherry trees blossom during the month of April. During its peak, thousands of people per day visit Branch Book Park to enjoy this magnificent sight.

This popular destination also features many other attractions including a roller rink. The park system's Administration Building and Senior Citizens Center are also located here.

**Brookdale Park**
Bellevue Avenue
Montclair and Bloomfield
Essex County
973-857-8530
Open sunrise to sunset
No entrance fee
121 acres

**Activities:** baseball, basketball, biking, fitness stations, picnicking, a playground, a running track, soccer, and tennis.

To early settlers, the area that would become Brookdale Park was known as "Stone House Plains." These Dutch immigrants, who settled the area in the early eighteenth century, cultivated the land for farming and grazing their herds. The park features a one-acre pond and a beautiful formal rose garden, which was planted by the North Jersey Rose Society.

**Eagle Rock Reservation**
Prospect & Eagle Rock Avenue
West Orange
Essex County
973-857-8530
Open sunrise to sunset
No entrance fee
408 acres

**Activities:** baseball, hiking, horseback riding, and picnicking.

Bald eagles nesting along the rocky cliffs on the eastern edge of the mountains were a common sight in the early nineteenth century, giving this reservation the name "Eagle Rock." Though most of this area is still in a pristine natural state, there are a number of hiking trails that wind through the red oak forests and maple wetlands. During the late 1890s, this area became a popular destination for picnickers due to its high elevation and magnificent views of the surrounding area. An Italian-style country dwelling, situated on the edge of a cliff, was built in 1911 and is home to the Highlawn Pavilion Restaurant.

## Grover Cleveland Park

Brookside Ave. & Runnymede Rd.
Essex Fells
Essex County
973-857-8530
Open sunrise to sunset
No entrance fee
42 acres

**Activities:** baseball, fishing, horseshoes, ice-skating, picnicking, a playground, and shuffleboard.

This park was named in honor of Grover Cleveland, the 22nd and 24th president of the United States, who was born in the nearby town of Caldwell. The land was once home to a sawmill, which would grind tanbark to manufacture paper. Now, only a footbridge near the far end of a pond marks the location of the sawmill. The heavily wooded area is perfect for long, peaceful walks.

## Irvington Park

Grove Street and Lyons Avenue
Irvington
Essex County
973-857-8530
Open sunrise to sunset
No entrance fee
24 acres

**Activities:** baseball, basketball, fishing, ice-skating, a playground, a running track, and tennis.

Irvington Park opened in 1913 and features a 1.65-acre pond with many beautiful trees including red oaks, mulberries and elms, lining the banks. A

**FACT:** *Aaron Burr Jr., an Essex County resident, was born in 1767. He served under General Washington and gained the rank of Major. After the Revolution, Burr became the attorney general of New York and later the Vice President of the United States. However, Aaron Burr is most noted in history for mortally wounding Alexander Hamilton in a duel at Weehawken on July 11, 1804.*

one and a half-mile jogging track encircles the pond, providing a full view of the natural beauty.

**Orange Park**
Center Street and Harrison Street
Orange
Essex County
973-857-8530
Open sunrise to sunset
No entrance fee
48 acres

**Activities:** baseball, basketball, fishing, a playground, and soccer.

Orange Park was once a marshy bog, unsuitable for most development. The Township of Orange, at the urging of its residents, purchased the land and made preparations to reclaim the open space and preserve it as a park. By 1899, the bog had been drained and excavated. A small, one and a half-acre pond was created and residents began planting beautiful flowers. Today, the colorful, formal flower garden is a main attraction for visitors.

**Riker Hill Art Park**
Beaufort Avenue
Livingston
Essex County
973-857-8530
Open sunrise to sunset
No entrance fee
205 acres

**Activities:** hiking.

A major portion of this park was a Nike missile tracking-base during the 1950s, but with the decommissioning of those missiles, the base was abandoned. The county purchased the land in 1977 and converted the barracks into art studios. This has become a cultural center for the county with artists, sculptors, and craftsmen all plying their skills in the studios. They conduct classes in such crafts as woodworking, glassblowing, painting, and also show their work to grateful audiences. There is also a geological museum and craft center for visitors to browse through. An impressive outdoor sculpture collection is displayed along the main road. The collection was a donation to the park and is valued at over $250,000. Located nearby is the 16-acre Dinosaur Park, the site of the smallest dinosaur tracks ever discovered.

## South Mountain Reservation

South Orange Ave and Cherry
    Lane
West Orange
Essex County
973-857-8530
Open sunrise to sunset
No entrance fee
2047 acres

**Activities:** an archery range, cross-country skiing, fishing, hiking, horseback riding, and picnicking.

Preserved in its natural state, this reservation includes dense woodlands, creeks, ponds, and the west branch of the Rahway River. A 25-foot waterfall, Hemlock Falls, is located in the woods by a pond. There are 19 miles of trails and 27 miles of carriage roads for jogging, horseback riding, and, weather allowing, cross-country skiing. The Turtle Back Zoo is located here and so is the South Mountain Arena with its two indoor ice-skating facilities. The roadway on Crest Drive is restricted to cars and used exclusively for walking. The area near Crest Drive was once the site of a signal station that was constructed during the Revolutionary War. This signal station was one of 23 beacons that General George Washington ordered to be built so British troop movements could be observed. It was from this outlook, on June 23, 1780, that local militias were warned of a British attack at the Hobart Gap, a natural pathway to Washington's troops camped at Morristown. The advanced warnings helped the Continental Army avoid a costly defeat. This signal system was also in service during the War of 1812.

## Vailsburg Park

South Orange Ave and Oraton
    Parkway
Newark
Essex County
973-857-8530
Open sunrise to sunset
No entrance fee
30 acres

**Activities:** baseball, basketball, bocce, picnicking, a playground, and soccer.

The Army used this area for training and recruiting, during World War I and World War II. In 1952, the Army established an anti-aircraft gun site on a small portion of this park, but it was demolished in 1960. Vailsburg Park features many athletic activities and a spacious picnic area. The park also has a senior citizens center.

**Verona Park**
Bloomfield Ave and Lakeside
    Avenue
Verona
Essex County
973-857-8530
Open sunrise to sunset
No entrance fee
54 acres

**Activities:** baseball, boating, bocce, fishing, a playground, and tennis.

The lake first formed in 1814, when the Peckman River was dammed to provide power for a gristmill. This artificial 13-acre lake, surrounded by weeping willows, became an ideal location for local residents even before it was designated an official park. An ornamental bridge over the lake is a popular site for taking wedding photographs. A boathouse, open during the summer, rents rowboats and paddleboats. Crafts shows and concerts are held around the gazebo.

**Watseeing Park**
Bloomfield Ave and Conger
    Street
Bloomfield
Essex County
973-857-8530
Open sunrise to sunset
No entrance fee
70 acres

**Activities:** baseball, basketball, a playground, and soccer.

Watseeing is a name derived from the combination of the Lenni-Lenape Indians words for hill (*Watschu*) and stone (*Assan*). A senior citizens building, a bandstand and a lawn bowling green, one of the few and considered the best in the state, are all located here.

**Weequahic Park**
Elizabeth Meeker Avenues
Newark
Essex County
973-857-8530
Open sunrise to sunset
No entrance fee
311 acres

**Activities:** baseball, basketball, picnicking, a playground, and tennis.

From 1900 to 1960, this park was known as the Waverly Fair Grounds. At that time, the 80-acre Weequahic Lake was a popular site for canoe races and amateur trotter racing was held at the half-mile long racetrack, attracting thousands of people who watched from the grandstand. Although the races have ceased and the grandstand is long gone, this area is still a popular place to visit. Runners now use the track and there is a beautiful, formal garden available for a leisurely stroll through.

**Greenwich Lake Park**
Tomlin Station Road
Gibbstown
Gloucester County
856-468-0100
Open sunrise to sunset
No entrance fee
75 acres

**Activities:** boating, fishing, picnicking, a playground, and swimming.

The 40-acre Greenwich Lake is stocked with trout and has a beach open for swimming, which is lifeguard supervised. The beach is open from April to November 30. There are a wide variety of plants and animals flourishing

**FACT:** *Attached to a private home located at 406 Swedesboro Road in Gibbstown, stands the Nothnagle Log Cabin. This cabin is believed to be the oldest standing wooden structure in North America.*

in the wetlands that surround the lake. A boat launch is open on weekends from the beginning of trout season to Memorial Day and then on a daily basis until Labor Day.

**James G. Atkinson Park**
Delsea Drive and Bethel Mill Rd
Sewell
Gloucester County
856-589-0047
Open sunrise to sunset
No entrance fee
60 acres

**Activities:** baseball, basketball, biking, fitness stations, picnicking, a playground, soccer, and tennis.

There are many activities to enjoy in this beautiful park. There is over a mile of biking and jogging trails. Free concerts are held every Sunday during June, July, and August and the picnic pavilion can accommodate reservations for large groups.

**Red Bank Battlefield Park**
100 Hessian Avenue
National Park
Gloucester County
856-853-5120
Open sunrise to sunset
No entrance fee
44 acres

**Activities:** picnicking and a playground.

After the Battle of Red Bank, which took place during the Revolutionary War, James and Ann Whithall's house served as the local hospital. This beautifully preserved house was built in 1748. It is open for visits free of charge, Wednesdays to Fridays from 9 A.M. to 4 P.M. and on the weekends from April through October from 1 P.M. to 4 P.M. The remains of Fort Mercer, where the actual battle took place, are in the northern section of the park. A 75-foot monument, erected near the house in 1905, is dedicated to the battle. The park also features picnic areas and numerous riverfront pathways, piers, and pavilions to enjoy.

## Scotland Run Park
2106 Clayton-Williamstown Road
Clayton
Gloucester County
856-881-0846
Open sunrise to sunset
No entrance fee
940 acres

**Activities:** boating, fishing, hiking, picnicking and a playground.

Scotland Run Park includes the 80-acre Wilson Lake, where boating and fishing are popular activities. A boat launch and a fishing pier are located in the northern portion of the lake. A beautiful arboretum, next to Wilson Lake, features several peaceful nature trails. The nature center, located across from the lake, sponsors many environmental and nature programs and displays artifacts from the early settlements of the South Jersey Area. The center is open Tuesdays to Thursdays from 8 A.M. to 2 P.M.

## Bayonne County Park
J.F. Kennedy Boulevard
Bayonne
Hudson County
201-915-1385
Open sunrise to sunset
No entrance fee
98 acres

**Activities:** bird watching, fishing, picnicking, a playground, and a running track.

This park provides a shade of green on the city. At 16 city-blocks long, it includes a running track and a picturesque walkway along the waterfront. It is an excellent location for observing the spring and fall bird migrations. A pier, extending out into Newark Bay, provides fishing opportunities.

**FACT:** *The town of National Park was originally referred to as "Roder Udden". This term, from the Swedish language, meaning Red Bank, arose from the reddish color of the soil in the high Delaware River bank.*

**James J. Braddock Park**
Kennedy Boulevard
North Bergen
Hudson County
201-319-3747
Open sunrise to sunset
No entrance fee
167 acres

**Activities:** bird watching and fishing.

Once known as North Hudson Park, this recreational facility is now named after a local boxer who was elected into the Boxing Hall of Fame in 1964. Nestled inside the park is Woodcliff Lake, which contains two small islands that are protected bird sanctuaries.

**Liberty State Park**
Morris Pesin Drive
Jersey City
Hudson County
201-915-3400
Open sunrise to sunset
No entrance fee
1,122 acres

**Activities:** biking, boating, fishing, picnicking, a playground, and swimming.

During the nineteenth and early twentieth centuries, before Liberty State Park existed, this was the site of a major waterfront industrial area with an extensive freight and passenger transportation network. The main terminal for the Central Railroad of New Jersey was built here in 1889 and helped serve the rush of immigration into the United States. At its peak, as many

**FACT:** *The inspiration for the blockbuster motion picture film, "Rocky", came while little known actor, Sylvester Stallone, was watching the Ali vs. Wepner fight. Chuck Wepner, born in Bayonne, was a liqueur salesman and a part time boxer. Wepner was given the opportunity of a lifetime when he was chosen to fight Muhammad Ali. Although Wepner lost the fight, he did manage to land a knockdown punch on Ali.*

as 28,000 people per day from nearby Ellis Island passed through this station on their way to a new life.

The southern portion of this area served as a munitions depot during
World War I and was the site of the infamous "Black Tom" explosion,
which happened in 1916. Freight cars loaded with munitions and other
supplies bound for Europe were waiting to be loaded onto nearby transport ships, when an explosion ripped through the site. It was believed to
have been an act of sabotage.

With the advancement in highways, bridges, and tunnels during the
1950s and 1960s, interstate-trucking companies began to outdo rail transportation in freight hauling, thus causing the railroad industry to rapidly
decline. The Central Railroad ceased operations and the land was abandoned and fell into ruin. The state purchased the land with the intention of
creating a public recreational facility, which officially opened in 1976.

The Interpretive Center (201-915-3409), located on Freedom Way, is an
environmental and educational facility featuring many exhibits. Sixty acres
of natural salt marshes adjacent to the building contain a nature trail and
observation points. Fishing and crabbing are permitted in the Hudson River
and a boat launch is open year-round during daylight hours. Picnic areas,
near the park's administration building, offer impressive views of the New
York Harbor. There is also a swimming pool, which is lifeguard supervised,
complete with a changing area and food concessions. A nominal fee for
pool usage is charged.

Ferry service, operating in the spring through late fall (201-269-5755) is
located near the old railroad terminal and transports passengers to nearby
Ellis Island and the Statue of Liberty.

The Liberty Science Center (201-200-1000) is located near the entrance
to the park. A small admission fee will get you in to see the world's largest
IMAX screen as well as 3-D laser-light shows, scientific demonstrations
and numerous hands-on exhibits that both children and parents will enjoy.

**Lincoln Park**
Kennedy Boulevard
Jersey City
Hudson County
201-915-1385
Open sunrise to sunset
No entrance fee
273 acres

**Activities:** fishing, picnicking, and a playground.

This is the oldest park in Hudson County and encompasses 273 acres of
lush, green foliage. A 15-acre lake provides a well-stocked place to fish. A
statue of Abraham Lincoln, erected in 1928, is near the entrance.

## Deer Path Park
West Woodschurch Road
Readington
Hunterdon County
908-782-1158
Open sunrise to sunset
No entrance fee
159 acres

**Activities:** baseball, cross-country skiing, fishing, fitness stations, hiking, horseback riding, horseshoes, picnicking, a playground, and soccer.

Deer Path is a beautiful park, consisting of rolling farmlands, meadows, open fields, and woods. The memorial gazebo and the gardens of Alois and Bertha Batz, the former owners of this land, are popular places for wedding ceremonies and picture taking. The nearby three-acre pond is a great place for fishing. A 55-acre section of land that contains horseback riding trails, pine forests, and panoramic views of the Southerland Mountains is located at the southern slope of Round Mountain. Access is from the parking area in Deer Path Park with trails leading west to Woodschurch Road.

## Echo Hill Environmental Area
Lilac Drive
Clinton
Hunterdon County
908-782-1158
Open sunrise to sunset
No entrance fee
76 acres

**Activities:** camping, cross-country skiing, fishing, hiking, picnicking, and a playground.

**FACT:** *Overlooking the Hudson River in Jersey City stands the Colgate Clock, the world's largest vertical face clock. It was produced in 1928 by the Seth Thomas Clock Company. The clock, which is 50 feet in diameter and 70 feet high, has hands that are 23 feet long and weigh nearly a ton each. The Colgate Clock is so large that it is visible at night from parts of lower Manhattan in New York City.*

Echo Hill was constructed in 1936, for use as a private summer camp for children. The county acquired the land in 1973 and converted the camp's dining hall into an activity center, which can be reserved. Two unfurnished cabins in a peaceful wooded area are also available for reservation. Echo Hill is part of the undeveloped 950-acre South Branch Reservation, which contains old farmlands, marshes, abandoned railroad right-of-ways, and old trestle bridges. Its many rivers are ideal for canoeing.

## Hunterdon County Arboretum
Route 31
Clinton
Hunterdon County
908-782-1158
Open sunrise to sunset
No entrance fee
73 acres

**Activities:** cross-country skiing, hiking, and picnicking.

Once a commercial nursery, now a beautiful arboretum with lush wetlands, streams, and fields, the Hunterdon County Arboretum is an ideal place to relax and enjoy nature. Wildlife is abundant here, as are numerous species of trees, which do not naturally grow in any other area of the state. There is a 20,000 square foot display garden with a newly renovated, bi-level, cedar gazebo as its centerpiece that visitors may enjoy. The gazebo, built in 1892, is a popular spot for wedding ceremonies and taking photographs. The main building, headquarters for the county park system, can be reserved for special occasions.

## Round Valley Recreation Area
1220 Lebanon Stanton Road
Lebanon
Hunterdon County
908-236-6355
Open sunrise to sunset
No entrance fee
5,291 acres

**Activities:** biking, boating, camping, canoeing, cross-country skiing, fishing, hiking, horseback riding, hunting, ice-skating, picnicking, a playground, scuba diving, sledding, and swimming.

The 4,000-acre reservoir featured in this recreation area is the deepest lake in the state at over 180-feet deep in some spots. The reservoir has a water capacity of 55 billion gallons. Swimming and fishing are permitted.

Round Valley is one of the few places that offer a real wilderness camping experience. The campsite can only be reached via a three-mile trail that begins in the parking lot. There are 85 family campsites, which can accommodate up to six people and eight group sites that can accommodate up to 25 people. All campsites are open from April 1 to October 31.

**Spruce Run Recreation Area**
One Van Syckel's Road
Clinton
Hunterdon County
908-638-8572
Open sunrise to sunset
No entrance fee
1,910 acres

**Activities:** basketball, biking, boating, camping, canoeing, cross-country skiing, fishing, hiking, hunting, picnicking, a playground, swimming, and volleyball.

The main feature of this all-season recreational area is the 1,290-acre reservoir with its 15 miles of shoreline. A seasonal boathouse (908-638-8234) rents out paddleboats and canoes and there are 70 tent and trailer camping sites complete with picnic tables and fire rings. The campgrounds are open April 1 to October 31.

**Voorhees State Park**
251 County Road (Route 513)
Glen Gardner
Hunterdon County
908-638-6969
Open sunrise to sunset
No entrance fee
640 acres

**Activities:** baseball, biking, camping, cross-country skiing, fishing, fitness stations, hiking, hunting, picnicking, and a playground.

This park is named after former New Jersey Governor Foster M. Voorhees, who, in 1929, donated his family's 325-acre farm to the state. Since then, the state has acquired additional land and has continued to make numerous improvements. Both a trail and a street in the park still bear the name "Hill Acres," the former name of the estate. The New Jersey Astronomical Association (908-638-8500) built an observatory here in 1965 and their 28-inch Newtonian reflector, one of the largest telescopes privately owned in the state, is located at the highest point of elevation in the park. A space exhibit inside the building offers tours and day and evening programs. For those who like to mix exercise and nature, there are 18 fitness stations scattered along a one and a half-mile hiking trail that encircles the park. There are 50 wooded campsites and two group-campsites, each near modern facilities. All campsites are open year round. There are also two group-picnic areas, which can be reserved for large parties and special occasions. Hunting is also permitted in designated and marked areas.

## Cadwalader Park
Parkside Avenue
Trenton
Mercer County
609-989-3632
Open sunrise to sunset
No entrance fee
146 acres

**Activities:** baseball, picnicking, a playground, and tennis.

This park was named in honor of Dr. Thomas Cadwalader, who vaccinated the population of Trenton for smallpox in the late 1740s. The land for Cadwalader Park was once part of an estate designed by John Notman, a noted architect who designed the State Hospital and was the architect-in-charge for the 1845 expansion of the State House as well. The estate's great house, an Italianate-style mansion, was built in 1848, to be the summer residence of Philadelphia lawyer Henry McCall, Sr. The City of Trenton purchased the land in 1888 and the estate was converted into a museum. Today, this museum displays the works of local and international artists and has exhibits on the history of Trenton's ceramic industry.

## Hamilton Veterans Park
2206 Kuser Road
Hamilton
Mercer County
609-581-4124
Open sunrise to sunset
No entrance fee
333 acres

**Activities:** baseball, hiking, soccer, and tennis.

Once a Civil War training camp, this park opened in 1977 to honor the town of Hamilton's veterans. The main entrance leads visitors to recreational facilities including a tennis complex and nearby food stand. The entrance near Klockner Road leads to numerous wooded trails and gardens, while the entrance near Whitehorse-Hamilton Square Road features a huge fountain with gardens and a boardwalk. This park is home to the Civil War and Native American Museum (609-585-8900), which is open on the weekends from Noon to 5 P.M. The museum emphasizes Central Jersey's role in the war and features regimental uniforms, weapons, and equipment. Native American artifacts, many dating as far back as 8,000 B.C, are also on display.

### Herrontown Woods Arboretum
Snowden Lane
Princeton
Mercer County
609-989-6530
Open sunrise to sunset
No entrance fee
142 acres

**Activities:** bird watching and hiking.

Professor Oswald Veblen donated this land to the county in 1957. It is now preserved in its natural state and includes over 30 species of trees and plants. There are also many trails that pass through the arboretum.

### John A. Roebling Park
Park Avenue
Hamilton
Mercer County
609-586-8160
Open sunrise to sunset
No entrance fee
257 acres

**Activities:** bird watching, boating, fishing, and picnicking.

Named after John A. Roebling, the designer of the Brooklyn Bridge, this park is mostly undeveloped and contains swamps, tidal marsh, shallow ponds, and creeks. A small picnic area is accessible from Schiller Avenue, which is located near the historic Watson House, the oldest house in Mercer County. The building, which was constructed in 1708, is now the head-quarters for the Daughters of the American Revolution. An 18-acre lake in the park offers fishing.

**Kuser Farm Park**
Kuser Road
Hamilton
Mercer County
609-890-3630
Open sunrise to sunset
No entrance fee
22 acres

**Activities:** tennis.

Kuser Farm Park was once a summer home for the Kuser family. They were a very wealthy and prominent family with numerous business connections. In 1915, Anthony R. Kuser loaned $200,000.00 to William Fox to form the Fox Film Corporation. In 1934, the family surrendered their shares of Fox in order to make possible a merger with 20th Century. This merger created one of the top film companies known today as 20th Century Fox. The Jersey Valley Model Railroad Club (609-890-3630) has a display in the basement of the museum, which features examples of local landscapes, including Veterans Park and the Hopewell train station.

**Marquand Park**
Lovers Lane
Princeton
Mercer County
609-921-9480
Open sunrise to sunset
No entrance fee
17 acres

**Activities:** baseball, bird watching, picnicking, and a playground.

In 1842, Judge Richard Field, a professor at Princeton University, purchased 30 acres of farmland for the purpose of building his residence. The next 10 years were spent designing the grounds and not much actual building took place. Another Princeton professor, Allen Marquand, purchased the land years later and he and his wife continued to make improvements. Mrs. Marquand lived in the house, now called Guernsey

Hall, until she died in 1950. Her heirs then donated a portion of the estate to the town. Since then numerous trees and shrubs have been planted. There are over 200 species of domestic and foreign trees, 11 of which are the largest of their kind in the state. This is a great place to take a peaceful walk and enjoy the natural surroundings.

**Mercer County Park**
Hughes Drive
West Windsor
Mercer County
609-989-6530
Open sunrise to sunset
No entrance fee
2,500 acres

**Activities:** baseball, basketball, boating, ice-skating, picnicking, a playground, soccer, tennis, and volleyball.

Mercer County Park is an athletics enthusiast's paradise. A 100-acre athletic complex features 12 baseball fields, 7 soccer fields, and 18 basketball half-courts (for league information call 609-989-6540).

**Boat Marina:** (609-484-4004, open May through October, off-season call 609-989-6538) Located on the 300-acre Lake Mercer, this marina features a boat ramp for small car top boats and a public dock that is available for daily use. Paddle and rowboats can be rented from the boathouse. The upper level is available for catered parties; call 609-890-9568 for information.

**Equestrian Center:** (Federal City Road, 609-730-9059) This training facility has the capacity to board 15 horses. Lessons and riding programs for the disabled are available.

**Ice Skating Center:** (Open daily from mid-November to mid-March, 609-371-1669) The center features an Olympic-sized rink where skating equipment can be rented and lessons are available. There is also a snack bar.

**Mercer County Park East Picnic Area:** (Off Dutch Neck-Edinburg Road, 609-989-6536) This picnic area will accommodate up to 225 people and can be reserved for special occasions. A five-mile trail connects this area to the tennis center and marina.

**Mercer County Park West Picnic Area:** (near the marina) This area features over 100 lakeside tables in wooded areas and a pavilion that can be reserved.

**Outdoor Tennis Center:** (South Post Road, 609-448-8007) This 19-acre complex features 26 tennis courts, 10 of which are lighted. A clubhouse nearby has lockers, showers, a snack shop, and a pro shop that provides professional instructors. A three-level observation desk overlooks the playing area and provides spectacular views of the tennis center.

**Valley Road Group Picnic Area:** (Valley Road) This picnic area, which is available for reservations, is within a 19-acre open space that can accommodate up to 300 people. A baseball field, basketball court, and volleyball court are nearby.

**Princeton Battlefield State Park**
500 Mercer Road
Princeton
Mercer County
609-921-0074
Open sunrise to sunset
No entrance fee
85 acres

**Activities:** bird watching, cross-country skiing, and hiking.

After General Washington crossed the Delaware with his troops and surprised the Hessians in Trenton, the Continental Army embarked to Princeton and defeated a force of British troops. The battle took place on January 3 1777, and gave Washington his first victory over British troops in the field. The battle was fought over a broad front, reaching present day Princeton University. The remains of the once tall, majestic Mercer Oak is close to where General Mercer fell. The nearby Clark House, built in 1772, was pressed into service as a hospital for General Mercer and for those who were direly wounded. General Mercer died nine days later. The house, furnished with colonial pieces, contains exhibits relating to the Revolutionary War. A hiking trail leads down to the Delaware and Raritan Canal.

**Rosedale Park**
Federal City Road
Hopewell
Mercer County
609-989-6532
Open sunrise to sunset
No entrance fee
472 acres

**Activities:** boating, canoeing, fishing, picnicking, and a playground.

The park's 38-acre lake is stocked with trout to ensure excellent fishing opportunities. Family and group picnic areas are located alongside the lake. The group area (609-989-6536) is available for reservation.

### Stony Brook-Millstone Watershed
31 Titus Mill Road
Pennington
Mercer County
609-737-3735
Open sunrise to sunset
No entrance fee
785 acres

**Activities:** hiking.

This is the largest private nature reserve in the state. There are ten miles of trails, a three-acre arboretum, and a three-acre pond. The Kate Gorrie Butterfly House is near the main entrance and contains native plant and butterfly species. The main office is open Mondays to Fridays from 9 A.M. to 5 P.M. The Buttinger Environmental Education Center is open Wednesdays to Fridays from 9 A.M. to 5 P.M. and Saturdays from 10 A.M. to 4 P.M. Attractions include an indoor discovery room with hands-on exhibits of the region's plants and animals. It also features a nature library with classrooms. The nature center provides 400 educational programs to over 125 schools around the state. The Watershed Organic Farm is open for visits Tuesdays to Saturdays from 10 A.M. to 5 P.M. The farm provides fresh vegetables to over 1,000 families in 85 communities. It also serves as a research and educational facility where people can learn all of the latest techniques on organic farming.

### Washington Crossing State Park
355 Washington Crossing-
Pennington Road
Titusville
Mercer County
609-737-0623
Open sunrise to sunset
No entrance fee
991 acres

**Activities:** biking, camping, cross-country skiing, fishing, hiking, horseback riding, and picnicking.

It was here on Christmas Eve, 1776, that the Continental Army, under the command of General George Washington, made its historic crossing of the Delaware River. A small ferry crossing had been established on this point in the early 1700's, to transport trade and passengers over the mighty river. Washington chose to cross here because the crossing was little used and not widely known. After his troops landed, they surprised the Hessian mercenaries at Trenton and then defeated the alerted British at the Battle of Princeton. This was the first time the Continental Army had won a pitched battle against the British and many historians consider these actions to be the turning point of the Revolution.

The park was established in 1912, with a little over 100 acres. Over the years, more land was acquired and newer facilities were built. The visitor's center (609-737-9303, open Wednesdays to Sundays) contains about 900 artifacts from the Revolutionary War, featuring pieces of equipment from both the British and American forces.

The Johnson Ferry House (609-737-2515) is where Washington and his staff stayed and finalized their strategy for the attack on Trenton, while the army regrouped. This eighteenth century house, once the ferry keeper's residence, is now furnished with authentic colonial pieces and offers living history demonstrations. The Nelson House (609-737-1783) is open for tours during the summer months. The house is believed to be a surviving section of the original ferry house and is located near the Delaware River, where the Continental Army camped after the successful crossing.

A 140-acre preserve is located in the northwest portion of the park and includes numerous trails and wildlife. The nature center (609-737-0609) is located in this preserve area and is open Wednesdays to Sundays. The center features many exhibits and informational displays.

There are three large picnic areas located at Washington's Crossing. The Green Grove section is available for large parties and accepts reservations. A group camping area is located in the Phillips Farm area, which has five miles of multi-use trails and a two and a half-mile trail used exclusively for horseback riding. Overall, there are almost 20 miles of trails in this park. Fishing is permitted in the Delaware River and the Raritan Canal. An open-air theater is located along a sloping hillside terrace and can accommodate around 900 people. It is a favorite venue for concerts and other musical performances. Call 609-737-1826 for information.

## Buccleuch Park
Easton Avenue
New Brunswick
Middlesex County
732-745-5094
Open sunrise to sunset
No entrance fee
78 acres

**Activities:** baseball, fitness stations, picnicking, a playground, soccer, and tennis.

This land was originally a working farm known as White House Farm. It was established in 1739 and owned and operated by Anthony Walton White and his wife, the daughter of Governor Lewis Morris. They entertained such guests as George Washington and Alexander Hamilton. In 1821, Colonel Joseph Warren Scott, a prominent New Jersey attorney, purchased the farmstead and changed its name to Buccleuch in honor of his ancestor, the Duke of Buccleuch of Scotland. His heirs donated the property to the city in 1911, which then designated the property as parkland. Restoration of the house soon began and the land was cleared and landscaped, taking full advantage of its natural beauty. The house is open to visitors June through October on Sundays from 2 P.M. to 4 P.M. There are many attractions in this park including open fields, a fitness course, a formal garden, and a gazebo that is a popular spot for pictures.

**Cheesequake State Park**
300 Gordon Road
Matawan
Middlesex County
732-566-2161
Open sunrise to sunset
No entrance fee
1,274 acres

**Activities:** basketball, biking, bird watching, boating, camping, canoeing, cross-country skiing, fishing, hiking, picnicking, a playground, sledding, and swimming.

This land was once the hunting grounds of the Lenni-Lenape tribe. The park is now a favorite recreational area. Swimming is permitted during the summer months in Hooks Creek Lake. Trails wind their way through a white cedar swamp and portions of the Pine Barrens. An Interpretive Center (732-566-3208), open Wednesdays to Sundays from 10 A.M. to 3 P.M., is accessible by trail and features exhibits on how the past inhabitants lived on this land. There are several picnic areas and 53 campsites located in the woodland settings, but with modern facilities nearby.

**FACT:** *Prior to becoming the Governor of New Jersey, James McGreevey served as the Mayor of Woodbridge from 1992 to 2001. Woodbridge, which is Middlesex County's sixth largest municipality, is the oldest original township in New Jersey; it was settled in the early autumn of 1664.*

**Davidson's Mill Pond Park**
Riva Avenue
South Brunswick
Middlesex County
732-745-3900
Open sunrise to sunset
No entrance fee
395 acres

**Activities:** boating, fishing, and hiking.

Primarily undeveloped, this park contains two beautiful ponds and a waterfall where a mill operation was once located. Fishing is permitted in the lake and in the two ponds. A boat launch is available for small, car-top boats.

**Donaldson Park**
Second Avenue
Highland Park
Middlesex County
732-745-3900
Open sunrise to sunset
No entrance fee
90 acres

**Activities:** baseball, basketball, boating, picnicking, a playground, and soccer.

There are many activities to enjoy here. A boat ramp provides access onto the Raritan River. Picnic areas are located in lightly wooded areas and one site features a covered pavilion.

**Johnson Park**
River Road
Piscataway
Middlesex County
732-745-3900
Open sunrise to sunset
No entrance fee
473 acres

**Activities:** baseball, biking, picnicking, a playground, soccer and tennis.

A recently renovated live animal area is a featured attraction in this park, complete with peacocks, deer, emu, llamas, and many other animals. There are two beautiful ponds situated on the banks of the Raritan River, and a two and a half-mile paved pedestrian and bicycle bath. East Jersey Old Town, a reconstructed antique village, was formed from historic buildings taken from various places across Central Jersey. The village can be toured and contains a visitor's center with additional information. Special exhibits and lectures are also held regularly. Another unique feature of this park is the horse-show area with private stables and a half-mile racing track.

**Joseph Medwick Park**
Post Boulevard
Carteret
Middlesex County
732-745-3900
Open sunrise to sunset
No entrance fee
82 acres

**Activities:** baseball, biking, hiking, in-line skating rink, picnicking, and a playground.

Located along the Rahway River, this park features two shaded picnic areas, an open grove, and a bicycle path.

**Merrill Park**
Middlesex Turnpike
Woodbridge
Middlesex County
732-745-3900
Open sunrise to sunset
No entrance fee
179 acres

**Activities:** baseball, basketball, hiking, picnicking, a playground, soccer, and tennis.

A small, live animal area is featured in this park along with several quiet picnic areas.

**Roosevelt Park**
Route 1
Edison
Middlesex County
732-745-3900
Open sunrise to sunset
No entrance fee
217 acres

**Activities:** baseball, basketball, biking, fishing, hiking, picnicking, a playground, and tennis.

Roosevelt Park is Middlesex County's oldest recreational area. It features an eight-acre lake and nature trails, which begin in the picnic area. There is also a small food concession stand located near the picnic area. The Stephen J. Capestro Theater hosts the county's "Plays in the Park" series, call 732-548-2884 for show times.

**Thompson Park**
Forsgate Drive
Monroe
Middlesex County
732-745-3900
Open sunrise to sunset
No entrance fee
675 acres

**Activities:** baseball, basketball, fishing, handball, hiking, picnicking, a playground, and tennis.

Thompson Park features the 30-acre Manalapan Lake, as well as a small live animal display, several hiking trails, and picnic groves.

**FACT:** *Middlesex County was the site where the first African American exercised his right to vote. On March 31st, 1870, one day after the adoption of the Fifteenth Amendment, Thomas Mundy Peterson cast his ballot in the City Hall of Perth Amboy, the oldest municipal building in the United States that is in continuous use. Perth Amboy's City Hall was also the site of the first state ratification of the first ten amendments to the United States Constitution, known as "The Bill of Rights," in November of 1789.*

**William Warren Park**
Florida Grove Road
Woodbridge
Middlesex County
732-745-3900
Open sunrise to sunset
No entrance fee
126 acres

**Activities:** baseball, basketball, biking, hiking, picnicking, a playground, soccer, and tennis.

William Warren Park is home to the "Kids-in-the-Park" summer theater camp, which give area youths a chance to display their talents. There are several hiking trails and numerous other activities to enjoy here.

**Allaire State Park**
Allaire Road (Route 524)
Farmingdale
Monmouth County
732-938-2371
Open sunrise to sunset
No entrance fee
3,061 acres

**Activities:** biking, camping, canoeing, fishing, hiking, horseback riding, hunting, picnicking, and a playground.

In 1882, James P. Allaire purchased a forge known as Monmouth Furnace. He renamed it Howell Works and began to manufacture castings and pig iron. The products were shipped to his foundry in New York, which built steamship engines and boilers. As the village grew, Allaire expanded the available housing for his workers and their families. Gristmills, saw mills, a general store, and a church were also added to the village. At its peak, the village population swelled to over 500. However, in 1848, with the discovery of high-grade iron ore in nearby Pennsylvania, it became too expensive to compete with the newer mining facilities, and the village started to decline.

Over the years, neglect and the elements began to take their toll on the buildings and the village fell into ruin. Fortunately, many local area residents recognized the historical importance of the abandoned village and through their efforts many of the structures have been saved. Those buildings that have been restored are open on the weekends throughout the summer season for tours. These buildings are now living museums and have costumed, historical interpreters who explain the activities that filled a normal day for a villager and demonstrate the many crafts that were essential for comfortable living. For more information call 732-938-2253.

The Pine Creek Railroad (732-938-5524) is open April through mid October and was established in 1953. It is the only narrow gauge steam railroad in the state.

The Manasquan River provides a scenic setting for fishing and canoe trips. Over 200 species of wild flowers, trees, and shrubs can be found in this park. This area is also located along the Atlantic Flyway and is an excellent spot for bird watching, especially during spring and fall migrations. The park's nature center (732-938-2003) is open Memorial Day through Labor Day and contains exhibits and information regarding the local area. Allaire State Park also contains several miles of trails and includes group campsites that can accommodate over 100 people.

**Dorbrook Recreation Area**
County Road 537
Colts Neck
Monmouth County
732-842-4000
Open 8 A.M. to sunset
No entrance fee
534 acres

**Activities:** baseball, biking, field hockey, flag football, hiking, horseback riding, horseshoe pits, an in-line hockey rink, rugby, soccer, swimming, and tennis.

The Monmouth County Park System acquired Dorbrook Recreation Area in 1985, from the estate of Murray Rosenberg, creator of Miles Shoe Stores. Dorbrook has many facilities for various sports and offers introductory clinics in golf, soccer, and basketball. The activity center also conducts classes in such activities as Tai Chi and arts & crafts. Most facilities in this park are connected by a paved two and a thirds-miles long trail. An outdoor-swimming

**FACT:** *Located in West Long Branch, Monmouth University's historic 'Woodrow Wilson Hall' was a major location site for the 1982 motion picture 'Annie'.*

pool is located near the visitor center and there is a picnic area, which accepts reservations and can accommodate groups of up to 75 people.

**Gateway National Recreation Area**
**Sandy Hook Unit**
Off State Highway 36
Atlantic Highlands
Monmouth County
732-872-5970
Open sunrise to sunset
Admission fee from Memorial Day through Labor Day
1,665 acres

**Activities:** biking, bird watching, fishing, hiking, picnicking, a playground, and swimming.

Sandy Hook is a barrier beach peninsula located at the northern tip of the New Jersey shore. The park features seven miles of ocean beaches, many hiking trails and a historic district. Over 300 species of birds have been identified at Sandy Hook, which is located along the Atlantic Flyway, making it one of the premiere bird watching spots along the coast. Swimming is allowed daily from 10 A.M. to 6 P.M. during the summer and the beach is lifeguard supervised. Concession stands are only a short walk from the beaches.

Because of its location, Sandy Hook has played a major role in both navigation and coastal defense. In 1870, the area was chosen to be the first U.S. Army Proving Ground, where various weapons and munitions were tested. In 1895, Fort Hancock was established as part of a system of defenses designed to protect New York Harbor.

**Visitor's Center:** The visitor's center serves as the main information station for the "Hook." It also contains a small a museum that features two main exhibits. The first is about nature and includes a display about local animals and their habitats. The second exhibit is on the United States Life Saving Service, the forerunner to the present day Coast Guard. It features a short video on the history of the service as well as photographs, uniforms and newspaper accounts of many sea rescues. Just outside the visitors center is the beginning of a one-mile long dune trail. *Hours:* Daily, 10 A.M. to 5 P.M.

**Fort Hancock:** This historic fort is one of two all concrete forts built in New Jersey (the other being Fort Mott in Salem County). It was built to protect New York Harbor from an attack by sea. Concrete was chosen because its sun-bleached appearance blended in with the natural landscape and could withstand a heavy shelling from enemy vessels. Fort Hancock has twelve six-inch guns that could launch a several hundred pound pro-jectile for miles. The fort was decommissioned in 1974, but many of the gun batteries and buildings still stand today. Exploration of the buildings is limited in most structures due to their neglected condition. Guided tours of the restored historic district are offered.

**Fort Hancock Museum:** This building was once a guardhouse, but it now features exhibits about the history of Fort Hancock. It also contains a small bookstore. *Hours:* Saturdays and Sundays from 1 P.M. to 5 P.M.

**History House:** Built in 1889, this was once the bachelor lieutenant's liv-ing quarters. The building is now used as a small museum that contains exhibits on everyday life at the fort. Inside, the museum also displays sets of period furniture, photographs, and documents detailing the history of the Hook. *Hours:* Saturdays and Sundays from 1 P.M. to 5 P.M.

**Lighthouse:** Built in 1764, this is the oldest continuously operating light-house in the country. During the Revolutionary War, it withstood cannon fire by colonists who were attempting to drive the occupying British forces away. The lighthouse was recently restored and guided tours are con-ducted during the summer months.

**Sandy Hook Museum:** This museum features a collection of weapons that were used at Fort Hancock. It also contains additional information about the lighthouse. *Hours:* Saturdays and Sundays from 1 P.M. to 5 P.M.

**United States Coast Guard Station:** Located at the northernmost tip of Sandy Hook, this Coast Guard Station is only open to visitors for pre-arranged tours. It is used as a training and recruiting center. *Phone:* 732-872-0326.

**Hartshorne Woods Park**
New Road
Middletown
Monmouth County
732-842-4000
Open 8 A.M. to sunset
No entrance fee
736 acres

**Activities:** biking, fishing, hiking, and horseback riding.

Richard Hartshorne bartered for this land with the local Native Americans in 1670. The land has remained in his family's possession ever since. Even today, several of his descendants still live on the bartered tract of land. The Rocky Point section of the park was one of several sites in the Highlands

Army Air Defense Site from 1940 until the mid-1970s. Fort Hancock, in nearby Sandy Hook, was also part of this coastal defense system. This area was an ideal location for the army because of its natural fortifications. During World War II, Battery Lewis housed two 66-foot long guns that were built for the Navy. The guns where phased out by the early 1950s and Rocky Point became a Nike-Hercules Missile control center. When the base was declared surplus property by the government, the county acquired the property with the intention of converting it into a park. This park, once a fortress for war and now a playground for peace, features many trails that are perfect for walking, bike riding, and horseback riding.

**Holmdel Park**
Longstreet Road
Holmdel
Monmouth County
732-842-4000
Open 8 A.M. to sunset
No entrance fee
375 acres

**Activities:** cross-country skiing, fishing, fitness stations, hiking, ice-skating, picnicking, a playground, sledding, and tennis.

Holmdel Park was originally known as Longstreet Farm. In 1806, Hendrick Longstreet purchased several small farms in the area and combined them to form a 495-acre homestead and farm. It was the most prosperous farm in the area. He owned livestock and produced grains, dairy, and potatoes. When the county acquired the property in 1967, a restoration process began in order to restore the buildings to their 1890s appearance. The buildings were opened for the public to enjoy by the early 1970s. A section of the park is still called Longstreet Farm and is now a living history farm. Employees are dressed in period costumes and recreate the area's turn-of-the-century agricultural life. The historic farm (732-946-3758) is open daily from 10 A.M. to 4 P.M. Hours are extended Memorial Day through Labor Day, daily from 9 A.M. to 5 P.M.

In this park there are many activities to pursue including fishing, playing tennis, and hiking on over eight miles of trails. Twenty acres of land are dedicated to the park's arboretum (732-431-7903), which contains an impressive collection of pines, spruces, dogwoods, magnolias, and hollies. The shelter building has a snack bar, which is open seasonally. There is also a large picnic area, which may be reserved and can accommodate groups of up to 125 people.

**Huber Woods Park**
Navesink River Road
Middletown
Monmouth County
732-872-2670
Open 8 A.M. to sunset
No entrance fee
258 acres

**Activities:** hiking and horseback riding.

Huber Woods was established in 1974, with a 118-acre gift from the Huber family and the J.M. Huber Corporation. Since then, the park has grown through additional acquisitions and donations. There are six miles of trails that are suitable for hiking, bicycle riding, and horseback riding. The environmental center features hands-on displays of plants and animals and includes classrooms, a weather station, and a bird viewing area. The park has a reptile house that is home to a variety of reptiles native to Monmouth County. A non-profit organization operates the park's equestrian center, which has facilities and access for both disabled and non-disabled riders. There are also classes offered to teach students how to ride and care for their horses.

**Manasquan Reservoir**
Windeler Road
Howell
Monmouth County
732-919-0996
Open April 1 to October 31, daily
    from 6 A.M. to sunset and
    November 1 to March 31,
    daily, 8 A.M. to sunset
No entrance fee
1,200 acres

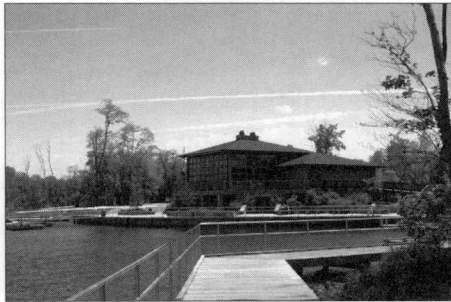

**Activities:** biking, boating, cross-country skiing, fishing, hiking, horseback riding, picnicking, and a playground.

The Manasquan Reservoir was completed in 1990, to provide clean water to local municipalities. It is part of a 1,200-acre area that includes a five-mile perimeter trail with adjacent wetlands and wooded areas. The Joseph C. Irwin Recreation building includes a large, warming fireplace, lounge area, snack bar, and observation deck complete with impressive views of the reservoir. Sailboats, kayaks, and rowboats may be rented at the lower level shop.

## Monmouth Battlefield State Park

347 Englishtown-Freehold Road
Manalapan
Monmouth County
732-462-9616
Open sunrise to sunset
No entrance fee
1,810 acres

**Activities:** cross-country skiing, hiking, horseback riding, hunting, picnicking, and a playground.

One of the largest battles of the American Revolution took place on these fields on June 28, 1778. After a desperate fight, the fledgling United States had won the field. This battle proved that the Continental Army could not only stand against the British on an open field but be victorious as well. Every year, the battle is reenacted to celebrate this turning point event. The Craig House, built in 1770, stands adjacent to the battlefield. It has been fully restored and furnished with authentic period pieces. It is open to the public on a limited basis. The visitor's center is open 9 A.M. to 5 P.M. and stands on top of Combs Hill, which was once commanded by the Continental Army artillery. It features a short video on the battle as well as displays of recovered artifacts. A gift shop and a snack bar are also located inside the building.

## Mt. Mitchell Scenic Overlook

New Ocean Boulevard
Middletown
Monmouth County
732-842-4000
Open 8 A.M. to sunset
No entrance fee
12 acres

**Activities:** picnicking.

Although it may be one of the smallest parks listed in this book, the awe-inspiring views just cannot be ignored. The overlook rises 260 feet above sea level and is the highest natural point on the Atlantic Coast in the United States. It features impressive views of the Sandy Hook region and the New York Skyline. A few scattered picnic tables offer visitors a chance to rest and enjoy.

## Owl Haven Nature Center
250 Englishtown-Freehold Road
Tennent
Monmouth County
732-780-7007
Open Tuesdays to Sundays,
    noon to 5 P.M.
No entrance fee
1 acre

**Activities:** biking, cross-country skiing, hiking, and horseback riding.

Owl Haven was established in 1980 and moved to its present location in 1983 from the historic Cobb House just across the street. It is located in Monmouth Battlefield State Park and has access to the battlefield's 25 miles of trails. The nature center has a bookstore, gift shop, and a museum with mounted specimens. Owl Haven also sponsors field trips and offers educational classes. Outside the building is a bird feeding station and butterfly garden, which are keen areas to visit and glimpse some of the beautiful things nature has to offer.

## Poricy Park
Oak Hill Road
Middletown
Monmouth County
732-842-5966
Open sunrise to sunset
No entrance fee
250 acres

**Activities:** hiking.

Joseph Murray, a local farmer, once owned this land. He, his wife Rebecca, and their four children lived in the little red house that still stands today. Joseph was an ardent supporter of the American independence movement and during the Revolutionary War he joined the Monmouth Militia. On June 8, 1780, while he was working in the cornfield behind the barn, British loyalists murdered Joseph Murray.

Today, you can walk through the beautiful meadows and woodlands and visit the house in which he lived. The nature center is open Mondays to Fridays from 9 A.M. to 4 P.M. and Sundays from 12:30 P.M. to 3:30 P.M. It features interactive educational displays in natural science and environmental studies. It is also the place to learn about park offerings, register for classes, and enjoy the work of local artists. The Poricy Brook Fossil Beds are well known to fossil collectors in the Northeast and are a unique place to spend a Sunday afternoon.

### Seven Presidents Oceanfront Park
Ocean Avenue
Long Branch
Monmouth County
732-229-0924
Open 8 A.M. to sunset
Fee charged from Memorial Day through Labor Day
36 acres

**Activities:** boating, fishing, fitness stations, picnicking, a playground, swimming, and volleyball.

Seven Presidents Park was named after the seven United States Presidents that had visited Long Branch in the late 1800s, when the area was a favorite summer resort. Presidents Grant, Hayes, Wilson, Garfield, Arthur, Harrison, and McKinley, each took advantage of the scenic beauty to relax from their duties as President. So popular was this area with Washington D.C.'s elite, that it began to be known as the summer capital. This park was also the site of "The Reservation," built by Nate Salsbury, a Long Branch businessman. Salsbury built the Reservation to be used for his Wild West Show, which featured appearances by such figures of the western frontier as Buffalo Bill Cody, Annie Oakley, and Chief Sitting Bull.

Today, the beach is still a favorite place to swim, relax, and enjoy nature. A seasonal snack bar and changing facilities are located not far from the water. Swimming season starts on Memorial Day and ends Labor Day, with lifeguards present daily, 10 A.M. to 5 P.M. An activity center on the grounds provides many shore-oriented programs to enjoy.

### Shark River Park
Schoolhouse Road
Neptune
Monmouth County
732-922-3868
Open 8 A.M. to sunset
No entrance fee
725 acres

**Activities:** biking, fishing, hiking, horseback riding, horseshoes, ice-skating, picnicking, a playground, and shuffleboard.

Opening in 1961, Shark River became the first park in Monmouth County. Its seven miles of trails are suitable for hiking, bicycle riding, and horseback riding. The park has a pond that is stocked with many types of fish and may be used for ice-skating in the winter months. The shelter building (732-922-4080) includes a kitchen and fireplace. It may be rented anytime except during ice-skating season, December 15 to March 15. Horseshoe and shuffleboard equipment may be rented inside this building.

**Tantum Park**
Red Hill Road
Middletown
Monmouth County
732-842-4000
Open 8 A.M. to sunset
No entrance fee
368 acres

**Activities:** biking, hiking, horseback riding, picnicking, and a playground.

This park was named after Charles Tantum, a local businessman, who in 1905 purchased this land for use as his summer residence. He wanted to be close to the glassware factories that he owned in the nearby towns of Keyport and Millville. The park's Holland Activity Center (732-842-4000) displays some of the glass pieces produced at the factories. It also provides facilities and equipment for sports and fitness programs. The meeting room may be rented and can accommodate up to fifty people.

The Red Hill Activity Center features workshops, seasonal performances, dance competitions, and summer theater programs for parents and children. In 1981, the Clinton and Mary Heath Wing opened. The addition was donated in honor of Clinton Heath, a freed slave from North Carolina, who became the first African American farmer to settle in Middletown. The wing contains a permanent display of memorabilia from Monmouth County's early African American community.

Tantum Park has many open fields and winding trails that cut through wooded areas. This is a great place to enjoy a picnic and relax in the natu-

**FACT:** *Bruce Springsteen, a Monmouth County resident, was born in the town of Freehold on September 23, 1949. Springsteen's most famous album, "Born in the U.S.A." was released in 1984 and sold more than 20 million copies. In 1994 Springsteen won four Grammys for the song "Streets of Philadelphia" for the movie "Philadelphia".*

ral surroundings. Cyclists and horseback riders are only permitted on the gravel service road.

**Thompson Park**
805 Newman Springs Road
Middletown
Monmouth County
732-842-4000
Open 8 A.M. to sunset
No entrance fee
665 acres

**Activities:** fishing, fitness stations, hiking, picnicking, a playground, soccer, and tennis.

This park is named after Geraldine Thompson who bequeathed her land, called Brookdale Farm, to the county in 1967. The park is the headquarters of the Monmouth County Park System whose offices are in the former family mansion.

Pottery and ceramic classes are held in the Craft Center year-round for all skill and age levels. An 18-station fitness trail runs through the park to the adjacent Brookdale Community College campus. The lake is stocked for fishing and allows easy access for small boats. A picnic area may be reserved and can accommodate groups of up to 125 people.

**Turkey Swamp Park**
Georgia Road
Freehold
Monmouth County
732-842-4000
Open 8 A.M. to sunset
No entrance fee
910 acres

**Activities:** an archery range, basketball, biking, boating, camping, canoeing, fishing, fitness stations, hiking, horseback riding, ice-skating, picnicking, a playground, soccer, and swimming.

Canoes, rowboats, and paddleboats may be rented at the boathouse on this seventeen-acre lake. Four miles of trails wind through pine and oak trees and offer great views of the rich wildlife at this park. Plants and animals native to the Pine Barrens are often sighted here. The shelter building has vending machines, a kitchen, and an inviting fireplace in the lounge.

Family campsites (732-462-7286) are open March 15 to November 30 and provide spaces for tents and travel trailers. There are also a few cabins that are available to rent.

### Wolf Hill Recreation Area
Eatontown Boulevard
Oceanport
Monmouth County
732-842-4000
Open 8 A.M. to sunset
No entrance fee
91 acres

**Activities:** baseball, biking, hiking, and sledding.

This recently opened recreation area was given its unique name because of the wolves that once roamed the area at night in search of hides from a tannery that was located on the hill. The park has many open fields and contains the remnants of a farm once operated by the Billings family. The Monmouth Park Race Track, located next to the park, once maintained the Billings' farmhouse as a trophy room.

### Alamuchy and Stephens State Park
180 Stephens State Park Road
Hackettstown
Morris County
908-852-3790
Open sunrise to sunset
No entrance fee
9,200 acres

**Activities:** biking, boating, canoeing, cross-country skiing, fishing, hiking, horseback riding, hunting, ice fishing, ice-skating, picnicking, a playground, and sledding.

The name of the park is derived from the name of the Delaware Indian chief, Allamuchahokkingen, whose name means, "place within the hills." This name was also given, in his honor, to the first settlement of Europeans in the area in 1715. The Rutherford and Stuyvesant families once owned the majority of the land in this area. These families were direct descendants of Peter Stuyvesant, the last Governor of New Amsterdam. In the early 1970s, the state began purchasing the land with the intention of preserving it.

Alamuchy Natural Area contains fifteen miles of trails suitable for hiking, bicycle riding, horseback riding, and cross-county skiing. Saxton Falls, a beautiful and peaceful spot, contains the remnants of one of the Morris Canal locks. The Musconetcong River is stocked with trout and provides great fishing opportunities. Picnic tables are scattered along the river. Family campsites are open April 1 to October 31 and are located in wooded areas, complete with fire rings, picnic tables, and spaces for tents.

Another feature of this park is Waterloo Village, a restored historical community located along the banks of the Morris Canal.

### Bamboo Brook Outdoor Education Center

170 Longview Road
Chester
Morris County
973-326-7600
Open sunrise to sunset
No entrance fee
100 acres

**Activities:** bird watching and hiking.

The Bamboo Brook Outdoor Education Center was once known as Merchiston Farm and was the home of William and Martha Brookes Hutcheson from 1911 to 1959. Mrs. Hutcheson designed the beautiful gardens located around the house. She was one of the first women to be trained as a landscape architect in the United States. Mrs. Hutcheson was a popular landscaper who plied her talents for estates located in Massachusetts, Long Island, and New Jersey. She is also the author of a 1923 book entitled *The Spirit of the Garden*. This unique area contains many native and foreign plant species and trails that lead through the many gardens and fields. Birds, butterflies, and an abundance of wildlife may be found here.

### Elizabeth D. Kay Environmental Center

200 Pottersville Road
Chester
Morris County
973-879-0566
Open sunrise to sunset
No entrance fee
233 acres

**Activities:** bird watching and hiking.

Beautiful meadows of wildflowers greet you as you drive down the road towards the environmental center. Nature trails will take you through many areas that feature flowering trees, shrubs, quiet streams, and a variety of wildlife. A forest of Eastern Hemlock trees near the Black River contains the stone ruins of an old summerhouse. The environmental center is open weekdays, September through June from 9 A.M. to 4:40 P.M. and seven days a week in July and August. It offers many environmental programs and organized nature walks.

### Frelinghuysen Arboretum
53 East Hanover Avenue
Morris Township
Morris County
973-326-7600
Open 8 A.M. to sunset
No entrance fee
127 acres

**Activities:** hiking.

Mathilda Frelinghuysen donated her Colonial-Revivalist-style house and the magnificently landscaped grounds to the county in 1969, so that the public may enjoy its beauty. Her house, built in 1891, is now the headquarters of the county's park system. The grounds are ideal for informal picnics and contain many trails that run through the forest, fields, and gardens. The education center is open Mondays through Sundays from 9 A.M. to 4:30 P.M. and features flower and plant shows, special events, exhibits, and horticulture classes. The gift shop is open Mondays through Saturdays from 10 A.M. to 4 P.M. and Sundays from 1 P.M. to 4 P.M. The shop has a wide range of items for sale. Free tours of the grounds are offered at 2 P.M. on Saturdays and Sundays in late April through the end of October.

### Great Swamp National Wildlife Refuge
Pleasant Plains Road
Basking Ridge
Morris County
973-425-1222
Open sunrise to sunset
No entrance fee
6,818 acres

**Activities:** bird watching, and hiking.

Native Americans gave this land to English colonists in 1708. During the 1840s, the woods were cleared and marshes drained in order for farmers to successfully grow crops. However, these small farms did not prosper and the forest gradually took back the land. In the late 1950s, a proposal for an airport in the Great Swamps was put forth. It was this threat of development that sparked an effort by local citizens to form a committee and raise money to purchase and preserve the land.

The Great Swamp includes over 200 species of birds and has a wide variety of other wildlife. There are also over eight miles of trails in this refuge. Office hours are Mondays through Fridays from 8 A.M. to 4:30 P.M.

The park also has a wildlife observation center located off Long Hill Road. It is an excellent area for observing the local wildlife and has over one mile of trails and several interesting interpretive displays.

### Great Swamp Outdoor Education Center

247 Southern Boulevard
Chatham
Morris County
973-635-6629
Open 8 A.M. to sunset
No entrance fee
40 acres

**Activities:** bird watching and hiking.

This education center is located east of the Great Swamp and contains two classrooms, an auditorium, a reference library, and an exhibit hall. In addition, several educational programs and organized nature walks are offered on weekends. The center is open daily, September through June

**FACT:** *In the 1800s, hauling freight by wagon was expensive and slow. The continuing growth and prosperity in New Jersey demanded a more viable means of transporting goods. Canals were the answer. The Morris Canal opened in 1832. This artificial waterway ran from the Delaware River at Phillipsburg and went out across the mountains of Morris County. By 1836 the canal was extended to Jersey City and measured 109 miles in length. Due to increased rail competition in the 1920s, the canal ceased to operate.*

from 9 A.M. to 4:30 P.M. There are over two miles of trails, which include a boardwalk, that take you through the swamp and woodlands. An abundance of wildlife can be found in this area including over 200 species of birds. The trail culminates with an observation deck that affords a great view of the surrounding area.

### Hacklebarney State Park

Hacklebarney Road
Chester
Morris County
908-638-6969
Open sunrise to sunset
No entrance fee
892 acres

**Activities:** bird watching, fishing, hiking, hunting, picnicking, and a playground.

Hacklebarney Park was established in 1924, with the donation of 32 acres of land from Adolphe E. Borie. A dense forest, consisting of 356 acres of Eastern Hemlock, includes several miles of trails and features many rare plant species. There are over 100 species of birds and many types of wildlife that make this area their home, including black bear, white-tailed deer, and several species on the endangered list. The Black River cuts through this park, as do the Rinehard and Trout Brooks. The two brooks empty into the Black River making several small waterfalls along the way. The area offers excellent bird watching opportunities, especially during the spring and fall migrations. Hunting is allowed, but restricted to a 260-acre tract within the park.

### Hedden County Park

124 Reservoir Avenue
Randolph
Morris County
973-326-7600
Open 8 A.M. to sunset
No entrance fee
285 acres

**Activities:** baseball, boating, cross-country skiing, hiking, ice-skating, picnicking and a playground.

This park is named after the Hedden family who donated the original 40 acres of land to the county in 1963. The entrance on Reservoir Avenue leads to a fishing pier and a group picnic shelter that can accommodate up to 200 people. The boathouse stands on the beach of a picturesque, six-acre lake and rents out paddleboats and rowboats. The boathouse is open weekends, Memorial Day through mid-June from 11 A.M. to 6 P.M. and from late-June through Labor Day, Wednesdays through Sundays from 11 A.M. to 6 P.M. At the Concord Road entrance, there are hiking trails that follow the Kasckon Brook as well as additional picnic areas.

**Hopatcong State Park**
Lakeside Boulevard
Landing
Morris County
973-398-7010
Open sunrise to sunset
No entrance fee
113 acres

**Activities:** basketball, boating, fishing, ice fishing, ice-skating, jet skiing, picnicking, a playground, sledding, snowmobiling, and swimming.

The 2,500-acre Lake Hopatcong is the largest lake in the state. It was formed in 1750 from the joining of two smaller, adjacent lakes, the Great Pond and the Little Pond. These ponds were combined when a dam was constructed to provide power for a local iron forge. During the mid 1800s, the Morris Canal and Banking Company built another dam across the river and the lake became the principal source of water for the Morris Canal. The Lake Hopatcong Historical Museum (973-389-2616) is located in the old canal lock-tender's house. It features a history of the canal as well as information and exhibits on the Native Americans, who once lived in this region. The museum is open Saturdays and Sundays from Noon to 4 P.M., beginning with the second weekend of April through the end of June and again with the second weekend of September through November.

During the summer months, swimming is allowed in the lake. It is lifeguard supervised and changing areas, a snack bar, and beach supplies are located nearby. Fishing is allowed on the lake and on the nearby Musconetcong River. There are many privately owned marinas located around Lake Hopatcong and there are no motor restrictions for boats. A public boat ramp is available at the lake.

**Lewis Morris County Park**
270 Mendham Road
Morris Township
Morris County
973-326-7600
Open 8 A.M. to sunset
No entrance fee
1,154 acres

**Activities:** baseball, boating, camping, cross-country skiing, fitness stations, fishing, hiking, picnicking, a playground, sledding, and swimming.

This park is named in honor of Lewis Morris who became the first Governor of New Jersey in 1738. There are several miles of trails throughout this park as well as a few camping sites. Swimming is allowed in Sunset Lake and is lifeguard supervised with changing areas provided nearby. A boathouse (973-267-4351), located on a pier, rents paddleboats and canoes.

**Loantaka Brook Reservation**
South Street
Morris Township
Morris County
973-326-7600
Open 8 A.M. to sunset
No entrance fee
574 acres

**Activities:** baseball, biking, cross-country skiing, hiking, horseback riding, picnicking, and a playground.

This linear park has over four miles of paved trails and features many acres of quiet woodlands. A group picnic area with a pavilion is available for reservations. Hiking and bike riding are allowed in the Helen Hartley Jenkins Woods area. This densely wooded area includes the peaceful Loantaka Brook and is one of the finest untouched forests in the nation. Adjacent to the park, on South Street, is the Seaton Hackney Stables (973-267-1372), which includes a one and a fifth-mile oval track. The stables provide a permanent shelter for horses (for a small boarding fee) and offer riding lessons to young and old alike.

**Mahlon Dickerson
Reservation**
995 Weldon Road
Jefferson
Morris County
973-663-0200
Open 8 A.M. to sunset
No entrance fee
3,200 acres

**Activities:** an archery range, baseball, biking, camping, cross-country skiing, fishing, horseback riding, horseshoes, ice-skating, picnicking, and a playground

Named in honor of the former New Jersey Supreme Court Justice and governor, this reservation is both the largest and has the highest elevation in Morris County. Headley Overlook is 1,300 feet above sea level and features a picnic area at its peak, affording an unmatched view. There are over 20 miles of peaceful, wooded trails that wind throughout this park. Camping areas are complete with modern facilities nearby and there is a picnic area with a shelter that can be reserved. A unique and popular feature of this park is a racetrack for radio-controlled cars.

**Morristown National Historic
Park**
Jockey Hollow Road
Morristown
Morris County
973-539-2085
Open 9 A.M. to 5 P.M
Entrance fee from Memorial Day
through Labor Day
1,675 acres

**Activities:** biking, cross-country skiing, hiking, and horseback riding.

During the winter of 1779-1780, Washington was determined to secure a defensive campsite for his troops. The land around Morristown was selected by General Washington to accommodate his camped army because it provided almost total protection from sudden attacks by British forces. The rugged mountains and broad swamps served as natural fortifications for the soldiers. At this vantage point, Washington could keep an eye on the nearby British troops that were located in New York. He could also guard the roads connecting New England with Philadelphia and react swiftly to any threat.

This was not the first time the Continental Army had camped for the winter at Morristown. Washington had previously settled his troops here during the winter of 1777. The army, then numbering around 5,000 soldiers, was quartered in the local townspeople's homes.

This time however, the local people did not want the army living with them. They complained about the soldiers' rude behavior and crude lifestyle. As the Continental Army arrived in Morristown, Washington ordered his men to begin construction of a city of log cabins to be located just outside the town. However construction was delayed as terrible winter weather forced the men to seek shelter in their small tents that provided little warmth against the cold. With seven blizzards that December alone, this was the worst winter of the century. Throughout all of December the men slept under whatever shelter they could find. Many had no covering at all. Many more froze to death or succumbed to starvation because the roads were closed and food supplies could not get through the snow. It was not until early February that all of the cabins could be completed.

Senior officers of the Continental Army had it much easier. Washington and his Aides-de-Camp stayed in the luxurious Georgian-style home of the widowed Mrs. Jacob Ford. Other officers lived in the private homes of the local townspeople. Still, conditions were cramped. Morristown at this time totaled just a little over 50 houses and had a population of less than 300 people.

More then 11,000 soldiers occupied the 2,000-acre tract known as Jockey Hollow. A total of 1,200 log huts were constructed for the men. The cabins measured 14-feet wide by 16-feet long by 6½-feet high. Twelve soldiers were quartered in each cabin.

On June 24, 1780, General Washington learned that the enemy had started to move towards Staten Island. This information freed him from having to continue to guard against an attack into Morris County. Washington ordered his troops to begin to move the next day.

Morristown National Historic Park became the first national historic park in the United States on March 2, 1932, when President Herbert Hoover signed the bill into law. The park includes over 27 miles of foot and horse trails in the Jockey Hollow section alone. Color-coded trail maps are available at the Jockey Hollow Visitor's Center.

**Ford Mansion:** This Georgian-style mansion was completed in 1774, by Jacob Ford Jr. Mr. Ford was a wealthy businessman who owned a forge and was also a colonel in the New Jersey Militia. His home was considered to be one of the finest houses in all of Morristown. When General Washington came to the town on December 1, 1777, this house was instantly

---

**FACT:** *Morris County was once a leading producer of iron in the United States. There were close to 200 iron mines, 100 forges, and more than a dozen furnaces in the county. In 1880, Morris County ranked third in the nation in the amount of iron that was mined, producing approximately 570,000 tons.*

chosen for his winter headquarters. Washington, his wife, and his Aides-de-Camp occupied two out of the eight rooms in the mansion. Today, visitors are offered guided tours of the Ford Mansion, which is decorated with original furniture and displays some of Washington's personal belongings. *Hours:* Tours are given hourly starting at 10:00 A.M.

**Fort Nonsense:** Rising 230 feet above Morristown, this site was the location of a fort built in 1777, by soldiers of the Continental Army. The stated mission of this fort was to protect the army's supplies and to keep watch for enemy movement. At this height, lookouts could scan for beacon fires that would warn of enemy troop movements out of New York City. Washington named the fortification the "upper redoubt."

The fort never saw any action and over the years the purpose for building it became unclear. A story slowly grew that Washington ordered the fort built in order to keep the soldiers busy and it served no practical purpose. Many people soon began referring to the structure as "Fort Nonsense."

Today, Fort Nonsense has long crumbled away. Only blocks of granite are visible, marking the outline of the fort's foundation. The Washington Association placed the blocks there in 1888.

**Washington Headquarters Museum:** This museum contains many artifacts and exhibits from the Revolutionary War. There is also a library that contains over 50,000 manuscripts including many rare books and diaries of soldiers. *Hours:* Daily, 9 A.M. to 5 P.M. *Phone:* 973-539-2085.

## Jockey Hollow Area

**Guerin House:** At the time of the winter encampment, a local farmer, Joshua Guerin, owned this eighteenth century farmhouse. The army's prolonged stay took a toll on Joshua's homestead. He was forced to apply for compensation from the Continental Army for theft of his sheep and other belongings taken by soldiers. Today, the house is restored and is now a private residence.

**Jockey Hollow Encampment Area:** This is the largest and most visited section of the park. It contains a visitor center, several reconstructed soldiers' huts, an eighteenth century farm, and several open fields where the army camped for the winter. This section is very popular for walkers and bicycle riders. A two-mile long loop road is accessible to automobiles and offers a great tour of the area.

**Jockey Hollow Visitor's Center:** The visitor's center contains information about the entire park. A short film is featured about the Revolution and depicts how the army struggled to survive in the freezing winter weather. *Hours* Daily, 9 A.M. to 5 P.M. *Phone:* 973-543-4030.

**Patriot's Path:** This trail connects Lewis Morris Park with the Jockey Hollow section of the Morristown National Historic Park. The path begins near the New Jersey Brigade Encampment Site and contains numerous parking areas and access points along the way.

**Wick House:** Henry Wick built this small Cape Cod style farmhouse set on 1,400 acres of land around 1750. During the winter encampment, General Arthur St. Clair and his aides occupied the house along with Henry's wife Mary and their 21-year-old daughter Temperance. Temperance received a note of fame from her efforts to hide her horse in the farmhouse so the army would not take it. At the time of the encampment, Henry, at age 72, was serving as a volunteer for the Morris County Calvary.

A tour of the farm also includes an herb garden and a horse barn. Park Rangers dress in colonial cloths and perform cooking demonstrations inside the house. *Hours:* Daily, 9 A.M. to 4:30 P.M.

**Mount Hope Historical Park**
Richard Mine Road
Rockaway
Morris County
973-326-7600
Open 8 A.M. to sunset
No entrance fee
438 acres

**Activities:** hiking.

This park was once part of a 6,271-acre tract of land originally purchased by John Jacob Faesch in 1772. He used the land to supply the nearby, large-scale iron mine that he owned and operated. Over the years, the land was divided into several pieces as different mining companies built facilities here.

The last of the mines ceased operations in 1958, but there are still many ruins left to explore. Visitors will enjoy the two miles of trails and abundance of wildlife in this undeveloped park. Of particular interest is the old rail bed of the Mount Hope Mineral Railroad that hauled ore through this once booming iron mine.

**FACT:** *The name Rockaway is based on the Indian word, "Rechouwakie," meaning "the place of sands." Rockaway Township was well known for its abundance of iron. When settlers came to the area in the early 1700s, the Lenape Indians showed them "succasunna" or "black stone."*

**Old Troy Park**
440 Reynolds Avenue
Parsippany-Troy Hills
Morris County
973-326-7631
Open sunrise to sunset
No entrance fee
96 acres

**Activities:** baseball, biking, cross-country skiing, hiking, horseshoes, picnicking, and a playground.

Old Troy is a beautiful park that includes a picnic area with a shelter and a pond. There are many trails to walk along through the woodlands and swamps.

**Passaic River County Park**
River Road
Chatham
Morris County
973-326-7600
Open 8 A.M. to sunset
No entrance fee
711 acres

**Activities:** baseball, cross-country skiing, fishing, hiking, ice-skating, picnicking, and a playground.

This park is located along the Passaic River and has approximately 5,000-feet of shoreline, which makes it a great fishing and recreation destination. The river is only a short walk from the parking lot.

**Pyramid Mountain Historic Area**
472 Boonton Avenue
Montville
Morris County
973-334-3130
Open 8 A.M. to sunset
No entrance fee
1240 acres

**Activities:** bird watching and hiking.

Surveyor markers and stonewalls still mark the foundations of the home-steads and farms of early European settlers that once lived in this area. The park's many trails take hikers through fields, forests, and wetlands. Along the blue trail are a few overlooks that provide great views of the New York Skyline and the surrounding areas. Along the white trail, visitors will encounter the famous Tripod Rock, a multi-ton boulder that is balanced on three smaller rocks. Pyramid Mountain is home to over 400 species of plants, 100 species of birds, and an abundance of other wildlife. The Big Cat and Little Cat Swamps were named for the native bobcats that still inhabit the caves and shallow depressions of the region. Bears, beavers, and wild turkeys may also be found roaming the area. The visitor's center is open Mondays through Saturdays from 10 A.M. to 4:30 P.M. and offers guided hikes beginning at 1 P.M. on the weekends.

### Schooley's Mountain County Park

91 East Springtown Road
Washington
Morris County
973-326-7600
Open 8 A.M. to sunset
No entrance fee
782 acres

**Activities:** baseball, biking, boating, fishing, hiking, horseback riding, horseshoes, ice-skating, picnicking, and a playground.

This park was named in honor of the Schooley family who were propri-etors of land in the 1790s. This was also once home to the Morristown YMCA's Camp Washington. The former lodge has spacious rooms available to rent for receptions, reunions, or other special occasions. There is a boat-house (973-326-7600) on a pond that is open Memorial Day through Labor Day and rents paddleboats and rowboats. The boathouse also has vending machines and a warm fireplace. This park has many hiking trails, a natural, outdoor amphitheatre and a group picnic area (973-326-7631) that includes a pavilion and may be reserved.

### Silas Condict County Park

100 Kinnelon Road
Kinnelon
Morris County
973-326-7631
Open 8 A.M. to sunset
No entrance fee
265 acres

**Activities:** baseball, cross-country skiing, fishing, hiking, horseshoes, ice fishing, ice-skating, picnicking, and a playground.

This park was named for the Revolutionary War patriot, Silas Condict. He was a local farmer, surveyor, politician, and a member of the committee that drafted the first New Jersey Constitution. Silias was also a member of the Continental Congress and was elected to the state house of assembly, serving as its speaker.

There are several scenic overlooks and many trails in this beautiful park. A boathouse, which rents paddleboats and rowboats, has a patio that overlooks the seven-acre lake. The building is available to rent for receptions or meetings. The boathouse has a bit of a history, as it was once known as the Casino and is rumored to have been a speakeasy in the days of prohibition.

**Tourne County Park**
40 McCaffrey Road
Boonton and Denville
Morris County
973-326-7600
Open 8 A.M. to sunset
No entrance fee
545 acres

**Activities:** baseball, biking, cross-country skiing, horseback riding, picnicking, and a playground.

The name Tourne was derived from the Dutch word meaning "lookout" and this park does live up to that name, featuring very impressive views of the surrounding area. Samuel Ogden, a local miner, built the park's entrance in 1767. He ran a mining operation that at one time hauled iron ore from the Hibernian mines to his ironworks in Boonton. During the Revolutionary War, this ironworks was a major producer of cannon balls for the Continental Army.

Today, Tourne Park has many winding trails that cross through wildflower fields and quiet woodlands. Along the trails, hikers will be fascinated by the strange rock formations. There is an abundance of plants and wildlife making this a great place to study nature.

## Willowwood Arboretum

300 Longview Road
Chester
Morris County
973-326-7600
Open 8 A.M. to sunset
No entrance fee
130 acres

**Activities:** hiking.

Named for the many willow trees that are concentrated in the area, this arboretum includes over 3,500 individual plants and trees. Once a farm, the main residence dates back to the 1790s and features two small formal gardens. Henry and Robert Tubbs further developed the grounds when they purchased the property in 1908. They collected and grew all kinds of native and exotic plant species. In 1980, the county took over the land, to preserve its natural beauty. Willowwood is adjacent to the Bamboo Brook Outdoor Education Center.

## Barnegat Lighthouse State Park

Broadway Avenue
Barnegat Light
Ocean County
609-494-2016
Open sunrise to sunset
No entrance fee
32 acres

**Activities:** bird watching, fishing, hiking, and picnicking.

Located on the northern tip of Long Beach Island, this state park was established in 1957 and is home to "Old Barney," as the lighthouse is affectionately know to the locals. Visitors may climb the lighthouse's 217 steps to the top and take in the views of the Barnegat Inlet and surrounding areas. The lighthouse is open daily, Memorial Day through Labor Day and on weekends from November through April. There are different schedules for the spring and fall; it is advisable to call the park office for current information. The picnic area has two shelters and is close to the 1,033-foot concrete walkway that follows the coastline, providing many great fishing opportunities. Hundreds of species of birds may be found in this park especially during the spring and fall migration seasons. A one fifth of a mile-trail loops through one of the last remaining maritime forests in the state. The forest's black cherry, sassafras, eastern red cedar, and American holly trees not only invite visitors with their natural beauty, they also provide vital nesting and feeding areas for migrating birds.

**Beaver Dam Creek County Park**
Bridge Avenue
Point Pleasant
Ocean County
887-627-2757
Open sunrise to sunset
No entrance fee
40 acres

**Activities:** baseball, basketball, picnicking, a playground, soccer, and tennis.

A boardwalk, built along the park's tidal wetlands, gives visitors a first hand look at the swamp and its wildlife. This park also includes a picnic area with a pavilion and a six-acre athletic playing field.

**Berkeley Island County Park**
Brennan Concourse
Berkeley
Ocean County
887-627-2757
Open sunrise to sunset
No entrance fee
25 acres

**Activities:** boating, crabbing, fishing, horseshoes, picnicking, a playground, swimming, and volleyball.

Berkeley Island is located at the end of a peninsula, which juts into Barnegat Bay. During the summer months, swimming is allowed and is lifeguard supervised. A 100-foot pier is always available and provides great fishing opportunities. There are two picnic areas with shelters that may be reserved and can accommodate up to 75 people each.

## Cattus Island County Park

1170 Cattus Island Boulevard
Toms River
Ocean County
732-270-6960
Open 8 A.M. to sunset
No entrance fee
497 acres

**Activities:** biking, bird watching, crabbing, cross-country skiing, fishing, hiking, picnicking, and a playground.

John V.A. Cattus, a prominent New York businessman, purchased this land in 1895, to use as his summer residence. Today, there is little evidence of his house and outbuildings, but the county has preserved the land that Mr. Cattus once owned for future generations.

There are over eight miles of trails, including a 1,500-foot boardwalk that provides easy access through the salt marsh and pine-tree forest. Guided nature walks are offered Sundays at 2 P.M. Close to 300 plant species grow in this park and provide food and shelter to hundreds of birds. This rich natural habitat is a great place for bird watching especially during the spring and fall migration seasons.

The 5,000-square foot Cooper Environmental Center is open from 9 A.M. to 5 P.M. in the summer and from 10 A.M. to 4 P.M. during the winter. It includes exhibits and a library and offers a variety of nature programs.

## Island Beach State Park

Central Avenue
Seaside Park
Ocean County
732-793-0506
Open sunrise to sunset
No entrance fee
3,002 acres

**Activities:** biking, canoeing, fishing, horseback riding, scuba diving, and swimming.

During colonial times, Island Beach was known as Lord Sterling's Island. Over the years, there have been attempts to turn this area into a seaside resort. Fortunately, they never materialized and the land has been preserved. The state purchased this land for preservation and public recreation purposes. The park officially opened in 1959 and is one of the few undeveloped barrier beaches left on the Atlantic coast.

With its sandy beaches and miles of trails, Island Beach is a perfect place to relax and enjoy the natural surroundings. Swimming is allowed from mid-June through Labor Day and is lifeguard supervised. Changing areas and a food concession stand are available close to the beach. The park's maritime forests, the last few remaining in the state, attract many birds and are great places for bird watching, especially during the spring and fall migration seasons. There are no picnic tables in the park but picnics are allowed on the beach. The interpretive center includes a nature trail and is open daily from October 1 to April 30.

**Lake Shenandoah County Park**
Route 88 Ocean Avenue
Lakewood
Ocean County
732-506-9090
Open sunrise to sunset
No entrance fee
143 acres

**Activities:** baseball, biking, boating, fishing, picnicking, a playground, and soccer.

Surrounded by tall oak and pine trees, the 100-acre Lake Shenandoah is the focal point of this park. The waters are stocked with trout and there are two fishing piers with a nearby bait and tackle shop (732-363-9678). A boathouse rents rowboats and paddleboats and there is a small boat launch on the lake.

**Mill Creek County Park**
Mill Creek Road & Chelsea
    Avenue
Berkeley
Ocean County
887-627-2757
Open 8 A.M. to sunset
No entrance fee
14 acres

**Activities:** basketball, hiking, picnicking, and a playground.

Mill Creek features several trails and a sheltered picnic area with adjoining playground.

## Ocean County Park
Route 88 Ocean Avenue
Lakewood
Ocean County
887-627-2757
Open 8 A.M. to sunset
No entrance fee
323 acres

**Activities:** baseball, biking, cross-country skiing, fishing, picnicking, a playground, shuffleboard, swimming, tennis, and volleyball.

This park was once John D. Rockefeller's summer vacation site. Near the entrance, there are many tall, white pines that were planted during the 1920s and 1930s. During this era, Rockefeller imported many trees from parks all over the world.

Picnic tables overlook the beautiful pond, which features a swimming area with nearby changing facilities. There is also an eight court tennis center with a pro shop (732-506-9090, ext. 211) that offers lessons during the spring and summer months. A unique feature of this park is an open field that is used as a golf ball driving range.

## S. Mary Grace Burns Arboretum
Georgian Court College
900 Lakewood Avenue
Lakewood
Ocean County
732-346-2200 ext. 285
Open 8 A.M. to sunset
No entrance fee
152 acres

**Activities:** bird watching and hiking.

More than 300 native and exotic trees can be found in this beautifully landscaped arboretum. In 1896, George Jay Gould, the millionaire son of railroad tycoon Jay Gould, purchased this land for his residence. Bruce

**FACT:** *Created in 1875, Berkeley Township was named after Lord Berkeley, one of the original proprietors of New Jersey.*

Price, a famous New York architect, was hired to design the grounds and he created three major gardens. When George died in 1923, his heirs sold the property to the Sisters of Mercy who, under the agreement, had to keep the name of the estate, Georgian Court. A year later the sisters opened the college of the same name on the land.

The arboretum's Classic Garden was inspired by the formal gardens of Italy and includes life size statues of Greek gods and goddesses. The Japanese Garden includes many Japanese maple and cherry trees. Sister Mary Grace Burns, the first chairperson of the biology department, maintained, identified, and labeled the trees on the campus.

**Sambol-Citta Arboretum**
Ocean County College
College Drive
Toms River
Ocean County
732-255-4000
Open 8 A.M. to sunset
No entrance fee
10 acres

**Activities:** bird watching and hiking.

Richard S. Sambol and Joseph A. Citta initiated the development of this arboretum to stimulate interest in environmental sciences and to enhance the beauty of the campus. A winding trail leads through the many pine, spruce, and cherry trees that are clustered throughout the campus grounds. A small, placid pond is located near the center of the arboretum.

**Stanley H. Seaman County Park**
120 Lakeside Drive, Route 9
Tuckerton
Ocean County
609-296-5605
Open 8 A.M. to sunset
No entrance fee
22 acres

**Activities:** baseball, basketball, biking, boating, fishing, fitness stations, horse-shoes, picnicking, a playground, shuffleboard, soccer, tennis, and volleyball.

Located on the shores of Lake Pohatcong, this park includes a small boat launch and features a large recreation area.

## Wells Mills County Park
Route 532
Waretown
Ocean County
609-971-3085
Open 8 A.M. to sunset
No entrance fee
910 acres

**Activities:** biking, canoeing, fishing, hiking, picnicking, and a playground.

Wells Mills, which is located in the Pine Barrens, features 16 miles of hiking trails that traverse through beautiful forests of pine and oak trees. It was named after James Wells who built a dam and a sawmill here in the late 1700s. There are many rare plants and an abundance of wildlife in this park. Most of the area consists of freshwater wetlands.

The nature center offers many environmental programs and features an observation deck with great views of the surrounding area. It is open daily from 10 A.M. to 4 P.M. Also, canoes may be rented at the nature center. A boat launch is located on Wells Mills Lake.

## Garrett Mountain Reservation
Valley Road
West Paterson
Passaic County
973-881-4832
Open sunrise to sunset
No entrance fee
575 acres

**Activities:** fishing, hiking, horseback riding, and picnicking.

On top of Garrett Mountain stands an old, 70-foot tower that was once used as an observatory by Catholina Lambert. He made a fortune in the silk industry and by 1890, owned one of the largest mills in the Paterson area.

**FACT:** *The Pine Barrens includes 1.1 million acres in New Jersey and occupies 22% of the states land area.*

This reservation includes a stable (973-345-0449) that boards and rents horses. There are also many trails to stroll down and a pond that is stocked with trout.

**Goffle Brook Park**
795 Lafayette Avenue
Hawthorne
Passaic County
973-881-4832
Open sunrise to sunset
No entrance fee
103 acres

**Activities:** baseball, boating, cross-country skiing, fishing, ice-skating, picnicking, and a playground.

This park features the serene, five-acre Goffle Brook and several miles of hiking trails.

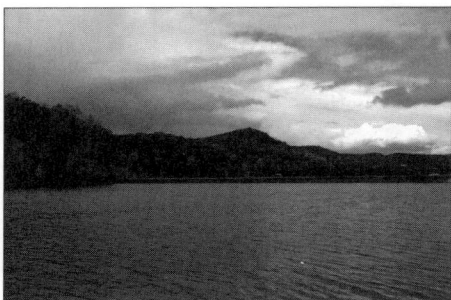

**Long Pond Ironworks State Park**
Route 511
West Milford
Passaic County
973-962-7031
Open sunrise to sunset
No entrance fee
1,725 acres

**Activities:** biking, bird watching, boating, canoeing, cross-country skiing, fishing, hiking, horseback riding, hunting, and ice-fishing.

**FACT:** *The 1903 film, "The Great Train Robbery", was mostly filmed in Passaic County by the Edison Film Company. The film, which was directed by Edwin S. Porter, is regarded as the first narrative film in history. It told a full story in just 14 silent, black and white scenes. During the filming, Porter used a number of innovative techniques, many of which were invented by Porter himself.*

This state park includes a boat ramp, which is open 24 hours a day, many miles of wilderness trails, and the remnants of an old ironworks factory, which is available for exploration. This is a very peaceful park and its natural surroundings provide great bird watching opportunities.

Long Pond Ironworks was founded in 1766, by German ironmaster Peter Hasenclever. He brought 500 workers and their families from Germany to construct this major ironworks operation, which included building a dam at "Long Pond," now known as Greenwood Lake. The dam provided the needed waterpower to operate the furnaces, which produced, among other products, greatly needed war materials during the Revolutionary War, the War of 1812 and the Civil War.

The ironworks shut down over 100 years ago, but many of the structures remain including the furnaces, the casting house, and the water-wheels. The area is currently undergoing a complete restoration. Tours of the furnace area and village are conducted and begin at the Long Pond Ironworks Historic District (973-657-1688).

### Ringwood Park Skylands Botanical

1304 Sloatsburg Road
Ringwood
Passaic County
973-962-7031
Open sunrise to sunset
No entrance fee
5,237 acres

**Activities:** biking, boating, canoeing, cross-country skiing, fishing, hiking, horseback riding, hunting, ice-fishing, ice-skating, picnicking, a playground, sledding, a shooting range, snowmobiles, and swimming.

This park was once part of a major ironworks plant that was developed in 1740, by the Ringwood Company. A dam was constructed on the Ringwood River to harness the water's power for the blast furnace and forges. This area was home to a number of ironmasters for nearly 200 years. During the Revolutionary War, this forge produced cannon balls for the Continental Army. In 1936, Erskine Hewitt donated the Ringwood Manor House and its grounds to the State of New Jersey.

The Ringwood River is stocked with trout and provides great fishing opportunities, while Bear Swamp Lake contains live bait and supplies.

**Ringwood Manor:** This large, country estate was once the home of the Hewitt family. Abram S. Hewitt, America's foremost ironmaster lived here. Inside, on display, is a large collection of nineteenth century American paintings and furniture. Free tours of the house are available. The parks main offices are also located in this building. *Hours:* Wednesdays to Sundays from 10 A.M. to 3:30 P.M. *Phone:* 973-962-7048

**Shepherd Lake:** This 74-acre lake features a boathouse (973-962-6999) that rents rowboats, canoes, and small sailboats. It is open weekends in the summer from 6 A.M. to 6 P.M. and weekdays from 8 A.M. to 6 P.M. In September, the hours for weekends change to 7 A.M. to 6 P.M. The swimming area is open daily Memorial Day through Labor Day and is lifeguard supervised. It is popular due to its fine sandy beaches and clear water. Changing areas and a food concession stand with beach supplies are located nearby. A concession-operated trap and skeet shooting range (973-962-6377) is located in this area and open throughout the year.

**Skylands Manor:** The building and grounds represent a historically accurate reproduction of an English mansion that was once common in the countryside nearly 400 years ago. In the 1920s, Clarence McKenzie, a New York stockbroker, built this house as his summer residence. Free tours of the manor are conducted and the landscaped grounds feature 1,100 acres of breathtaking gardens including a lilac garden, a wild flower garden, and a perennial garden. *Hours:* Sundays from 1 P.M. to 4 P.M. *Phone:* 973-962-7527.

**Weis Ecology Center**
150 Snake Den Road
Ringwood
Passaic County
973-835-2160
Open 9 A.M. to sunset
No entrance fee
160 acres

**Activities:** camping and hiking.

In 1974, Walter and May Weis purchased this land and opened the Weis Ecology Center. It is used primarily for environmental education purposes and offers a variety of classes and workshops on the subject. The center is open Wednesdays to Sundays from 8:30 A.M. to 4:30 P.M. Inside the building is a store that sells bird feeders, hiking supplies, and other nature related items. Cabins are located near the nature center and may be rented. In 1995, the Weis Ecology Center merged with the New Jersey Audubon Society.

**Colonial Park**
Metlars Road
Franklin
Somerset County
908-873-2695
Open 8 A.M. to sunset
No entrance fee
568 acres

**Activities:** baseball, biking, boating, cross-country skiing, fishing, fitness stations, hiking, ice-skating, picnicking, a playground, and tennis.

The Millstone River and the Delaware and Raritan Canal flow through this beautiful park. Two picnic areas, which may be reserved, can accommodate over 100 people each. The arboretum features many flowering shrubs, evergreens, and shade trees. The Rudolf W. van der Goot Rose Garden displays more than 3,000 roses from late spring through early autumn. A fragrance and sensory garden encourages visitors to touch and smell the many beautiful plants. The Perennial Garden, which occupies four beautifully landscaped acres, is centered on a gazebo.

A boathouse (908-873-8585) is located on Powder Mill Pond and rents paddleboats. The nearby wildlife refuge contains many trails and is a great place to get in touch with nature. The park also includes a tennis center (908-722-1200 ext. 226) that features eight tennis courts and a pro shop, which offers lessons. A unique feature at this park is a mini-putting course with holes 25- to 70-feet long.

**FACT:** *During the winter of 1777, while General Washington and his soldiers were stationed at Morristown, Lord Charles Cornwallis and his British troops were camped for the winter in New Brunswick. Washington sent General Benjamin Lincoln with a force of 500 American soldiers to Bound Brook in order to guard the town against enemy raids. On April 13, 1777, the Battle of Bound Brook took place with 4,000 British soldiers attacking the post. The British eventually captured the town and all its supplies.*

**Delaware and Raritan Canal**
625 Canal Road
Somerset
Somerset County
732-873-3050
Open sunrise to sunset
No entrance fee
3,785 acres

**Activities:** biking, bird watching, boating, canoeing, cross-country skiing, fitness stations, fishing, hiking, horseback riding, and picnicking.

The days of hauling freight along the canal are long gone, but fortunately with the creation of this park, most of the canal system is still intact. The Delaware and Raritan Canal State Park is a 70-mile linear park famous for its canoeing, hiking, and bicycle riding. This extremely picturesque park features many nineteenth century bridges, historic structures, and the remains of abandoned canal locks. Canoes may be rented at public places in the towns of Griggstown and Princeton and from private rental facilities located nearby.

The main section of the Delaware and Raritan Canal starts at Trenton and goes all the way up through the town of New Brunswick. A feeder canal travels close to the Delaware River and goes through such riverside towns as Lambertville, Stockton, and Frenchtown.

Delaware and Raritan Canal State Park offers many fishing and bird watching opportunities. There have been over 160 species of birds identified in this area.

**Blackwells Mills:** This area features a Bridge Tender's House, a wooden bridge, and an old mill. There are nearby picnic tables with grills and great views of the Millstone River. *Location:* Canal Road, Franklin.

**Cook Natural Area:** This 26-acre section contains dense clusters of woods and trails. There are also many small ponds in this undisturbed, natural setting. *Location:* Route 522, Kingston.

**Griggstown:** Griggstown features a wooden canal bridge, the Mule Tender's Barracks Canal Museum, a Bridge Tender's House, and the Griggstown Mill. Canoes are available for rent at this section of the park. Picnic tables and a food concession stand are located nearby. *Location:* Canal Road and River Road, Franklin.

**Prallsville Mills:** Prallsville Mills is a very picturesque nineteenth century mill complex. A trail passes through the restored village and over a bridge that overlooks a small waterfall. *Location:* Route 29, Stockton, Mercer County.

**Duke Island Park**
Park Drive off Old York Road
Bridgewater
Somerset County
908-722-7779
Open 8 A.M. to sunset
No entrance fee
332 acres

**Activities:** baseball, bird watching, boating, cross-country skiing, fishing, hiking, ice-skating, picnicking, and a playground.

The Raritan River and Raritan Power Canal both run through this park. There are five picnic areas with one area featuring a pavilion that can accommodate up to 250 people. In the summer, a series of free concerts are held at the park each Sunday evening during the months of June, July, and August. The park's many trails offer a peaceful getaway and a chance to view nature up close. A visitor center is located near the main parking lot.

**Lord Sterling Park**
259 South Maple Avenue
Basking Ridge
Somerset County
908-766-2489
Open 8 A.M. to sunset
No entrance fee
897 acres

**Activities:** bird watching, boating, cross-country skiing, fishing, hiking, and horseback riding.

The environmental education center is an 18,000-square foot building that includes an auditorium, an art gallery, a gift shop, and a library that features materials on natural history and environmental topics. Just outside the building is a boardwalk that runs along the river and provides outstanding views of the surrounding area.

The park's stables (908-766-5955) are situated on a secluded 450-acre section of the park with access to over 10 miles of trails. Several clinics are held annually. The facilities include indoor and outdoor trotter-rings. Horses are available to rent by the hour. The main office is open daily from 9 A.M. to 5 P.M.

**North Branch Park**
Milltown Road
Bridgewater
Somerset County
908-722-1200
Open 8 A.M. to sunset
No entrance fee
170 acres

**Activities:** baseball, bird watching, boating, cross-country skiing, fishing, horseback riding, picnicking, a playground, and soccer.

This park includes two picnic areas that may be reserved and has several tables scattered along the North Branch of the Raritan River. A unique feature of this park is the model aircraft and rocket fields, where visitors may enjoy their aerial hobbies without obstruction. North Branch Park is the home of the Independence Day Family Festival in July and the annual 4-H fair during August. The main offices of the Somerset County Park Commission are located here as well.

**High Point State Park**
1480 State Route 23
Sussex
Sussex County
973-875-4800
Open sunrise to sunset
No entrance fee
14,218 acres

**Activities:** biking, boating, camping, cross-country skiing, fishing, hiking, horseback riding, hunting, ice-skating, picnicking, a playground, snowmobiles, and swimming.

High Point State Park is located along the crest of the Kittatinny Mountains. Colonel Anthony and Susie Dryden Kuser donated this land to the state. This park has over 50 miles of trails, with the longest trail measuring 18-miles. Its lakes are stocked with trout and there are boat launches located at Sawmill Lake and Stennykill Lake.

For picnics, few other parks can compete. A group picnic area may be reserved and there is a 50-tent site with fire rings and picnic tables located along the 20-acre Sawmill Lake. The group site is open April 1 to October 31. There are also two smaller group campsites that are open May through October 15. Located along the eastern shore of the Steenykill Lake are two furnished cabins that contain a living room, fireplace, three bedrooms, kitchen with refrigerator, and a bathroom. They can accommodate up to 6 people each. These cabins are available from May 15 to October 15. There is also a larger group cabin that can hold up to 28 people and is available from May 15 to October 15.

**Dryden Kuser Natural Area:** This untouched natural area contains over 800 acres of land and rises 1,500 feet above sea level. Its Atlantic-white cedar swamp is the highest elevation swamp of its kind in the world. The area includes many miles of trails and an abundance of wildlife, including some endangered species.

**High Point Monument:** This monument was funded by the Kusers to honor New Jersey's Veterans. It is located on the highest point in the state, 1,803 feet above sea level. Visitors may climb the stairs of this 220-foot structure to the observation deck. The Pocono Mountains can be seen to the west, the Catskill Mountains to the north and the Wallkill River to the southeast.

**Lake Marcia:** This 20-acre lake includes lifeguard-supervised swimming during the summer months. Changing facilities and a food concession stand are located nearby. During the winter months the High Point Cross-Country Ski Center (973-702-1222) offers 24 miles of skiing trails throughout the park. Equipment may be rented in the pro shop, which includes a fireplace.

**Nature Center:** At the Nature Center, visitors have the opportunity to take part in many different interpretive programs and nature walks. *Hours:* June through October, weekends from 11 A.M. to 5 P.M.

**Parvin State Park**
701 Almond Road
Pittsgrove
Sussex County
856-358-8616
Open sunrise to sunset
No entrance fee
1,135 acres

**Activities:** biking, boating, canoeing, fishing, hiking, picnicking, and a playground.

Parvin State Park is situated along the edge of the Pine Barrens. Its forests are comprised mostly of pine and hardwood swamps. There are over 200 kinds of flowering plants located throughout the area. Several miles of trails run through the park and offer great wildlife viewing opportunities. Swimming is permitted in Parvin Lake and is lifeguard supervised. Changing facilities and a food concession stand are nearby.

There are 56 tent and trailer sites, each containing a fire ring and a picnic table. Modern facilities are located nearby. On the south shore of Parvin Lake, there is a group campsite that includes 15 cabins. Each cabin can accommodate up to four people and contains a furnished living room, a fireplace, a bathroom and a kitchen with a refrigerator. The cabins are available March 1 to November 30.

## Swartswood State Park

Route 619
Swartswood
Sussex County
973-383-5230
Open sunrise to sunset
No entrance fee
1,357 acres

**Activities:** basketball, biking, boating, canoeing, cross-country skiing, fishing, hiking, horseback riding, hunting, ice fishing, ice-skating, picnicking, a playground, sledding, swimming, and volleyball.

This park started in 1914, with a donation of 12½-acres of land from George M. Emmans. Swartswood Lake is stocked with trout and is one of the best fishing lakes in the state. Swimming is allowed in the lake from Memorial Day through Labor Day and is lifeguard supervised. A concession food stand and changing facilities are located nearby. A boathouse (973-383-4200) is located on the lake and rents rowboats, canoes, paddleboats, and kayaks. There are 75 campsites, each with a fire ring, picnic area, and space for a tent. Three group sites can accommodate up to 25 campers. Each group site includes modern facilities and a boat launch. A group picnic area may be reserved.

## Wawayanda State Park

885 Warwick Turnpike
Hewitt
Sussex County
973-853-4462
Open sunrise to sunset
No entrance fee
13,422 acres

**Activities:** biking, bird watching, boating, canoeing, cross-country skiing, picnicking, a playground, snowmobiles, and swimming.

Along the northern shore of the 255-acre Wawayanda Lake are the remnants of an iron-smelting town called Double Pond. It was a small factory town that operated during the last half of the nineteenth century. Only the blast furnace and the foundations of the village's buildings remain today.

The park is home to many species of plants and animals and even a few endangered species. There are over 40 miles of hiking trails, one of which is a section of the Appalachian Trail. Swimming is allowed in the lake when lifeguards are present. Changing facilities and a snack bar are located nearby and picnic areas are located near the shore of the lake. Canoes, paddleboats, and rowboats may be rented at the boathouse (201-764-1030). There are also three group campsites, which are open April 1 through October 31, located in this park.

**Briant Park**
Park Drive
Summit
Union County
908-527-4900
Open sunrise to sunset
No entrance fee
30 acres

**Activities:** fishing, fitness stations, ice-skating, picnicking, and a playground.

This park was once the estate of William Briant. During the mid 1800s, Briant constructed a dam, which created the present day lake. He ran a milling operation and also supplied the local citizens with ice during the winter months. In 1930, caretakers of the estate sold the property, including a ten-bedroom mansion, to the Union County Park System. Today, Briant Park contains several miles of trails and has a picnic area that may be reserved.

**Echo Lake Park**
Mountain Avenue
Mountainside
Union County
908-527-4900
Open sunrise to sunset
No entrance fee
144 acres

**Activities:** baseball, boating, fishing, fitness stations, ice-skating, picnicking, a playground, and sledding.

This pristine lake and park have recently undergone several improvements and renovations. Overlooking Echo Lake is a boathouse (908-232-9819) where visitors may rent rowboats and paddleboats. The boathouse is open daily, April through October. There is also a large picnic area that may be reserved.

### Nomahegan Park
Springfield Avenue
Cranford
Union County
908-527-4900
Open sunrise to sunset
No entrance fee
95 acres

**Activaties:** baseball, biking, fishing, ice-skating, picnicking, a playground, and soccer.

This park offers a paved trail that follows the shoreline of the lake, giving a splendid view of the surrounding area. There is also a picnic area that may be reserved.

### Reeves-Reed Arboretum
165 Hobart Avenue
Summit
Union County
908-273-8787
Open sunrise to sunset
No entrance fee
13 acres

**Activities:** bird watching and hiking.

This arboretum dates back to the Revolutionary War, when the land was originally a farm. In 1899, John Horner Wisner built the mansion that now serves as the administrative center. Wisner used this site for his country estate and had the property beautifully landscaped and maintained. His wife planted the original group of daffodils, which are now a major attraction during the month of April.

In 1916, Mr. and Mrs. Richard Reeves purchased the property and began to add to the collections and gardens. They designed a rose garden with a connecting rock-pool garden and hired Italian masons to lay the stone steps near the house.

Charles L. Reed purchased the property in 1968 and added the herb garden and enlarged the woodland trails. He was the last private owner of the estate.

In 1974, local citizens met with representatives from the town of Summit and agreed to raise money to purchase the land and preserve it. Today, this beautifully landscaped arboretum features incredible gardens, open fields, and nature trails.

The mansion and office are open Mondays, Tuesdays, Thursdays, and Fridays from 9 A.M. to 3 P.M. The formal garden peaks in mid-June. The education center includes a library and gift shop, and sponsors periodic events and seasonal programs.

The arboretum's garden shop is open Mondays through Saturdays from 10 A.M. to 4 P.M. It has a large selection of fine crafts that reflect the beauty of nature and can find a place in any home. If you love birds you will want to stop in and check out the shop's birdhouse kits, selection of birdseed, and books about these feathered creatures. The garden shop also sponsors many educational programs for children such as field trips, summer camps, and workshops. There are also field trips for adults, as well as many different gardening classes.

**Warinanco Park**
Linden Road
Roselle
Union County
908-298-7850
Open sunrise to sunset
No entrance fee
204 acres

**Activities:** baseball, basketball, biking, boating, cricket, fishing, fitness stations, handball, horseshoes, ice-skating, picnicking, a playground, a running track, shuffleboard, soccer, and tennis.

**Boathouse:** *Location:* St. Georges Avenue. *Phone:* 908-289-1899. *Hours:* Summer Months.

**Ice Skating Center:** *Location:* Thompson Avenue. *Phone:* 908-298-7849.

**Tennis Courts:** *Location:* Park Street and Jersey Avenue. *Phone:* 908-245-2288. *Hours:* Mid-April through mid-October.

**Watchung Reservation**
452 New Providence Road
Mountainside
Union County
908-789-3670
Open sunrise to sunset
No entrance fee
2,000 acres

**Activities:** baseball, bird watching, cross-country skiing, fishing, hiking, horseback riding, ice-skating, picnicking, and a playground.

Located along the first and second ranges of the Watchung Mountains, this reservation features over 13 miles of trails and scenic picnic areas, which may be reserved (908-527-4900). Surprise Lake, Seeley's Pond, and the Blue Brook are stocked with trout and provide great fishing opportunities.

**Deserted Village of Feltville:** This historic village features 10 buildings that date from the mid 1800s. It is contained on a large tract of land. Walking tours are conducted frequently from April through October.

**Nature and Science Center:** Inside this educational center is a natural history gift shop, ever-changing exhibits, an auditorium that can accommodate up to 259 people, and a 550-volume library. Near the main entrance of the building is an exhibit on the deserted village of Feltville. During January and February, cross-country skiing lessons are offered. *Location:* Coles Avenue and New Providence Road, Mountainside. *Hours:* Daily, 1 P.M. to 5 P.M. *Phone:* 908-789-3670.

**Trailside Museum:** This center opened in 1941 and is New Jersey's first nature center. Inside are exhibits on animals and birds that can be found throughout the reservation. There are also displays of animal tracks, trees, and fossils. *Hours:* Daily, 1 P.M. to 5 P.M. Closed Mondays to Fridays from the last week in November through the last week in March.

**Trailside Planetarium:** This planetarium, which contains an 18-foot diameter dome and a Nova Star projector, can accommodate up to 40 visitors. *Hours:* Shows start Sundays at 2 P.M. for ages 6 and up, 3:30 P.M. laser shows for ages 10 and up, and 3:30 P.M. weekly show for ages 4-6.

**Visitor's Center:** The Visitors Center contains exhibits on both the history of the early settlers and the natural history of the area. It also includes a gift shop, a bird attraction area, and herb and wildflower gardens.

**Watchung Stables:** These stables offer both children and adults the opportunity to ride a horse along the more than 26 miles of trails. Horses may be rented by the hour. Lessons are available as well as dedicated riding sessions for the disabled. *Location:* 1160 Summit Lane. *Phone:* 908-789-3665. *Hours:* Mondays through Fridays from 9 A.M. to 12 P.M. and again from 1 P.M. to 5 P.M. Saturdays and Sundays from 8:30 A.M. to 12 P.M. and again from 1 P.M. to 5 P.M.

## Wheeler Park
Wood Avenue
Linden
Union County
908-527-4900
Open sunrise to sunset
No entrance fee
19 acres

**Activities:** baseball, basketball, picnicking, a playground, soccer, and swimming.

This park is named after John Russell Wheeler, the first Marine from New Jersey that lost his life in World War I. This park features a pool (908-862-0977), which is open throughout the summer months.

## Delaware Water Gap
Route 80
Warren County
570-588-2435
Open sunrise to sunset
No entrance fee
67,205 acres

**Activities:** biking, bird watching, boating, canoeing, cross-country skiing, fishing, hiking, horseback riding, hunting, picnicking, a playground, and swimming.

During the nineteenth century, this area was a popular resort. Large hotels were opened and they catered to affluent businessmen and their families. Many people flocked to this region because of the quality of the air, the coolness of the breezes, and other perceived health benefits. For most of the vacationing urbanites, this was a drastic change from the hot and polluted cities.

Today, most of the large hotels are gone and people only come here for short stays rather than the week and month-long vacations of old. However, the air is still crisp and the views are just as spectacular as they ever were.

There are more than 200 miles of roadways winding through the scenic valleys, over ridges, and past historic structures. Old Mine Road is the main road into the park and is particularly pleasant to travel. There are a number of waterfalls in this park and more than 60 miles of trails, including a 25-mile section of the Appalachian Trail. Mount Tammany (1,527 feet) and Mount Minsi (1,463 feet) provide unique climbing experience and awesome views of the Delaware Water Gap. Swimming is allowed along the 40 miles of shoreline of the Delaware River and on the sandy beaches at the Milford and Smithfield recreation areas. The Water Gap is a great place for avid naturists and bird watchers. Hawks and Bald Eagles are common sights in the sky and there are other animals, including deer, black bears, and beavers, that are abundant.

**Appalachian Trail Camping:** Camping along the trail is permitted for hikers who are on extended hikes more than one day in duration. For safety, camping is restricted to within 100 feet from the trail. *Hours:* Open all year. *Phone:* 570-588-2451.

**Bushkill Visitors Center:** The Bushkill Visitor's Center offers insights about the animals that are most commonly found in the park. Visitors have the opportunity to learn more about the activities of such animals as bats and bears and why beavers build their dams. Inside the building is an exhibit on the history of the Water Gap area and a display of what flowers are currently blooming in the park. A short hike, conducted by park rangers, gives visitors the opportunity to learn about the geology of one of the more impressive natural sights, the Dingmans Falls. The center also includes a store that sells mementos and other park-related items. *Location:* Route 209, Bushkill, P.A. *Hours:* Daily, 9 A.M. to 5 P.M. *Phone:* 570-588-7044.

**Dingmans Campgrounds:** This private campground is operated under permit from the National Park Service. *Location:* Route 209, Dingmans Ferry, P.A. *Hours:* April 1 through October 15. *Phone:* 570-828-2266.

**Dingmans Falls Visitor's Center:** This center offers many nature programs and conducts guided walks along the Dingmans Falls Trail. Daily ranger led programs are offered at 10 A.M. and at 2 P.M. These programs give visitors an introduction to the recreational activities available in the park and offer a history of the native plants and wildlife. A boat launch and picnic area are located near the building. *Location:* Johnny Bee Road, off Route 209, Dingmans Ferry, P.A. *Hours:* Daily, 9 A.M. to 5 P.M.

**Group Camping:** This camping area is available to non-profit groups and organizations. *Location:* Hidden Lake, Bushkill, P.A. and Rivers Bend, Millbrook, N.J. *Hours:* Open all year. *Phone:* 570-588-2440.

**Kittatinny Point Visitor's Center:** Located near Mount Tammany, this visitors center features a natural history display about the park. *Location:* Off Route 80, Columbia, N.J. *Phone:* 908-496-4458.

**Millbrook Village:** In 1832, Abram Garris built a mill that would become the nucleus of a village. Buildings were constructed around the mill including a hotel, general store, and a church. The village flourished and reached its peak during the late 1800s, declining thereafter, during the turn of the century. This nineteenth century community is now re-created and brought back to life through costumed interpreters who demonstrate trades such as blacksmithing and woodworking. Select buildings are staffed on weekends from 9 A.M. to 5 P.M., from May through late October. *Location:* Old Mine Road. *Phone:* 908-841-9531.

**Mohican Outdoor Center:** This facility is located along the Appalachian Trail and provides a place for weary hikers to rest. It is run by the Appalachian Mountain Club and offers recreation programs and educational workshops. Guests are welcome to enjoy the available cabins and have fun swimming and canoeing in the lake. Hikers may also buy various supplies and souvenirs in the gift shop. *Location:* 50 Camp Road, Blairstown, N.J. *Phone:* 908-362-567.

**Old Mine Road:** This scenic road travels along the Delaware River and is one of the earliest roads in the region. Dutch settlers constructed this route in the 1600s, for the purpose of transporting goods and supplies. Later, the road was a main thoroughfare for transporting copper and slate from the mines and quarries in the area.

**Peters Valley Craft Center:** This art education center has eight studio areas (blacksmithing, ceramics, fiber, fine metals, photography, weaving, woodworking, and special topics) that offer classes taught by skilled craftspeople. Peters Valley Store & Gallery (973-948-5202) is the main interpretive center for the valley and displays work made by the craftspeople and local artisans. It includes information on the valley and feature ever changing displays that highlight selected points of interest. There are also several theme shows held throughout the year and an annual craft fair. *Location:* 19 Kuhn Road, Layton, N.J. *Phone:* 973-948-5200.

**Pocono Environmental Education Center:** Located in a former Pocono honey moon resort, this education center offers study programs and workshops that are ideal for schools, churches, youth groups, and anyone else who is interested in learning about the natural world in a beautiful and informal setting. The campus includes a library, craft center, darkroom, store, indoor pool, offices, and meeting areas for presentations and dances. There are 12-miles of trails located near the center and during the winter, the trails are excellent for cross-country skiing. Guests are housed in one of the 47 cabins, which can comfortably sleep from two to 14 people. The cabins are heated and have modern conveniences. Meals are prepared and served buffet style in the Dining Hall. This is the largest residential center for environmental education in the Western Hemisphere. *Location:* Briscoe Mountain Road, Dingmans Ferry, P.A. *Phone:* 570-828-2319.

**River Camping:** River camping consists of primitive camping areas that are located along the shores of the Delaware River. They are designed for boaters who are traveling between access points. These camps are located every eight to 10 miles along the river and are limited to a one night stay with availability on a first come first serve bases. No permit is needed and there are no fees. *Hours:* Open all year. *Phone:* 570-588-2451.

**Slateford Farmhouse:** This 170-acre farmstead includes a farmhouse and various outbuildings. Tours are conducted and are dedicated to exemplifying the early-American farming life. *Location:* Off route 611, P.A.

**Van Campen Inn:** This impressive, two-story, stone house was built around 1746 and has been restored by the National Park Service. It is one of the oldest homes in the Water Gap area. The house was once a rest stop for people traveling along the Old Mine Road. *Location:* Old Mine Road. *Hours:* May through October, Sundays from 1 P.M. to 5 P.M. *Phone:* 973-729-7392.

**Walpack Center:** Walpack was once a thriving farming community with a post office, general store, church, and several homes. Today, there are only a few of these buildings remaining. The Walpack Historical Society maintains an office and small museum in this historic village and conducts scheduled tours of the buildings. *Location:* Old Mine Road. *Phone:* 973-729-7392.

**Walpack Valley Environmental Education Center:** This education center caters to students in grades 5 through 12. The programs offered vary in length from one to five days and combine classroom activities with various chores in order to promote environmental awareness to the students. The focus is on natural science, history, and sensory activities. The programs cover wildlife habitats, forest succession, geology, and unique pond and stream studies. Field study includes wildlife ecology, earth sciences, wetland investigations, water quality, and astronomy. The education center is open to all schools and environmentally related organizations. *Location:* Old Mine Road. *Phone:* 973-948-5749.

**Jenny Jump State Forest**
State Park Road
Hope
Warren County
908-459-4366
Open sunrise to sunset
No entrance fee
2,427 acres

**Activities:** biking, boating, camping, canoeing, cross-country skiing, fishing, hiking, hunting, ice fishing, picnicking, and a playground.

The Minsi tribe of the Lenni-Lenape Indians once inhabited the area around the forest. They were a relatively peaceful tribe compared to their Iroquois neighbors to the north. However, there were several violent clashes with the early European Settlers. It was in this environment of fear and hatred that Sven Roseen, a Swedish missionary, recorded the legend of Jenny Jump in 1747. The legend told a tale of young Jenny, who was gathering berries in the forest with her family. Her father saw Indians approaching and, fearing the girl's fate, yelled for Jenny to jump from the ridge, believing that to be a more painless death.

The United Astronomy Club of New Jersey has leased a portion of forest off Farview Road and uses it as an observatory site. The Greenwood Observatory was completed in 1995 and includes an education center and a museum. The observatory is open Saturday evenings, April through October from 8 P.M. to 10 P.M. The observatory features a 28-inch Newtonian-Cassegrain Telescope, which is one of the largest in the state.

There are 22 tent and trailer sites located in a large, wooded campground area. Modern facilities are located nearby. Campers may purchase firewood at the main office from April 1 through October 21. There are also two smaller group campsites, which are open April 1 through October 31. For those who choose not to rough it entirely, there are eight cabins open year round, located near the top of Jenny Jump Mountain. Each cabin can accommodate up to four people and includes a living room and a wood burning stove.

Picnic tables are located at the Orchard Picnic Area. Fishing is allowed at Ghost Lake, which also features a boat launch. Nine miles of trails traverse through wooded areas and mountainous terrain. The park's Summit Trail reaches an elevation of 1,090 feet and offers great views of the Pequest Valley below.

**Merril Creek Reservoir**
116 Montana Road
Washington
Warren County
908-454-1213
Open sunrise to sunset
No entrance fee
940 acres

**Activates:** bird watching, boating, canoeing, cross-country skiing, fishing, hiking, and hunting.

> **FACT:** *Warren County, named for Dr. Joseph Warren, a Major General in the Revolutionary War, died in Charlestown, Massachusetts on June 17th, 1775 during the Battle of Bunker Hill.*

This 650-acre reservoir was constructed to hold water for the release into the Delaware River during periods of low flow. The lake has a maximum depth of 255 feet and includes more the five miles of shore land. It is stocked with trout and features a boat launch.

Merril Creek Visitor's Center includes a classroom, an auditorium, and also features exhibits of animals that live near the reservoir and the surrounding area. It is open daily from 8:30 A.M. to 4:30 P.M. Trails start just outside the building and wind through fields, woodlands, and old farm ruins.

**Oxford Furnace Lake Park**
Kauffman Drive
Oxford
Warren County
908-453-3098
Open sunrise to sunset
No entrance fee
711 acres

**Activities:** boating, fishing, picnicking, a playground, soccer, and swimming.

This park was the site of the first hot-blast furnace in America. It was a major producer of cannon balls during the French and Indian War and the American Revolution. In its time, from 1741 to 1884, this ironworks was the longest continuously operating iron producer in America. Today, only the ruins remain.

Joseph Shippen Jr. acquired the title to the land in 1741. His family built the ironworks and the Shippen Manor House (908-453-4381) located on nearby Belvidere Avenue. The manor has been restored and now serves as a museum and a cultural center. Costumed interpreters conduct guided tours during the first and second Sundays of each month from 1 P.M. to 4 P.M.

Swimming is allowed in the nearby lake from late June through Labor Day and is lifeguard supervised. A picnic area with a shelter is also located near the lake.

**Pequest Trout Hatchery**
Route 46
Oxford
Warren County
908-637-4125
Open 10 A.M. to 4 P.M.
No entrance fee
1,600 acres

**Activities:** hiking and picnic tables.

Located in the Pequest Wildlife Management Area, this center demonstrates to visitors how more than a half million trout are raised each year for stocking in the public waters of New Jersey. A brief, 15-minute video documents this operation, beginning with the egg gathering all the way through the stocking of the waters. A self guided tour takes visitors to the waters where the trout are raised. The average trout from this facility grows to be 10½ inches long and is stocked in one of over 200 bodies of water.

The exhibit hall contains live fish as well as a display of mounted local wildlife specimens. Workshops are offered on fishing education and pond ecology. There is also a nature trail and a picnic area nearby.

**Worthington State Forest**
Delaware Water Gap
Old Mine Road
Warren County
908-841-9575
Open sunrise to sunset
No entrance fee
5,878 acres

**Activates:** biking, boating, camping, canoeing, cross-country skiing, fishing, hiking, hunting, and snowmobiles.

The village of Brotzmanville once stood where the park's campground is located. The village had a post office, several residences, a sawmill, a gristmill, and a school. During the 1890s, Charles Worthington, an industrialist, purchased large tracts of land in the area, including the village. He had the village abandoned and removed, leaving only bare land. He called his 8,000-acre country estate "Buckwood." It featured a private game preserve and enough land to support the breeding of cattle and raising pheasants.

Today, the park features the 41-acre Sunfish Pond, which is encircled by a wooded trail. There are over 14 miles of trails, which pass by many scenic overlooks including one that climbs up to Mount Tammany. At 1,527 feet above sea level, this mountain offers the most impressive views of the Delaware Water Gap. A six-mile section of the Appalachian Trail also runs through the park, giving hikers an added bonus.

There are 69 tent and trailer sites, complete with picnic tables and fire rings. Modern facilities are located nearby. Three group sites, with a capacity for 35 people each, are also located in the park. The campsites are available from April through the end of December.

# Country Life

*Fosterfields Living Historical Farm*

From historic country villages to rich, cultural city centers, New Jersey is a state with a unique bond to its past. The people of New Jersey are proud of the state's long history and agricultural heritage. They share in the bond between past and present, working to maintain the continuing production of fresh fruits and vegetables, which are among the most valued in the world, and promoting the state's long and colorful history.

But even though New Jersey is known as the Garden State, the development of open land is increasing at an alarming rate due to suburban sprawl. To stem this tide, in 1998, the residents of New Jersey approved the commitment of nearly one billion dollars to fund a massive farmland and open space preservation program that will preserve thousands of acres of farmland for future generations.

This section lists the sites that are linked to the state's agricultural history and reveal how people lived and worked in that bygone era when New Jersey was truly the "Garden State."

**Barclay Farmstead:** Since Joseph Cooper, a descendent of the founder of Camden, built this farmhouse in 1816, six generations of his family have made it their home. Visitors may tour the farmhouse, which is furnished with original nineteenth century pieces, and observe demonstrations of skilled crafts. The historic grounds also include a tool shed, corncrib, blacksmith shop, and an orchard. *Location:* 209 Barclay Lane, Cherry Hill, Camden County. *Hours:* Year round, Tuesdays through Fridays from 9 A.M. to 4 P.M. *Phone:* 856-795-6225. *Admission Fee:* Free.

**Church Landing Farmhouse:** Daniel Garrison and his wife Rebecca built this farmhouse in 1860. Visitors may tour the building to experience how typical families of that era lived. Each room is accurately decorated in authentic period furnishings. *Location:* 86 Church Landing Road, Pennsville, Gloucester County. *Hours:* Wednesdays and Sundays from 1 P.M. to 3 P.M. Closed in February. *Phone:* 856-678-4453. *Admission Fee:* $2 adults, $1 seniors, and children are free.

**Cooper Mill:** Nathan A. Cooper built this mill in 1826 to harness the power of the Black River. Visitors may witness demonstrations of the millstone grinding grains into flour and corn meal. Other demonstrations include blacksmithing and cider pressing. *Location:* 66 Route 513, Chester, Morris County. *Hours:* Grounds are open daily 10 A.M. to 5 P.M., mill is open July through August, Fridays through Tuesdays from 10 A.M. to 5 P.M. and May through June and September through October on weekends from 10 A.M. 5 P.M. *Phone:* 908-897-5463. *Admission Fee:* $3 adults, $2 seniors, and $1 children.

**Dr. William Robinson Plantation:** Doctor Robinson, who practiced natural healing through plants and herbs, once owned this farm that sits on an acre of property. Built in 1690, it has since been meticulously restored. An herb garden, smoke house, corncrib, and barn also occupy the grounds. Visitors may view the doctor's medicine room as well as many other rooms, which are complete with period furnishings. *Location:* 593 Madison Hill Road, Clark, Union County. *Hours:* April through December on the first Sunday of the month from 1 P.M. to 4 P.M. *Phone:* 732-381-3081. *Admission Fee:* Free.

**Fosterfields Living Historical Farm:** This working farm is complete with live animals and workers attired in period costumes. The highlight of this farmstead is the nineteenth century Gothic Revival mansion that was built by the grandson of Paul Revere. *Location:* 73 Kahdena Road, Morristown, Morris County. *Hours:* April through October, Wednesdays to Saturdays from 10 A.M. to 5 P.M. and Sundays from 12 P.M. to 5 P.M. Tours of the mansion are held Thursdays to Sundays from 1 P.M. to 4 P.M. *Phone:* 973-326-7645. *Admission Fee:* $4 adults, $3 seniors, and $2 children.

**Garretson Farm:** Six generations of the Garretson family lived on this farm from 1719 to 1950. Here visitors may observe demonstrations of colonial cooking and a collection of antique farming equipment on display in the barn. *Location:* 402 River Road, Fairlawn, Bergen County. *Hours:* Grounds are open weekdays from 9 A.M. to 4:30 P.M. House is open from March to mid-June and from mid-September to November on Sundays from 1 P.M. to 4 P.M. *Phone:* 201-797-1775. *Admission Fee:* Free.

**Hamilton House Museum:** Visitors may tour this nineteenth century restored farmhouse, which is furnished with period pieces from the Colonial, Federal, and Victorian eras. The house depicts the lives of the ordinary people who worked and lived in the Passaic area. *Location:* 971 Valley Road, Clifton, Passaic County. *Phone:* 973-744-5707. *Hours:* Open only by appointment. *Admission Fee:* Free.

**Holcombe-Jimison Farmstead:** This is the oldest known farm in Hunterdon County. The farmstead, which has been restored, is a showcase for the history of Hunterdon County's agricultural heritage. Visitors may tour the farmhouse, blacksmith shop, print shop, and woodworking shop. The museum contains a wide range of farming equipment and many interesting exhibits. *Location:* 1605 Route 29, Lambertville, Hunterdon County. *Hours:* May through October on Sundays from 1 P.M. to 4 P.M. and on Wednesdays from 9 A.M. to 12 P.M. *Phone:* 609-397-2752. *Admission Fee:* Free.

**Holmes-Hendrickson House:** Built in 1754, this Dutch-style farmhouse reflects the lifestyle of a prosperous farming family of this era. A tour of the rooms features authentic period furnishings and decor. *Location:* 62 Longstreet Road, Holmdel, Monmouth County. *Hours:* May through September on Tuesdays, Thursdays, Fridays, and Sundays from 1 P.M. to 4 P.M. and on Saturdays from 10 A.M. to 4 P.M. *Phone:* 732-462-1466. *Admission Fee:* $2 adults, $1.50 seniors, and $1 children.

**Howell Living History Farm:** Life on the farm during the early 1900s is recreated here. Re-enactors dress in period costume and demonstrate many crafts and skills. Visitors may tour the farmhouse and various outbuildings for a revealing look at turn-of-the-century farm life. *Location:* Valley Road, Howell, Mercer County. *Hours:* Saturday from 10 A.M. to 4 P.M., April through November on Sundays from noon to 4 P.M., February through November, Tuesdays through Fridays from 10 A.M. to 4 P.M. *Phone:* 609-737-3299. *Admission Fee:* Free.

**Littell-Lord Farmstead:** The Lord Family purchased this farmhouse, built by a local farmer named Andrew Littell, in 1867. The rooms and furnishings reflect the family's Victorian-era tastes and style. Visitors may tour the parlor, kitchen, and bedrooms. Re-enactors are on hand, dressed in period costume and demonstrating various crafts. *Location:* 31 Horseshoe Road, Berkeley Heights, Union County. *Hours:* March through June and September through December on the third Sunday of each month from 2 P.M. to 4 P.M. *Phone:* 908-464-0961 *Admission Fee:* Free.

**Longstreet Farm:** Hendrick Longstreet built this farm in 1806. Now restored to its 1890 appearance, this working farm is complete with animals and costumed re-enactors. The farmhouse includes many rooms with period furnishings and offers the visitor a glimpse of farming life in the late nineteenth century. *Location:* Longstreet Road, Holmdel, Monmouth County. *Hours:* Daily, 10 A.M. to 4 P.M., Memorial Day through Labor Day, 9 A.M. to 5 P.M., the farmhouse is open weekends, March through December from Noon until 3:30 A.M. *Phone:* 732-946-3758. *Admission Fee:* Free.

**Miller-Cory House Museum:** Costumed re-enactors guide visitors through this farmhouse, originally built in 1740. Crafts are demonstrated and the daily life of an eighteenth century farm family is recreated. *Location:* 614 Mountain Avenue, Westfield, Union County. *Hours:* Mondays to Fridays from 9 A.M. to 12 P.M. *Phone:* 908-232-1776. *Admission Fee:* $2 adults and $0.50 children/students.

**New Sweden Farmstead:** These reconstructed log cabins, exact replicas of a seventeenth century Swedish-style farmstead, contain authentic furnishings and farm equipment of Swedish origin. The village includes a blacksmith shop, storehouse, threshing barn, stable, main residence, and a smokehouse. *Location:* Bridgeton City Park, Bridgeton City, Cumberland County. *Hours:* May through September, Saturdays from 11 A.M. to 5 P.M. and Sundays from 12 P.M. to 5 P.M. *Admission Fee:* $3 adults, $2.50 seniors, $1.50 children.

**Prallsville Mills:** In 1794, John Prall Jr. purchased a small wooden gristmill. From this modest investment, his business grew into a thriving commercial center. The mill is the main attraction for touring and is complete with original working machinery. Other buildings include a sawmill, wagon shed, and a grain silo. This village also features the picturesque Delaware and Raritan Canal as its backdrop. Special events are held during the year, including concerts, art exhibits, and antique shows. *Location:* Route 29, Stockton, Hunterdon County. *Hours:* Grounds open daily, sunrise to sunset, building hours vary. *Phone:* 609-397-3586. *Admission Fee:* Free.

**Saltbox Museum:** Two separate houses (one built in 1790 and the other in 1844) were combined in the late nineteenth century to form this house. The first floor of the museum is furnished to represent a typical farmhouse of the mid-1800s. Re-enactors are costumed in period garb and display the functions of everyday life in that time period. *Location:* 1350 Springfield Avenue, New Providence, Union County. *Hours:* First and third Sundays of each month from 1 P.M. to 3 P.M. Closed in December. *Admission Fee:* Free.

**Volendam Windmill:** This windmill, which is 60-feet tall, is a replica Dutch-design windmill. Visitors may explore the inner workings and observe demonstrations of flour being ground. A climb to the top of the windmill features outstanding views of the surrounding countryside. The gift shop has interesting items of Dutch origin for sale. *Location:* 231 Adamic Hill Road, Holland, Hunterdon County. *Hours:* May through September on Saturdays and Sundays from 12 P.M. to 4:30 P.M. *Phone:* 908-995-4365. *Admission Fee:* Free.

**Walnford:** Richard Waln established this farming village during the 1700s. His family once owned hundreds of acres in the area and employed many of the local population. Now restored, this 36-acre farmstead includes a farmhouse, gristmill, carriage house, and various outbuildings. *Location:* Walnford Road, Allentown, Monmouth County, *Hours:* Grounds are open from 8 A.M. to sunset. Building hours vary. *Phone:* 609-259-6275. *Admission Fee:* Free.

**Wortendyke Barn:** This is a perfect example of a new world Dutch barn. Originally built in 1770, it has since been restored. Various artifacts, photographs, and exhibits that describe Bergen County's agricultural history are on display. *Location:* 13 Pascack Road. Park Ridge, Bergen County. *Hours:* May through October on Wednesdays and Sundays from 1 P.M. to 5 P.M. *Phone:* 201-646-2780. *Admission Fee:* Free.

# Wildlife
# Management Areas

*Salem River*

# Atlantic County

**Absecon (3,688 acres):** This area is mostly a salt marsh. It is a good place for waterfowl hunting, saltwater fishing, crabbing, clamming, and bird watching. There is a public boat launch at Faunce Landing Road and water skiing is allowed. The northern half of the old Brigantine Bridge is open as a fishing pier. *Location:* Routes 87, 30, and 9.

**Lester G. MacNamara (12,377 acres):** Established in 1933, this is one of the oldest wildlife management areas in the state. The main office is located off Tuckahoe-Marmora Road. The grounds include a dog-training area, a hunter-training area, clay bird shooting range, and an archery range. A boat ramp is located on the Tuckahoe portion of the tract and provides access to the Great Egg Harbor River and Bay. This is a fantastic area for bird watching, fishing, trapping, and hunting for waterfowl, deer, and other upland game. *Location:* Route 50.

**Makepeace Lake (7,458 acres):** Fishing is a favorite recreation on the 300-acre Makepeace Lake. Other activities include bird watching, trapping, and hunting for waterfowl. Small, car-top boats may be launched from Elwood-Weymouth Road. There is also a shooting range in the area. *Location:* Elwood-Weymouth Road near Egg Harbor City.

**Pork Island (197 acres):** This is a good place for saltwater fishing, crabbing, and hunting for waterfowl. *Location:* Jerome Avenue, Margate.

**Port Republic (755 acres):** Three quarters of this area is salt marsh, with the remainder considered upland-field habitat. Hunting is allowed for upland game, wild turkey, and deer. Fishing is allowed in the Mullica River. In cold weather, Collins Cove may be used for ice fishing. Launching ramps and rental boats are available throughout the surrounding areas. *Location:* Clarks Landing Road.

# Burlington County

**Medford (214 acres):** This is a favorite location for hunters, with plenty of upland game. *Location:* Ark Road, Medford Township.

**Swan Bay (1,529 acres):** Recreational activities abound this scenic wildlife area. Hunting is allowed but limited for upland game, waterfowl, and deer. Fishing is allowed in the Mullica River. *Location:* Turtle Creek Road, off Route 542.

# Camden County

**Winslow (6,566 acres):** This is a mostly wooded area, with hunting allowed for upland game, deer, and waterfowl. A facility for archery and shotgun training is located on the grounds, and there are two ponds for fishing. The district office is located on New Brooklyn/Blue Anchor Road in Sicklerville. *Location:* Piney Hollow Road.

# Cape May County

**Beaver Swamp (2,800 acres):** Hunting for upland game, wild turkey, deer, and waterfowl is allowed. Clint Mill Pond provides many spots for fishing. *Location:* Swainton, Court House-South Dennis Road.

**Cape May Wetlands (11,332 acres):** Activities in this largely, salt marsh area include boating, fishing, crabbing, trapping, and hunting for waterfowl and upland game. This is a great place for bird watching especially during the spring and fall migration seasons. One boat ramp is located at Corson's Inlet and another at Strathmere. *Location:* Ocean Drive, Roosevelt Boulevard.

**Dennis Creek (5,400 acres):** This is a good spot for bird watching, especially during the spring and fall migration seasons. Watchers may even spot a bald eagle or two. Boat ramps are located at Jakes Landing Road and Bidwells Ditch. Fishing, crabbing, and hunting for deer, waterfowl, and upland game are allowed. *Location:* Route 47, Marmora.

# Cumberland County

**Bear Swamp (2,000 acres):** Activities include bird watching, hiking, cross county skiing in the winter, mountain biking, and hunting for upland game, deer, wild turkey, and waterfowl. Fishing is allowed in several of the ponds. *Location:* Hampton and Franklin Townships, Routes 521 and 633.

**Cedarville Ponds (42 acres):** These ponds are a great place to fish, but it is only allowed along the perimeter of the pond. *Location:* Sawmill Road and Route 533, Cedarville.

**Clarks Pond (78 acres):** Three ponds make up this area and provide a good spot for fishing. Small, car-top and electric boats may navigate the waters. *Location:* Route 698 (Millville Road).

**Dix (2,643 acres):** This area is mostly marshland with a few wooded and open areas. Hunting is allowed for waterfowl, deer, and upland game. The streams, creeks, and nearby Delaware River provide excellent fishing spots. *Location:* Black Neck Road.

**Edward G. Bevan (12,000 acres):** The grounds include a dog-training area and a rifle and archery range. Hunting is allowed for upland game, deer, wild turkey, and waterfowl. Fishing is allowed in Shaw's Mill Pond. An office is located in Mauricetown between Millville Road and Mauricetown Road. *Location:* Routes 555 and 629.

**Egg Island (8,540 acres):** This area is mostly tidal marsh. Hunting is allowed for upland game and waterfowl. Activities include bird watching, fishing, and crabbing. Boat launches are located on Hansey Creek Road. *Location:* Off Route 533.

**Fortescue (900 acres):** This wildlife area is comprised of salt marsh and small plots of open land. Fishing and crabbing are allowed in the Delaware Bay. Hunting is allowed for upland game and waterfowls. This area is excellent for bird watching. In the winter, this area attracts many thousands of snow geese. *Location:* Fortescue Road, Fortescue.

**Heislerville (5,700 acres):** Hunting is allowed for upland game, deer, and waterfowl. The Maurice River provides many places to fish. Crabbing is allowed in the Delaware Bay and a boathouse is located on the river. The area's two ponds attract thousands of migrating birds, including wintering snow geese. *Location:* Matts Landing, East Point, and Thompson Beach Roads.

**Menantico Ponds (295 acres):** A series of ponds with depths of up to 40 feet support many species of fish. Car-top boats with electric motors are allowed. Launching ramps are located off Route 49. *Location:* Off Route 49, Millville.

**Nantuxent (916 acres):** This marsh has just a small upland portion. Hunting is allowed for waterfowl, upland game, and deer. Trapping is also allowed. *Location:* Bay Point Road.

**New Sweden (1,409 acres):** The Delaware Bay provides many enjoyable fishing locations and attracts flocks of birds, especially during the spring and fall migration seasons. Trapping and hunting for waterfowl is allowed. *Location:* Accessible by boat from private marinas at Husted Landing and Bay Point.

**Peaslee (17,988 acres):** This is one of the largest wildlife management areas in the state. It consists of pine and oak woodlands, with a few other woods mixed in. Hunting is allowed for deer, upland game, wild turkey, and waterfowl. The many lakes and streams also provide great fishing opportunities. *Location:* Route 49.

**Union Lake (4,677 acres):** Union Lake is the largest lake in Southern New Jersey. It is almost 900 acres in surface area, with a maximum depth of 30 feet. This is the only lake in the state that allows boats with gas-powered motors, though there is a limit of 10-horsepower imposed upon the power of the motors. Activities include sailing, recreational boating, fishing, and hunting for upland game and deer. *Location:* Route 55.

# Gloucester County

**Glassboro (2,337 acres):** This area is a combination of woodlands and fields. Its many features include a dog-training center, and hunting, which is allowed for upland game and deer. *Location:* Route 47, Glassboro and Clayton Townships.

**Harrisonville Lake (37 acres):** This 30-acre lake has a maximum depth of seven feet and only small, car-top boats are allowed on it. Fishing is allowed on some portions of the shoreline. *Location:* Harrisonville.

**Logan Pond (12 acres):** This small area includes a four and a half acre pond, which is open for fishing. *Location:* Gibbstown Road, Gibbstown.

# Hunterdon County

**Amwell Lake (22 acres):** Amwell Lakes provides many locations for prime fishing opportunities. Only small, car-top boats are allowed on the lake. *Location:* Off Route 31.

**Capoolong Creek (61 acres):** This creek has a fine reputation among fishing enthusiasts. *Location:* Kingstown-Sidney Road, Pittstown, Kingstown, and Sidney.

**Clinton (1,475 acres):** This is one of the best-known and most widely used wildlife management areas. It is comprised of woodland and open fields. The area includes a dog-training facility and archery and shotgun ranges. Hunting is allowed for waterfowl, deer, and upland game. Fishing is allowed in Spruce Run Reservoir, where motorboats are allowed but limited to 10-horsepower. *Location:* Van Syckel's Road.

**Ken Lockwood Gorge (260 acres):** This is a wooded area with gaps of open fields sprinkled about. Hunting is allowed for deer and upland game. The Raritan River runs through this area, providing plenty of opportunities and locations to cast a line. *Location:* Raritan River Road.

# Mercer County

**Baldwin Lake (37 acres):** Eighteen-acre Baldwin Lake is a great location for easy fishing and has access for small, car-top boats. *Location:* A quarter of a mile north of the intersection at Mount Rose Road.

# Monmouth County

**Assunpink (5,600 acres):** This outdoorsman's recreation area includes well-maintained shotgun and archery ranges. Fishing is allowed in Stone Tavern Lake and 225-acre Lake Assunpink. Boat launches are available for trailer-towed boats as well as small, car-top boats. Hunting is allowed for upland game and deer. There are many good bird watching opportunities here. *Location:* Imlaystown Road, Upper Freehold Township.

**Turkey Swamp (2,457 acres):** This area is mostly pine and oak forest. Hunting is allowed for deer and upland game. An archery range is also located on the grounds. *Location:* Turkey Swamp Road.

# Morris County

**Berkshire Valley (1,830 acres):** Hunting is allowed for upland game, wild turkey, deer, and waterfowl. The Rockaway River is an excellent source for fishing opportunities. *Location:* Berkshire Valley Road, Roxbury Township.

**Black River (3,057 acres):** The grounds include a hunter-training area, ranges for clay pigeon shooters and archers, and a dog-training area. Hunting is allowed for upland game, deer and waterfowl. There are limited fishing opportunities and access to the Black River is difficult, although there are several small ponds in the area. *Location:* North Road (Route 513), Chester.

# Ocean County

**Butterfly Bogs (103 acres):** This forested area contains many varieties of pine and oak trees. Hunting for upland game and deer is allowed. Three lakes provide good opportunities for fishing. *Location:* Butterfly Road, Jackson Township off of Route 527.

**Colliers Mills (12,250 acres):** This expansive pine and oak forested area features a white cedar swamp. Hunting is allowed for waterfowl and upland game. A dog-training facility and shooting range are also located on the grounds. The ponds and creeks provide plenty of good fishing spots. *Location:* Hawkins Road, Colliers Mills.

**Great Bay Boulevard (3,965 acres):** This wildlife management area is mostly salt marsh. Activities include fishing, crabbing, and clamming. Hunting is permitted for waterfowl only. This is a great place for bird watching, especially during the spring and fall migration seasons. Car-top and trailer-towed boats are allowed on the waters. *Location:* Great Bay Boulevard, Tuckerton.

**Greenwood Forest and Pasadena (27,298 acres):** Pine, oak, and white cedar make up the thousands of acres of forest in this area. Hunting is permitted for waterfowl, deer, upland game, and wild turkey. Fishing is allowed in each of the three lakes located here. *Location:* Route 536.

**Manahawkin (965 acres):** Hunting is allowed for upland game, deer, and waterfowl. Fishing is permitted at Cedar Creek with access provided from Stafford Avenue. *Location:* Stafford Avenue, Stafford Township.

**Manasquan River (753 acres):** This area provides a dog-training facility between May 1 and August 31. Hunting is permitted for limited upland game, and fishing is allowed on the river. *Location:* Ramshorn Drive, Brick and Wall Townships.

**Manchester (2,376 acres):** This heavily wooded area features many varieties of pine and oak and a white cedar swamp. Hunting is permitted for deer, upland game, and wild turkey. *Location* Beckerville Road, Horicon Road.

**Prospertown Lake (125 acres):** Fishing is permitted in the 80-acre lake and a pier extends out into the lake to augment the limited bank fishing. Only car-top boats are allowed. *Location:* Route 537, Jackson Township.

**Sedge Islands (175 acres):** On these secluded sandy islands, hunting is permitted for waterfowl. Fishing and crabbing is allowed in Barnegat Bay. A public boat launch is located at the northern end of Long Beach Island providing access to the islands. *Location:* Off the southwestern end of Island Beach State Park, access to the islands is by boat only.

**Stafford Forge (7,288 acres):** The area's four ponds provide excellent opportunities for fishing. Hunting is permitted for upland game, deer, and waterfowl. The area includes a dog-training facility and a shotgun range. *Location:* Off Route 539, Eagleswood and Little Egg Harbor Townships.

**Whiting (1,200 acres):** This wildlife area consists of acres of pine and oak forests. Hunting is permitted for upland game, wild turkey, and deer. Fishing is allowed in Bauer Pond. *Location:* Manchester Township, off Route 530.

# Passaic County

**Wanaque (2,277 acres):** Hunting for upland game, wild turkey, and deer is permitted. The Wanaque River and the 45-acre Green Turtle Pond provide many ideal fishing opportunities. Trailer and car-top boats are permitted on the pond with access provided by a boat launch located at the northern end. *Location:* East Shore Road or Awosting Road.

# Salem County

**Mad Horse Creek (7,670 acres):** This area of tidal marsh has small portions of upland habitat. Activities include trapping and hunting for upland game and waterfowl. A boat ramp, located at Mad Horse Creek, provides access to the Delaware Bay. Fishing is permitted in the bay. *Location:* Stow Neck Road.

**Maskells Mill Pond (47 acres):** This 33-acre pond has a maximum depth of five feet and offers good fishing opportunities. Only small, car-top boats are permitted on the lake. *Location:* Route 58, Lower Alloways Creek Township.

**Salem River (250 acres):** The area along this idyllic river allows for many recreational activities. Hunting is also permitted for waterfowl and upland game. *Location:* Off Route 47, Mannington Township.

# Sussex County

**Flatbrook-Roy (2,334 acres):** This area includes a hunter training range and archery and rifle ranges. Activities include bird watching and cross-county skiing when weather permits. Hunting is allowed for upland game, wild turkey, deer, and waterfowl. Fishing is permitted in the Big Flat Brook and the Little Flat Brook, which are two of New Jersey's most famous trout streams. *Location:* Route 615.

**Hainesville (282 acres):** The area's 30-acre pond and the nearby Little Flat Brook provide excellent fishing opportunities, especially for trout. The grounds include a dog-training facility specializing in training water dogs. Hunting is permitted for upland game, wild turkey, deer, and waterfowl. *Location:* Red Hill Road.

**Hamburg Mountain (2,442 acres):** This wildlife management area consists of both forests and mountains. Fishing is permitted at Franklin Pond Creek. Hunting is allowed for upland game, wild turkey, and deer. *Location:* Route 23 and Route 517, Hardyston and Vernon Townships.

**Walpack (387 acres):** The Big Flat Brook, one of the states most famous trout streams, flows through this wildlife area and provides excellent fishing opportunities. Hunting is permitted for deer, waterfowl, upland game, and wild turkey. *Location:* Route 615.

**Whittingham (1,514 acres):** Hunting is permitted for upland game, deer, and waterfowl. The area also features a dog-training center. *Location:* Springdale Road and Route 609, and Springdale Road and Tranquility Road, Fredon and Green Townships.

# Warren County

**Columbia Lake (55 acres):** Paulinskill River Watershed provides a large shoreline and offers excellent fishing opportunities. Limited waterfowl hunting is allowed on this shallow lake. This is a good place for bird watching, especially during the spring and fall migration seasons. Car-top and trailer boats may be launched at a boat launch located off of Warrington Road. *Location:* Off of a dirt road from Route 46 in Columbia, or from Warrington Road off Route 94.

# Beaches

*Seven Presidents Oceanfront Park*

# Monmouth County

**Keansburg:** *Location:* Beachway. *Beach Fee:* None. *Parking:* Municipal lot off Bay Avenue and street parking. *Phone:* 732-787-0215. *Lifeguards:* Swim at your own risk. *Facilities:* Restrooms, small boardwalk, and a snack bar.

**Sandy Hook:** *Location:* Gateway National Recreation Area. *Beach Fee:* None. *Parking:* $10 daily, $50 season. *Phone:* 732-872 5970. *Lifeguards:* Yes. *Facilities:* Restrooms, showers, and a snack bar.

**Highlands:** *Location:* South Bay Avenue, Miller Street and Snug Harbor Avenue. *Beach Fee:* None. *Parking:* Street parking and lot parking. *Phone:* 732-872-1959. *Lifeguards:* Yes. *Facilities:* Snug Harbor has restrooms available only during the week.

**Middletown:** *Location:* Ideal Beach, Leonardo Beach, Bayshore Waterfront Park (Port Monmouth Road) and Port Monmouth (Port Monmouth Road). *Beach Fee:* None. *Parking:* Free lots. *Phone:* 732-615-2660. *Lifeguards:* Bayshore Waterfront Park and Port Monmouth are unguarded. Ideal Beach and Leonardo Beach are guarded. *Facilities:* Ideal Beach has a playground, restrooms, and a snack bar; Leonardo has restrooms.

**Sea Bright:** *Location:* Ocean Avenue. *Beach Fee:* $5 daily, $75 season, $35 season for seniors, children 12 and under are free. *Parking:* $5 municipal lot, metered and street parking. *Phone:* 732-842-0215. *Lifeguards:* Yes. *Facilities:* Restrooms.

**Monmouth Beach:** *Location:* Ocean Avenue. *Beach Fee:* $5 daily, $60 season, children under 12 are free. *Parking:* $3 daily. *Phone:* 732-229-5296. *Lifeguards:* Yes. *Facilities:* Snack bar, and restrooms.

**Long Branch:** *Location:* Broadway to Brighton Avenue. *Beach Fee:* $5 daily, $3 ages 12 to 17, $35 season, $30 season ages 12 to 17, free for children under 12. *Parking:* Metered and street parking. *Phone:* 732-571-6545. *Lifeguards:* Yes. *Facilities:* Boardwalk, changing area, restrooms, snack bar, restrooms, and volleyball.

**Seven Presidents Oceanfront Park:** *Location:* Joline Avenue. *Beach Fee:* $5 daily, $42 season, $32 ages 12 to 16, $16 for seniors, children 12 and under are free. *Parking:* $4 daily, $40 season. *Phone:* 732-229-0924. *Lifeguards:* Yes. *Facilities:* Boat launch, fitness area, playground, restrooms, snack bar, and volleyball.

**Deal:** *Location:* Ocean Avenue. *Beach Fee:* $5 daily, $6 weekends, $75 season, $50 age 12 to 17, children under 11 are free. *Parking:* Street parking. *Phone:* 732-531-1454. *Lifeguards:* Yes. *Facilities:* Playground, snack bar, and volleyball.

**Allenhurst:** *Location:* Between Corlies and Allen Avenue. *Beach Fee:* $5 daily, children under 13 are free. *Parking:* Street and lot. *Phone:* 732-531-2700. *Lifeguards:* Yes. *Facilities:* Restrooms, and a snack bar.

**Loch Arbor:** *Location:* Euclid Avenue. *Beach Fee:* $5 daily, Children under 13 are free, $80 season, $50 for seniors *Parking:* Metered and street parking *Phone:* 732-531-4740. *Lifeguards:* Yes *Facilities:* Restrooms, snack bar, and volleyball.

**Asbury Park:** *Location:* Deal Lake Drive. *Beach Fee:* $3 daily, $4 weekends, children 12 and under are free, season passes are $20 for adults, $10 for teens ages 13 to 17 and $10 for seniors. *Parking:* Metered parking. *Phone:* 732-775-0900. *Lifeguards:* Yes. *Facilities:* Restrooms and a snack bar.

**Ocean Grove:** *Location:* Ocean Avenue. *Beach Fee:* $5.50 daily, $10 weekends, $27.50 weekly, $60 season for adults, $54 season for seniors, $33 season ages 13 to 17, children under 12 are free. *Parking:* Metered. *Phone:* 732-531-9283. *Lifeguards:* Yes. *Facilities:* Restrooms.

**Bradley Beach:** *Location:* Cliff Lake Avenue though Third Avenue. *Beach Fee:* $6 daily, $50 season, $25 season for seniors, children 13 and under are free. *Parking:* Street. *Phone:* 732-776-2998. *Lifeguards:* Yes. *Facilities:* Boardwalk, gazebo, restrooms, and a snack bar.

**Avon:** *Location:* Lakeside to Washington Avenue. *Beach Fee:* $5.75 daily, $60 season, $25 season ages 12 to 18, $25 season for seniors, children under 12 are free. *Parking:* Street parking ocean avenue, municipal lot at East End Avenue. *Phone:* 732-502-4508. *Lifeguards:* Yes. *Facilities:* Restrooms and a snack bar.

**Belmar:** *Location:* First to 20th Avenues. *Beach Fee:* $5.50 daily, $40 season, $10 season for seniors, children 14 and under are free. *Parking:* Street. *Phone:* 732-681-1176. *Lifeguards:* Yes. *Facilities:* Boardwalk, restrooms, and a snack bar.

**Spring Lake:** *Location:* South Boulevard to Brown Avenue. *Beach Fee:* $6 daily $73 season, children 11 and under are free. *Parking:* Free parking on Ocean Avenue. *Phone:* 732-449-8005. *Lifeguards:* Yes. *Facilities:* Boardwalk, restrooms, and a snack bar.

**Sea Girt:** *Location:* Beacon Boulevard to Seaside Place. *Beach Fee:* $6 daily, $60 season, $50 season for seniors, children 11 and under are free. *Parking:* Street. *Phone:* 732-449-9335. *Lifeguards:* Yes. *Facilities:* Restrooms.

**Manasquan:** *Location:* Manasquan Inlet to Sea Girt Boundary. *Beach Fee:* $5 daily, $47 season, $20 ages 12 to 16, $15 for seniors, children under 11 are free. *Parking:* $3 daily, $8 weekends, $47 a season for municipal lots on Second, Third, Fourth and Pompano Avenues. *Phone:* 732-223-1221. *Lifeguards:* Yes. *Facilities:* Restrooms and a snack bar.

# Ocean County

**Point Pleasant Beach:** *Location:* Jenkinson's. *Beach Fee:* $5 daily, $6 weekends, $1.50 for children ages 5 to 11, $70 season for adults, $50 season for seniors, $45 season for children ages 5 to 11. *Parking:* Metered streets and lots. *Phone:* 732-899-2424. *Lifeguards:* Yes. *Facilities:* Boardwalk.

**Bay Head:** *Location:* East Avenue. *Beach Fee:* $5 daily, $55 season, children under 12 are free. *Parking:* Street and lot. *Phone:* 732-892-4179. *Lifeguards:* Yes. *Facilities:* None.

**Brick:** *Location:* Off Route 36. *Beach Fee:* $3 daily, $25 season, free children under 12. *Parking:* $4 daily, $35 season. *Phone:* 732-262-1075. *Lifeguards:* Yes. *Facilities:* restrooms, and a snack bar.

**Lavallette:** *Location:* Dover Avenue to Bryn Mawr Avenue. *Beach Fee:* $5 daily, $15 weekly, $35 season for adults, $10 season for seniors, and children under 12 are free. *Parking:* Two municipal lots available. *Phone:* 732-793-2100. *Lifeguards:* Yes. *Facilities:* Boardwalk.

**Dover Township:** *Location:* Ortley Beach, Shelter Cove and Monkey Island. *Beach Fee:* $4 weekdays, $5 weekends, $40 season. *Parking:* Street. *Phone:* 732-341-1000. *Lifeguards:* Yes. *Facilities:* Ortley Beach has a small boardwalk; Shelter Cove and Monkey Island have restrooms.

**Seaside Heights:** *Location:* Ocean Avenue. *Beach Fee:* Free Wednesdays and Thursdays, $3 Monday, Tuesdays and Fridays, $5 Saturday and Sunday, $35 season, children under 12 are free. *Parking:* Street, metered and lot. *Phone:* 800-732-7467. *Lifeguards:* Yes. *Facilities:* Boardwalk.

**Seaside Park:** *Location:* Ocean Avenue. *Beach Fee:* $6 daily, $17 weekly, $37 season for adults, $15 season for seniors, and children under 12 are free. *Parking:* Metered. *Phone:* 732-830-2100. *Lifeguards:* Yes. *Facilities:* Boardwalk, restrooms, snack bar, and volleyball.

**Berkeley:** *Location:* White Sands Beach, South Seaside Park. *Beach Fee:* $3 daily, $4 weekends, $15 weekly, $25 season for adults, seniors and children under 12 are free. *Parking:* Metered. *Phone:* 732-269-4456. *Lifeguards:* Yes. *Facilities:* Restrooms.

**Island Beach State Park:** *Location:* Central Avenue. *Beach Fee:* None. *Parking:* $6 per car on weekdays and $7 per car on weekends. *Phone:* 732-793-0506. *Lifeguards:* Yes. *Facilities:* Picnic tables, restrooms, snack bar, trails.

**Barnegat Light State Park:** *Location:* 30th to Fourth Streets. *Beach Fee:* $3 weekdays $4 weekends, $10 weekly, $25 season, $7 season for seniors and children under 11. *Phone:* 609-494-9169. *Lifeguards:* Yes. *Facilities:* Restrooms.

**Long Beach Township:** *Location:* Long Beach Boulevard. *Beach Fee:* $5 daily, $10 weekly, $20 season, seniors and children under 12 are free. *Parking:* Street. *Phone:* 609-361-1200. *Lifeguards:* Yes. *Facilities:* Restrooms.

**Harvey Cedars:** *Location:* William Street to 86th Street. *Beach Fee:* $5 daily, $10 weekly, $22 season for adults, $8 season for seniors, and children under 12 are free. *Parking:* Street. *Phone:* 609-494-6906. *Lifeguards:* Yes. *Facilities:* Baseball, fitness area, a playground, restrooms, and volleyball.

**Surf City:** *Location:* North 25th Street to South Street. *Beach Fee:* $5 daily, $12 weekly, $23 season for adults, seniors and children under 13 are free. *Parking:* Street. *Phone:* 609-494-3064. *Lifeguards:* Yes. *Facilities:* Restrooms.

**Ship Bottom:** *Location:* South Third Street to 31st Street. *Beach Fee:* $4 weekdays, $5 weekends, $12 weekly, $22 season for adults, $12 season for seniors, children 11 and under are free. *Parking:* Street and metered. *Phone:* 609-494-1614. *Lifeguards:* Yes. *Facilities:* Restrooms.

**Beach Haven:** *Location:* 12th Street to Nelson Avenue. *Beach Fee:* $5 daily, $10 weekly, $20 season for adults, seniors and children under 12 are free. *Parking:* Street. *Phone:* 609-494-7211. *Lifeguards:* Yes. *Facilities:* Restrooms.

# Atlantic County

**Brigantine:** *Location:* Brigantine Avenue. *Beach Fee:* $15 season, $10 weekly, and $10 daily. *Parking:* Street. *Phone:* 800-847-5198. *Lifeguards:* Yes. *Facilities:* Restrooms and volleyball.

**Atlantic City:** *Location:* Pacific and Atlantic Avenues. *Beach Fee:* Free. *Parking:* Street and metered. *Phone:* 609-348-7100. *Lifeguards:* Yes. *Facilities:* Boardwalk, snack bar, and restrooms.

**Ventnor City:** *Location:* Atlantic Avenue. *Beach Fee:* $10 season and $5 daily. *Parking:* Street and metered. *Phone:* 609-823-7900. *Lifeguards:* Yes. *Facilities:* Boardwalk and restrooms.

**Margate City:** *Location:* Atlantic Avenue. *Beach Fee:* $10 season and $3.50 weekly. *Parking:* Street and lots. *Phone:* 609-823-6473. *Lifeguards:* Yes. *Facilities:* Restrooms and volleyball.

**Longport:** *Location:* Longport Boulevard. *Beach Fee:* $15 season and $5 weekly. *Parking:* Street. *Phone:* 609-822-6503. *Lifeguards:* Yes. *Facilities:* Restrooms.

# Cape May County

**Ocean City:** *Location:* Central Avenue. *Beach Fee:* $16 season, $8 weekly, and $4 daily. *Parking:* Metered and lots. *Phone:* 800-232-2465. *Lifeguards:* Yes. *Facilities:* Boardwalk, restrooms, and a snack bar.

**Sea Isle City:** *Location:* Ocean Drive. *Beach Fee:* $15 season, $8 weekly, and $4 daily. *Parking:* Street and metered. *Phone:* 609-263-8687. *Lifeguards:* Yes. *Facilities:* Boardwalk, restrooms, and a snack bar.

**Avalon:** *Location:* Third Avenue. *Beach Fee:* $17 season, $8 weekly, and $4 daily. *Parking:* Street. *Phone:* 609-967-3936. *Lifeguards:* Yes. *Facilities:* Restrooms and volleyball.

**Wildwoods:** *Location:* Pacific and Central Avenues. *Beach Fee:* Free. *Parking:* Metered. *Phone:* 800-992-9732. *Lifeguards:* Yes. *Facilities:* Boardwalk, restrooms, a snack bar, and volleyball.

**Cape May:** *Location:* Beach Avenue. *Beach Fee:* $17 season, $10 weekly, and $4 daily. *Parking:* Metered. *Phone:* 609-884-5508. *Lifeguards:* Yes. *Facilities:* Restrooms and volleyball.

**Cape May Point:** *Location:* Cape May Point State Park, Lighthouse Avenue. *Beach Fee:* None. *Parking:* $15 season, $10 weekly, and $10 daily. *Phone:* 609-884-8468. *Lifeguards:* Yes. *Facilities:* Boardwalk, restrooms, a snack bar, and volleyball.

# Museums and
# Historic Sites

*Dey Mansion*

### Atlantic County Historical Society

907 Shore Road
Somers Point
Atlantic County
609-927-5218
Open Wednesdays to Saturdays
from 10 A.M. to 3:30 P.M.
Free admission

Founded in 1913, the Atlantic County Historical Society collects and pre-serves items of special interest and historical significance to southern New Jersey. The exhibits feature elements of local life, displays of important per-sons, and memorabilia and images of the cities and towns. The upstairs room, called the Nautical Room, devotes a large display to Commodore Richard Somers. He was a local Navy hero who died in Tripoli Harbor fighting the Barbary Pirates. Since his death, the U.S. Navy has kept his memory alive by christening several ships with his name. Pictures off all six Navy ships that were named after him are on display in the museum. A monument of Commodore Somers also stands at the Navel Academy in Annapolis, Maryland.

### Lucy the Elephant

9200 Atlantic Avenue
Margate
Atlantic County
609-823-6473
Open mid-June through Labor
Day, daily from 10 A.M. to
4:30 P.M. Labor Day through
October and April through
Mid-June weekends only,
from 10 A.M. to 4:30 P.M.
$3 per person

In 1881, James Vincent de Paul wanted to sell the land he owned around the town of Margate but he had difficulty attracting buyers. The problem was people were more interested in the booming area of Atlantic City. Being an inventor and engineer, James constructed a 65-foot elephant. He named it Lucy and hoped that it would cause a sensation and attract property buyers to his real estate holdings. It worked! People traveled many miles just to see this strange creation. In fact, it was such a wondrous sight that two more elephants were built, one in Cape May and another on Coney Island. Only the original remains to this day, however.

As the years went on, Lucy was used for many things including a summer home, business office, beach cottage, and a tavern. It survived many disasters ranging from a fire to a fierce nor'easter, which left the elephant standing knee-deep in sand.

Lucy was moved to its present location in the 1970s, when a developer wanted to purchase the land it sat on. Concerned local citizens and town officials banded together and relocated the elephant to city owned land.

Today visitors may tour the inside of this beloved landmark. The entrance leads to a huge reception room that features an observation deck. The inside of the elephant is set up to be a mini-historical museum with many items and photographs of the area.

## Noyes Museum

Lilly Lake Road
Oceanville
Atlantic County
609-652-8848
Open Tuesdays to Saturday 10
    A.M. to 4 P.M. and Sunday
    Noon to 5 P.M.
$3 adults, $2 seniors, and
    children are free

The Noyes Museum collects, preserves, and exhibits American fine art with an emphasis on New Jersey artists. This attractive exhibit space showing contemporary paintings, photography, and sculptures is continuously updated and changing, always displaying a fresh, new look with each visit. The museum also offers lectures, workshops, and classes in addition to a host of special events. Pottery, textiles, and jewelry crafted by local artisans may be purchased in the gift shop.

## Somers Mansion

1000 Shore Road
Somers Point
Atlantic County
609-927-2212
Open Wednesdays to Saturdays
    from 10 A.M. to 4 P.M. and
    Sundays from 1 P.M. to 4 P.M.
Free admission

John Somers, an English Quaker, came to Atlantic County in 1693. He purchased 3,000 acres of land located along the Great Egg Bay, which became known as the Somers Plantation. He also operated a ferry across the bay, which linked his plantation to nearby Cape May County.

The mansion, a Dutch-style colonial, was built in 1720 and is the birth-place of John's great grandson Commodore Richard Somers. Commodore Somers served in the Navy and died at Tripoli Harbor on September 4, 1804. He and 12 men who died with him are buried in an unmarked grave in Libya. His courageous deeds are immortalized in the words of the Marine Corps song ". . . from the halls of Montezuma to the shores of Tripoli."

The State of New Jersey acquired the 16-room mansion in 1941. The building was renovated and all non-original portions that were added to the structure throughout the years were removed. The house is restored to its 18th century appearance of only three rooms.

**African Art Museum**
23 Bliss Avenue
Tenafly
Bergen County
201-894-8611
Open daily from 10 A.M. to 5 P.M.
Free admission

The African Art Museum is operated by the S.M.A. fathers and is part of a larger church complex. The museum's exhibits serve to highlight Western African art and include many artifacts such as masks, sculptures, and religious symbols. The museum also features a main exhibit that changes periodically.

**Aviation Hall of Fame of New Jersey**
Teterboro Airport
400 Fred Wehran Drive
Teterboro
Bergen County
201-288-6344
Open Tuesdays to Sundays from 10 A.M. to 4 P.M.
$5 adults, $3 seniors and children

This museum is dedicated to the preservation of New Jersey's aviation and space heritage. Visitors are especially drawn to a room that features some of the greatest names in aviation history, which are linked with New Jersey. There is a theater that can seat up to 55 people and offers short films on aviation subjects. Children can get hands on experience as air traf-

fic controllers by directing air traffic while listening to actual radio communications between Teterboro Tower and dozens of airplanes. Outside the
museum is a M.A.S.H. exhibit that is dedicated to the veterans of the
Korean War. It is the only one of its kind in the United States.

## Hermitage

335 North Franklin Turnpike
Ho-Ho-Kus
Bergen County
201-445-8311
Grounds are open Mondays to
    Fridays from 9 A.M. to 5 P.M.
Tours held Wednesdays to
    Sundays
$3 adults, and children are free
Admission is for mansion tours
    only

Located on five acres of land and surrounded by century-old trees, the
Hermitage was a frequent place for early American leaders including General Washington, Marquis de Lafayette, and James Monroe, to visit. This 14-
room Gothic Revival mansion was built for Elijah Rosencrantz Jr. and his
family in 1847. The house incorporated portions of an historic Colonial-era
home that was built around 1750.

Visitors may tour the mansion Wednesdays through Sundays at 1:15 P.M.,
2:15 P.M., and 3:15 P.M. The museum shop, which features changing exhibits
from the Hermitage collection, is a must see stop after the tour.

## Hiram Blauvelt Art Museum

705 Kinderkamack Road
Oradell
Bergen County
201-261-0012
Open Tuesdays to Thursdays
    from 10 A.M. to 4 P.M.
Free admission

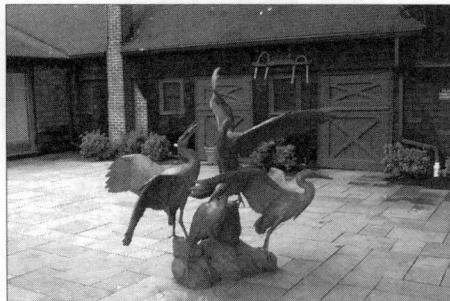

Hiram Blauvelt was an early conservationist who collected wildlife art.
From his contributions, he hoped to promote the value of nature on everyday culture and the need for conservation. The museum is located in the
former carriage house of his estate, which was built in 1893. The museum
follows its founder's ideals, bringing awareness to issues facing the natural
world and showcasing the artists who are inspired by it. The museum

focuses on artwork representing wildlife and features many exhibits including one on extinct birds from different parts of the world.

**New Jersey Navel Museum**
78 River Street
Hackensack
Bergen County
201-342-3268
Open weekends 10 A.M. to 5 P.M.
$4.50 adults, $3 children, for
	submarine tour only

Available for viewing on the grounds are several small boats, missiles, mines, and torpedoes. The museum houses many exhibits including photographs and memorabilia that serve to illustrate the lifestyle of the men at sea. The main attraction is the USS *Ling,* a *Balao* class fleet submarine that entered service during World War II. Tickets may be purchased inside the museum. The last tour starts at 4:00 P.M.

The *Ling* was built by the Cramp Shipbuilding Company of Philadelphia, Pennsylvania and was commissioned on June 8, 1945. It was assigned to the Atlantic Fleet and made one patrol before the war ended. It was decommissioned on October 16, 1946. During the 1960s, the *Ling* was reactivated and served as a training vessel. The submarine arrived on loan to the museum in 1973.

The tour of the USS *Ling* will take you through all of the compartments on board the submarine including the Torpedo Room, Control Room, and Main Engine Room.

**Air Victory Museum**
South Jersey Regional Airport
68 Stacy Haines Road
Medford
Burlington County
609-267-4488
Open weekends 10 A.M. to 4 P.M.
$4 per person

The exhibits of the Air Victory Museum focus on the technological breakthroughs in flight, from balloons to planes, throughout the history of the United States. Particularly interesting displays are the replicas of the Wright Brother's plane and the Spirit of St. Louis. There are also vintage military and commercial planes on display and countless artifacts ranging from clothing to full-motion flight simulators. The collection is periodically rotated, ensuring visitors will learn something new with every visit. Visitors may also stop by the museum's library and explore the approximately 3,000 books covering topics ranging from early flight to space exploration.

### Burlington County Historical Society

475 High Street
Burlington City
Burlington County
609-386-4773
Open Mondays to Thursdays
     from 1 P.M. to 4 P.M. and
     Sundays from 2 P.M. to 4 P.M.
$5 per person

Home of the Burlington County Historical Society, this building was constructed in 1780. It is famous for being the birthplace of James Fenimore Cooper, author of the *Last of the Mohicans*. James was born on September 15, 1789 and was the eleventh of twelve children. When he was one year old, his family moved to Lake Otsego, New York, where his father established a settlement that was to become modern day Cooperstown.

The house contains four rooms that feature displays of Cooper artifacts and furniture. It also features objects from the estate of Joseph Bonaparte, Napoleon's brother who settled not far from the town of Burlington after the battle of Waterloo.

Behind the house is the society's research library, which is open Mondays, Tuesdays, Thursdays, and Fridays from 1 P.M. to 4 P.M. Wednesdays from 10 A.M. to 4 P.M., and Sundays from 2 P.M. to 4 P.M. The library's hours are extended on the first Friday of the month from 6 P.M. to 9 P.M. In addition to the volumes of books the library has, there are photographs, maps, manuscripts and newspapers about the county.

The Burlington County Historical Society also conducts tours of several historic houses and landmarks in the town.

**Fort Dix Military Museum**
Fort Dix
Pennsylvania Avenue, Building
     6501
Burlington County
609-562-2334
Open Mondays through Fridays
     8 A.M. to 4 P.M.
Free admission

Fort Dix was named after Major General John Adams Dix, who served with distinction in the War of 1812 and the Civil War. During his distinguished public career, he was a Minister to France, a United States Senator, and Governor of New York.

Construction began on the fort in 1917 and expanded rapidly as the fort became the main basic training facility and debarkation point on the East Coast for soldiers during World War II. During the Vietnam War, a mock Vietnamese village was recreated to enhance the training soldiers received before going oversees. In 1990, Fort Dix was chosen to be the site where select Kuwaiti citizens were trained in basic military skills. These citizens later took part in the liberation of their county. In December 1995, soldiers deploying troops for the Bosnia Peace Mission were taught crowd control and search and seizure tactics at the fort. Today the fort is a major regional training and mobilization center for the Army Reserve and Army National Guard.

The Fort Dix Military Museum includes vintage military vehicles and other memorabilia on display about the grounds. Inside the museum are uniforms, firearms, equipment, and photographs. Each exhibit is rich in detail and tells a story of dedication and sacrifice.

**Prison Museum**
128 High Street
Mount Holly
Burlington County
609-265-5858
Tours are held May through
     September, 4th weekend of
     every month from 10 A.M. to
     4 P.M.
Free admission

When the last prisoner left the jail in 1966, the prison at Burlington County had been the oldest prison in continuous use in the United States. Construction began in 1808, following the blue prints of noted architect

Robert Mills. He later designed outstanding buildings in Richmond, Virginia, but is most-famously known for designing the Washington Monument, the Treasury Building, and the old Patent Office, in the late 1830s.

In the design of the jail, Mills proposed radical changes to the medieval concept of prison construction frequently used at the time. His insights and innovations made the Burlington County Prison a prototype for the prisons of today. Today, the prison has been converted into a museum where visitors may tour the cells and corridors and see the unique designs that made this facility so cutting-edge.

### Smithville Mansion

Smithville Road
East Hampton
Burlington County
609-261-3780
Grounds are open 8 A.M. to
    Sunset, tours are held May
    through October on Sundays
    and Wednesdays
$5 adults, $3 seniors and children

In 1776, Joseph Parker purahsed a 37-acre tract of land from Solomon Southwick. A few years later, he built a gristmill and a sawmill on the land. Then a dam was constructed on the nearby creek to provide the mill with power. The site became known as Parker's Mill.

In 1831, two brothers, Jonathan and Samuel Shreve, purchased the original tract of land plus an additional seven acres. They had plans to construct a cotton-cloth manufacturing center on the site. By 1850, the workers' houses, the mansion, and an enlargment of the mill pond had all been built. They even built a canal to nearby Mount Holly for the transportaion of goods. The site had grown into a small village with over 200 workers employed and living there full-time. The village was known as "Shreveville" and included a school, general store, 50 workers houses, and the mansion. The cloth manufacturing center was very successful. However, in the late 1850s, a nation-wide depression devastated the cotton industy and the brothers had to mortgage their property. The coming of the Civil War made matters worse as cotton became increasingly difficult to

**FACT:** *Burlington County is the site of New Jersey's first public school. It was opened in Bordentown in 1852 by Clara Barton. Barton, who worked as a nurse during the Civil War, later founded the American Red Cross in 1881.*

get. The town was nearly abandoned and well on its way to becoming a forgotten place.

In 1865, Hezekia Bradley Smith, a successful machinery production entrepreneur from Massachusetts visited the area, looking for a new place for his business. He rediscovered the village of Shreveville and purchased it, thinking it was a good location for his business because it was close to major cities and included a transportation system. He began the task of converting the near deserted village into a major indutrial center. The mill pond was enlarged and machine shops were built from the old buildings. The H.B. Smith Machine Company would eventualy manufacture over 150 different types of machines and many woodworking items. Hezekia renamed the town Smithville and brought in more workers, renovating the workers' houses and built new ones. In 1870, he bought the surrounding farmland, totalling more than 300 acres, in order to make the village more self-sufficient.

During the 1880s, the company developed a mechanical means of self-transportation and the bicycle was created. The bicycle quickly became the center's most produced item. The most famous edition of the bicycle built by the company was the "Star" bicycle.

Decendants of the Smith family lived in the mansion until 1962, when the land was donated to the state. Tours of the mansion and grounds are offered. The Smithville Mansion is presently the home of the Burlington County Cultural & Heritage Department (609-265-5068).

**Camden County Historical Museum**
Park Boulevard and Euclid
  Avenue
Camden
Camden County
856-964-3333
Open Sundays from 1 P.M. to 5
  P.M. and Tuesdays to
  Thursdays from 12:30 P.M. to
  4:30 P.M., closed during
  August
$2 adults, children are free

Founded in 1899, the Camden County Historical Society is dedicated to the collection and preservation of the area's history. The main building contains a library that holds over 19,000 volumes of books, including an outstanding map collection and the most complete grouping of historical newspapers about Camden County. The museum features permanent and changing exhibits that demonstrate nineteenth century life in the Camden area. Exhibits include information about blacksmithing, candle making, coopering and weaving. There is also a display on early-

American glass and various firefighting equipment, toys, and household implements.

Adjacent to the museum is Pomona Hall, a beautiful eighteenth century Georgian-style mansion that was built by Joseph Cooper. It has been restored to its 1788 appearance and includes a fine collection of eighteenth and nineteenth century furnishings. Tours are conducted with costumed interpreters, who demonstrate the activities of day-to-day life for the people of that time. As an added feature once per month, open-hearth demonstrations are performed.

### Greenfield Hall

343 Kings Highway East
Haddonfield
Camden County
856-429-7375
Open Wednesdays to Fridays
    from 1 P.M. to 4 P.M. and the
    first Sunday of the month
    from 1 P.M. to 4 P.M.
Free admission

John Gill IV had Greenfield Hall built in 1841. The land belonged to his ancestors since the early 1700s, when John Gill I purchased the property from his cousin, Elizabeth Haddon Estaugh, the founder of Haddonfield.

Today, Greenfield Hall is maintained by the Historical Society of Haddonfield and is furnished much as it would have been when members of the Gill family resided in it. Inside visitors will find a wide collection of furniture, needlework, dolls, costumes, glass, and china.

### Indian King Tavern Museum

233 Kings Highway East
Haddonfield
Camden County
856-429-6792
Open Wednesdays to Saturdays
    from 10 A.M. to 12 P.M. and
    Sundays from 1 P.M. to 4 P.M.
Free admission

Indian King Tavern was originally constructed in 1750. During these times it was both a tavern and a local meeting hall. During the revolution, as the British and Continental armies engaged in battles near the Trenton area, the New Jersey legislature abandoned Trenton and fled south to a safer haven in the village of Haddonfield. Once at Haddonfield, they reconvened in a room on the second floor of this tavern. It was during this session that the New Jersey General Assembly officially passed legislation to create an independent state and adopted its seal.

Francis Hopkinson, a local attorney and a signer of the Declaration of Independence designed the Great Seal of New Jersey. New Jersey's state seal is comprised of symbols representing important aspects of daily life in 1777.

In 1903, Indian King became New Jersey's first state historic site. It stands today as an outstanding example of eighteenth century colonial architecture.

## Walt Whitman House
328 Mickle Boulevard
Camden
Camden County
856-964-5383
Open Wednesdays to Saturdays
from 10 A.M. to 1 P.M. and
Sundays from 1 P.M. to 4 P.M.
Free admission

During the 1870s, Walt Whitman came to Camden and lived with his brother's family in a house located on Stevens Street. Walt Whitman is considered one of America's greatest poets and during the time he spent in Camden, many famous authors such as Charles Dickens and Oscar Wilde would come to visit him.

Whitman grew to enjoy the area so much that even after his brother moved to the countryside; Walt stayed on in the city. With the success of his 1883 edition of *Leaves of Grass,* he was able to purchase his own home. This building was the only house Whitman would ever own in his life.

Walt Whitman spent the last years of his life in this house. He previously had a stroke and could not get around much on his own. Many of the items in his house were given to him by friends in order to make life easier. In 1892, Whitman died in this house at the age of 72.

Today, the building has been restored to its original appearance. Inside, visitors will find books, letters, and other personal belongings of Whitman's. Even the notice of his death that was nailed to his door has been preserved.

**Cape May Historical Museum**
504 Route 9
Cape May Courthouse
Cape May County
609-465-3535
April through December,
    Tuesdays through Saturdays
    9 A.M. to 3 P.M., January
    through March, Saturday 9
    A.M. to 3 P.M.
$2 adults and $.50 children

Located in the John Holmes House, which dates back to the eighteenth century, the Cape May County Historical and Genealogical Society operates a museum and a research library that is open to the public. The kitchen and bedroom contain authentic period furnishings and visually illustrate early country life in America. The more modern Victorian-style dining room is furnished with early eighteenth century pieces and contains many interesting artifacts. The house's other rooms include collections of china, furniture, and glass, which date from the late seventeenth to early twentieth centuries.

The museum's Medical Room displays many exhibits on the advancement of surgical instruments and techniques during the eighteenth and nineteenth centuries. There is also a collection of military artifacts dating from the Revolutionary War to the present time. The museum's prize possession is the original flag taken from the Confederates States ironclad, the *Merrimac*.

In the back of the house stands an old barn. It contains such exhibits as a hunting-decoy collection, a stagecoach, and a peddler's wagon.

**Discovery Sea Shell Museum**
2717 Asbury Ave
Ocean City
Cape May County
609-398-2316
Open daily from 10 A.M. to 5 P.M.,
    Memorial Day to December,
    Mondays to Saturdays from
    10 A.M. to 8 P.M. and Sundays
    from 12 P.M. to 6 P.M.
Free admission

This museum features a collection of seashells that were gathered from around the world. Visitors will see many rare seashell specimens including the astonishing *Glory of India*. An unusual exhibit features "freaks of nature," which includes the only Siamese-Twin Helmet shell known to exist. The museum also has a gift shop with many different shells and shell-craft items for sale. In the Shell Yard, more than 10,000 varieties of seashells may be found, as well as different types of coral and carved shells. The most unusual specimen is the mysterious air plants that grow inside shells without the need of soil.

**Emlen Physick Estate**
1048 Washington Street
Cape May
Cape May County
609-884-5404
Open daily, April through
    December and weekends,
    January through March
$8 adults and $4 children

This Victorian-style, 18-room mansion was built in 1879 for Emlen Physick Jr. He and his extended family, which included his widowed mother, Frances Ralston, and his aunt, Emilie Parmentier, lived in this house. Mr. Physick, who never married, was descended from a very famous and wealthy Philadelphia family. His grandfather, Dr. Philip Syng Physick, was considered the father of American surgery and was famous for implementing new surgical procedures and inventing numerous medical instruments, which are still in use today. Emlen followed in his grandfather's footsteps and graduated from medical school, but he never actually practiced medicine. Instead, Emlen preferred to be a farmer and eventually owned two tenant farms. He bought and sold a great deal of real estate in the Cape May area and even took an active interest in local politics by voicing his opinions at city council meetings.

Following Emlen Physick's death in 1916, the mansion and the grounds passed through a variety of different owners and eventually fell into a state of disrepair. During the 1960s, the estate was acquired by a group of developers who planned to tear down the house and put up a housing development. Fortunately, local citizens decided to save this historic structure. They formed the Mid-Atlantic Center for the Arts (MAC) in 1970 and delayed the demolition process long enough to allow the City of Cape May to purchase the property and preserve the estate.

Today, the MAC, who has begun a major restoration of the property, leases the mansion and grounds from the city. The money raised from the guided tours of the Cape May region, which are conducted by the MAC, largely funds the maintenance of the house.

Visitors may tour the mansion and the outbuildings on the estate's four acres of property. The mansion contains changing exhibits that showcase the luxury that the Physick family lived in. The Gallery Shop features many tea and tea-rated accessories, including unusual teapots, silver-plate servings, china, and cookbooks.

At the Twinings Tearoom, located in the 1876 carriage house, visitors may enjoy an afternoon tea or luncheon. The menu includes sandwiches, salads, pastries, and breads, not to mention the large selection of superb teas.

**Tea Luncheon:** Includes tea sandwiches, salads, breads, pastries, scones, and beverages. *Hours:* Available daily from 11:30 A.M. *Admission:* $15 per person.

**Elegant Afternoon Tea:** Includes finger sandwiches, pastries, scones, and beverages. *Hours:* Available daily from 2 P.M. *Phone:* 609-884-5404 extension 138, reservations required. *Admission:* $12.50 per person.

**Cumberland Historical Museum**
Ye Greate Street
Greenwich
Cumberland County
856-455-4055
Open April through mid-
    December, Tuesdays through
    Saturdays from 12 P.M. to
    4 P.M. and Sundays from
    2 P.M. to 5 P.M.
Free admission

The Cumberland County Historical Society uses this historic building as a museum. Nicholas Gibbon, an English textile merchant who traded with the colonies, had this house built in 1730. His intention, once settling in America, was to construct a replica of a certain London townhouse that he admired back home.

The mansion is filled with different artifacts from every period of Cumberland County history. The rooms of the house are decorated with eighteenth and nineteenth century furniture. Demonstrations of colonial-style, open-fire cooking techniques are held daily in the kitchen. The second floor contains the bedrooms, which include a collection of children's toys, nineteenth century furniture, and a display cabinet that features artifacts from the famous Greenwich journalist and patriot, the Reverend Philip Vickers Fithian.

A small museum shop sells post cards, gifts, and a collection of books on the history of Greenwich.

Adjacent to the house is the Barn Museum, which includes a vast display of tools that were used by early farmers of this region.

**Delaware Bay Museum**
1727 Main Street
Port Norris
Cumberland County
856-785-2060
Open April through October,
    Saturdays and Sundays from
    1 P.M. to 4:30 P.M.
Free admission

This museum contains a number of interesting artifacts and photographs depicting the history and culture of the Delaware Bay region. Exhibits focus on the oyster farming and shipbuilding industries of South Jersey. This area was once considered the oyster capital of the world and had, at the time, the highest number of millionaires per capita in the nation. However, in 1957, the oyster industry crashed with the sudden appearance of a dangerous parasite.

The main attraction of the Delaware Bay Museum is the *A.J. Meerwald*, an oyster schooner built by the Meerwald family of South Dennis. The vessel was launched in 1928 and was part of a fleet of hundreds of similar boats constructed along the bay. Over the years, the *Meerwald* has been converted several times to accomplish different tasks, including being a part of the United States Coast Guard. The schooner was donated to the museum in 1989 and has since been restored to its original specifications. It now serves as a monument and reminder of the Bay area's once proud days of shipbuilding and oyster farming.

**FACT:** *Located in Cumberland County, the town of Greenwich was founded in 1675 by John Fenwick. Greenwich has the distinction of being one of five "tea-party" towns in America, the others being Annapolis, Charleston, Princeton, and Boston. On the evening of Thursday, December 22, 1774, about forty people, disguised as Indians, stole the cargo of the British vessel the "Greyhound". The cargo, which contained many chests of tea, was taken to a field and burned to protest the oppression of British rule.*

**Edison National Historic Site**
Main Street and Lakeside Avenue
West Orange
Essex County
973-736-0550 ext. 42
$2 adults and children are free

## *Hours*

| | |
|---|---|
| Wednesdays to Fridays: | Weekends: |
| Visitor's Center: 2 P.M. to 5 P.M. | Visitor's Center: 9 A.M. to 5 P.M. |
| Laboratory Tours: 12:30 P.M. to 4 P.M. | Laboratory Tours: 10 A.M. to 4 P.M. |
| Glenmont Tours: 12:30 P.M. to 4:20 P.M. | Glenmont Tours: 11:30 A.M. to 4:20 P.M. |

# *West Orange Laboratories*

Thomas Edison started his long career as an inventor by tinkering with telegraphic technology. He soon made small improvements in the field and found that he had a talent and a passion. With these improvements Edison was awarded several patents. He used the money that he received from his patents to open a small lab in Menlo Park.

Edison and his small team of engineers would work long hours out of this tiny laboratory, pursuing advancements in sound and electrical technology. He achieved world fame with his invention of the phonograph and by implementing the first practical use of the incandescent lamp. Thomas Edison used each success as a means to invest further in his laboratory. He was determined to create the ultimate research center, a place that could be devoted to the rapid and inexpensive development of his inventions.

A new laboratory, which was located in West Orange, was completed in 1887. Edison once boasted that this laboratory could build anything from a lady's watch to a locomotive. Nearly 200 workers were employed including many scientists and engineers with backgrounds in chemistry, physics, and mathematics.

Edison spent many hours each week performing administrative duties and improving the then-current technologies. He loved his career and would often work 100-hour weeks. Edison treated his employees with respect and listened to their solutions and approaches for various problems. He stocked his library with over 10,000 volumes of books and supplied his laboratories with every conceivable substance so that his workers would have both the information and materials they needed. Out of the West Orange laboratories came many inventions including a movie camera and improved battery storage.

After Thomas Edison's death in 1931, the lab remained in operation for a few years more. The facility at West Orange is considered the first modern research and development laboratory. The Bell and Westinghouse laboratories, two of the worlds largest, were modeled after Edison's facility, which in itself was one of his greatest inventions. During his lifetime, Edison was awarded over 1,000 patents. He arguably contributed more to technological progress then any other person in United States history.

## *Glenmont*

Glenmont was America's first private, landscaped, residential area. In 1886, Thomas Edison bought this Queen Ann-style mansion, which included 13.5 acres of land. He and his wife moved into the house after their honeymoon in Florida. His wife was in charge of the house and made several changes to it over the years. She also hired a staff of people to help maintain the house and grounds. Many guests were entertained at the house including President Herbert Hoover, Helen Keller, Orville Wright and the Edison's personal friends, Henry Ford and Harvey Firestone.

Today the 23-room mansion contains many of the family's personal belongings such as furniture, paintings, and books. Tours of both the West Orange Lab and the Glenmont mansion are conducted. Tickets are sold at the Visitor's Center of the West Orange Laboratory.

**Grover Cleveland Birthplace**
207 Bloomfield Avenue
Caldwell
Essex County
973-226-0001
Open Wednesdays to Fridays
from 9 A.M. to 6 P.M.,
Saturdays from 9 A.M. to 5
P.M., and Sundays from 1 P.M.
to 6 P.M.
Free admission

Stephen Grover Cleveland was born on March 18, 1837. He was the son of the Reverend Richard Cleveland and his wife Ann. Stephen was the fifth of nine children and was named after the first ordained pastor of the First Presbyterian Church at Caldwell. Four years after Stephen's birth, the Cleveland family moved to New York.

In 1859, Stephen received his law degree and entered into local politics, becoming mayor of Buffalo in 1882. One year later, he successfully ran for Governor of New York. Cleveland soon set his sights on the presidency. After a whirlwind campaign, in 1885, Cleveland was sworn in as the 22$^{nd}$ President of the United States. However, Cleveland did not win re-election for a second term four years later. Although he won the popular vote he didn't gain enough support in the Electoral College to win. Determined to be president again, he led a grass-roots campaign and won the election of 1892 and became the only United States President to serve two non-consecutive terms.

Visitors may tour this house, the birthplace of our 22$^{nd}$ and 24$^{th}$ President, and see the humble roots of one of our greatest leaders. The house was originally constructed in 1832 and was used as the pastor's residence from the beginning. Over the years the building was enlarged and remodeled several times. Most of the first floor has been restored to its late 1830s look. Inside are many artifacts and memorabilia that once belonged to the family.

### Israel Crane House

110 Orange Road
Montclair
Essex County
973-744-1796
Open Mid-September to mid-
    June, Sundays from 2 P.M. to
    5 P.M.
$3 adults and $1 children

This Federal-style mansion was home to three generations of the Crane family. Israel Crane, a successful merchant, established this homestead in 1796. The mansion has been restored to its original look and displays an outstanding collection of period furnishings. Visitors may watch and even participate in demonstrations of open-hearth cooking and, at special times of the year, demonstrations are conducted in quilting, basket making, and blacksmithing. The outside garden is lovingly maintained and kept fresh and beautiful with blossoms of rare, eighteenth century vintage flowers and herbs.

Behind the Crane House is the County Store and Museum Shop, which was built in the 19$^{th}$ century by Nathaniel Crane. It stands as a fine example of a modest home during this period. Today, a visitor will find this gift shop stocked with pot-pourri, baskets, and other crafts.

Adjacent to the mansion is a late nineteenth century residence that is the home of the Montclair Historical Society, which oversees the maintenance of all three buildings. This home is also used as a library, which contains information about the town of Montclair. The society maintains a total of five buildings.

**Montclair Art Museum**
3 South Mountain Avenue
Montclair
Essex County
973-746-5555
Open Tuesdays through
    Saturdays from 11 A.M. to
    5 P.M. and Sundays from
    1 P.M. to 5 P.M.
$5 adults, $4 seniors and students

Opening in 1914, the Montclair Art Museum is situated on three and a half acres of carefully landscaped property. The museum's grounds include the Van Vleck Arboretum, which features a collection of native and rare plant species. The museum's 25,000 square feet of space house seven galleries. The Montclair Art Museum focuses on collecting and preserving American and Native American art. Its collection comprises of over 15,000 works in a variety of media dating as far back as the eighteenth century.

On the museum grounds is the Yard School of Art. The school offers year-round programs for both children and adults. The LeBrun Library contains over 14,000 volumes of books, 4,000 bound periodicals, and 20,000 slides. The library serves as an art reference resource for both its members and the general public.

A small museum store (973-746-5555, extension 237) is located on the first floor. Its hours are Tuesdays through Saturdays from 11 A.M. to 5 P.M. and Sundays from 1 P.M. to 5 P.M.

**Newark Museum**
49 Washington Street
Newark
Essex County
201-596-6550
Open Wednesdays through
    Sundays from noon to 5 P.M.
Free admission

One can spend the entire day viewing and learning from the exhibits at the Newark Museum. The museum includes a wide selection of American-style paintings and sculptures that date from as far back as the eighteenth century. There is also a collection of glass, ceramics, textiles, and furniture, which represents the prime examples of the city's major manufacturing periods.

The Newark Museum also contains a wide range of classical art from Egypt and Greece. Artwork is also on display from Africa, Japan, China, and India. An exhibit on Tibet features a Buddhist altar that was consecrated in 1990 by the 14th Dalai Lama.

Many objects from the Victorian era are on display at the adjoining Ballantine House, a restored 17-room mansion that was built in 1885. John H. Ballantine, owner of Newark's most famous brewery, once owned this house.

In addition, the Newark Museum also contains a planetarium, a recreated one-room schoolhouse circa 1784, a collection of coins and paper money, which is the largest such public collection in New Jersey and a café that offers lunch Wednesdays to Sundays from 12 P.M. to 3:30 P.M.

**New Jersey Historical Society**
52 Park Place
Newark
Essex County
973-596-8500
Open Tuesdays through
    Saturdays from 10 A.M. to
    5 P.M.
Free admission

The New Jersey Historical Society was founded in 1845 and moved to this building in 1997. Inside are three floors of displays and exhibits about New Jersey that focus on the cultural and historical heritage of the Garden State. The museum includes books, furniture, paintings, and sculptures from all time periods. The society's library is a great place to research family history and contains many photographs and newspapers preserved on microfilm, which date as far back as the colonial times.

**Gloucester County Historical
    Society**
58 North Broad Street
Woodbury
Gloucester County
856-848-8531
Open Mondays, Wednesdays, and
    Fridays from 1 P.M. to 4 P.M.
Closed July and August
$2 adults and $1 children

This 18-room mansion was constructed in 1765 and was originally the home of John Sparks. In 1792 Andrew Hunter purchased the estate. He was a chaplain in the Revolutionary War and one of the "Tea Burners" of Greenwich. Six years later the house became the home of John Lawrence. John's younger brother James also lived in the house and received his education at the nearby Woodbury Academy. James achieved posthumous fame during the War of 1812, when he was mortally wounded while commanding his battleship. He last words "Don't give up the ship" have since become the watchword of the U.S. Navy.

Today, the Gloucester County Historical Society maintains the mansion as a museum. A small gift shop sells many fine reproductions of South Jersey glass and other unique items. The society also maintains a research library (856-845-4771) on 17 Hunter Street. The library includes newspapers, deeds, cemetery data, and over 800 volumes on genealogy. It also features maps, photographs, and newspapers relating to Gloucester County. The library's hours are Mondays to Fridays from 1 P.M. to 4 P.M. There are additional hours on Tuesdays and Fridays from 6 P.M. to 9:30 P.M. It is also open on the first Saturday of the month from 10 A.M. to 5 P.M., and on the last Sunday of the month from 2 P.M. to 5 P.M.

**Heritage Glass Museum**
High and Center Streets
Glassboro
Gloucester County
609-881-7468
Open Saturdays from 11 A.M. to
    2 P.M.
Free admission

In 1779, the Stanger family established a glass works in Gloucester County. The quality of the sands, the abundance of trees for fuel, and the proximity of the Philadelphia market made this area ideal for their new

**FACT:** *Gloucester County was home to the nation's first federal government installation. On July 5th, 1776, land was purchased (in the present day town of Paulsboro) for the creation of Fort Billings. General George Washington himself inspected the fort on August 1st, 1777. However, Fort Billings did not stand long. A few months later, on October 3rd of the same year, the British broke the chevaux-de-frise below the fort and landed on the shore. The Americans abandoned the fort, burning most of it as they fled.*

venture. The glass industry at Glassboro was once the nation's most extensive and best equipped, producing the greatest variety of styles and colors. The Stanger Glassworks had managed to become very successful in a short time. However, the company was forced to close in 1781, due to devalued currency as a result of the Revolutionary War. Ownership of the company changed hands for several years until, finally, the Whitney Brothers Glass Works acquired the property.

The Heritage Glass Museum is housed in a former bank building on property that once belonged to the Whitney Brothers Glass Works. The museum contains many fine examples of historic bottles and glass related items.

### Matchbox Road Museum
17 Pearl Street
Newfield
Gloucester County
800-976-7623
Open Mondays to Fridays from
    8 A.M. to 4 P.M.
Free admission

This unique museum is a toy car collector's heaven. There are over 20,000 Matchbox vehicles on display and for sale.

### Afro-American Historical
    Society
Greenville Library
1841 Kennedy Boulevard
Jersey City
Hudson County
201-547-5262
Open Mondays through Saturdays
    from 10 A.M. to 5 P.M., closed
    Saturdays during the summer
Free admission

This museum focuses is on the African American experience in this country. There are exhibits on the civil rights movement, famous athletes, and cultural artifacts including those from historic African American churches. There are also quilts dating back to the early 1840s. Selections of African art are also on display.

**Jersey City Museum**
350 Montgomery Street
Jersey City
Hudson County
201-413-0303
Open Wednesdays and Fridays
    from 11 A.M. to 5 P.M.,
    Thursdays from 11 A.M. to
    8 P.M. and weekends from
    12 P.M. to 5 P.M.
$4 adults, $2 seniors and children

Just recently opened, the Jersey City Museum contains 30,000 square feet of space and includes a 152-seat auditorium, a computer based resource room, and a museum shop with a café. The exhibits focus on nineteenth and twentieth century American artwork. The museum also displays several industry-related collections including a group of over 500 examples of advertising and product designs featuring many items from Jersey City's industrial heritage.

**Hunterdon Historical Museum**
56 Main Street
Clinton
Hunterdon County
908-735-4101
Open April through October,
    Tuesdays to Saturdays from
    10 A.M. to 4 P.M. and Sundays
    from noon to 5 P.M.
$4 adults, $3 seniors, and $1
    children

On the picturesque banks of a 200-foot wide waterfall stands one of the most photographed structures in all of New Jersey. The Old Red Mill, built around 1810, was once the center of a thriving village and was used for processing wool, grist, talc, and even generating electricity. The roofline

**FACT:** *In June of 1967, Glassboro was host to the United States Presidential Summit of President Lyndon Johnson and Soviet Premier Aleksei N. Kosygin. The summit was held at the historic Hollybush Mansion, located on the Rowan University Campus. Although no formal agreements were reached, the talks did lead to improved relationships between the two countries.*

extension, which was added to accommodate new machinery in 1908, gives the mill its distinctive appearance.

Today, the old mill serves as a historical museum and its four floors contain nearly 40,000 artifacts showcasing Hunterdon County's rural, agricultural, and commercial heritage. The museum also includes a county gift shop that sells fine examples of local craft.

Visitors may also tour several other structures on this nine-acre complex, including a blacksmith shop, general store, an 1860 one-room school house, and a reproduction of a nineteenth century log cabin complete with an herb garden and a stone spring house. There are also various carriage sheds that display a variety of wagons, carriages, and other nineteenth century transportation and agricultural equipment.

A significant portion of the grounds incorporates the Mulligan Quarry. This limestone quarry was first opened in 1848, by three Irish immigrant brothers and remained in their family until the early 1960s. The quarry's 150-foot limestone cliffs provide the backdrop for the museums special events such as educational programs, tours, concerts, living history reenactments, and craft shows. The rolling terrain, which rises above the riverbanks, provides relaxing lawn seating against the dramatic sheer wall backdrop.

Other structures included in the quarry are the quarry office, tenant house, blacksmith shop, and rock-screening house. These buildings date from the 1850s to the early twentieth century.

### Hunterdon Museum of Art
7 Lower Center Street
Clinton
Hunterdon County
908-735-8415
Open Tuesdays to Saturdays
    from 11 A.M. to 5 P.M.
Free admission

The Hunterdon Museum of Art is housed in a historic, stone gristmill that was built in 1836. The mill is located directly across from the Hunterdon Historical Museum and sits near the bank of the south branch of the Raritan River. The museum, which was established in 1952, contains more than 9,000 square feet of space and features many paintings, sculptures, and ever-changing exhibits. Approximately 12 exhibitions are held each year, which focus on the work of emerging artists.

The museum's education department offers in-depth classes for both children and adults in a variety of subjects. Experienced art teachers staff three studios, which function as classrooms with facilities to meet the needs of every student, from children and teens, to seniors, and to people with special needs.

**Lebanon Museum**
57 Musconetcong River Road
New Hampton
Hunterdon County
908-537-6464
Open Tuesdays and Thursdays
from 9:30 A.M. to 5 P.M. and
Saturdays from 1 P.M. to 5
P.M.
Free admission

This Greek-revival-style structure was originally built in 1823 and used as a one-room schoolhouse. During the 1870s, a second story was added to the structure. Today it serves as a museum and features a recreated nineteenth century schoolroom with period furnishings and changing exhibits on the second floor.

**Marshall House**
62 Bridge Street
Lambertville
Hunterdon County
609-397-0770
Open April through October and
weekends from 1 P.M. to
4 P.M.
Free admission

This two-story, Federal-style brick building, located on the main commercial street in Lambertville, was the boyhood home of James Wilson Marshall. Marshall, a skilled carpenter, was working for California land developer John Sutter, building a sawmill in Coloma Valley near Sacramento. While working, Marshall discovered gold on the property and the news of his find sparked the famous California gold rush of 1849.

The Lambertville Historical Society now maintains the house as a

**FACT:** *Hunterdon County was the site of the famous Lindberg kidnapping trial. On January 1935, at the Flemington courthouse, Bruno Richard Hauptmann went on trial for kidnapping and killing the 20-month-old first-born son of Charles Lindberg. Lindberg became an American icon when he was the first person to fly solo across the Atlantic Ocean on May 21, 1927, Hauptmann was tried and convicted in 1935 and, after exhausting appeals, he was executed in 1936.*

museum. Although the furniture in the house never belonged to the family, the pieces do reflect the tastes and times that they lived in.

At the entrance to the building is a friendship quilt, which was made in 1843 and contains the names of the 27 leaders of Lambertville's founding families. The museum also features a 30-minute film depicting the history of the town of Lambertville and a small gift shop, which sells books specific to the area.

The Marshall House is the starting point for guided walking tours of Lambertville. Tours are held every fourth weekend, beginning at 2 P.M. and cost $5 per person.

## Hopewell Museum

28 East Broad Street
Hopewell
Mercer County
609-466-0103
Open Mondays, Wednesdays,
    and Saturdays from 2 P.M. to
    5 P.M.
Free admission

The Hopewell Museum preserves the image of typical village life in America from the early Colonial days to the present through its many displays and exhibits. Inside are rooms with period furnishings such as the Colonial Parlor and the Victorian Parlor. On display are collections of china, glass, and early kitchen utensils. The museum also contains a display of antique guns and swords. There is a great display of photographs and memorial dedicated to the local area.

## Morven

55 Stockton Street
Princeton
Mercer County
609-683-4495
Open Wednesdays from 11 A.M.
    to 3 P.M.
Free admission

In 1754, attorney Richard Stockton, who was later a signer of the Declaration of Independence, acquired 150-acres of land and, together with his wife, the well regarded poet, Annis Boudinot, established the family home on the property. It was Annis, who named the house *Morven* after a mythical Gaelic kingdom in the poems of Ossian. Throughout the next two decades, Richard and Annis worked hard to expand and improve their beautiful Georgian-style house and formal gardens. By 1780, their estate had grown to over 300 acres.

Hard times fell on the family during the Revolutionary War, as British soldiers occupied *Morven*. Though the Stockton family fled to Monmouth County, Richard was captured and imprisoned. He died in 1781, soon after his captivity. Annis returned to the estate after the occupation and continued to live there for several years after her husband's death. When the Continental Congress convened at Princeton in 1783, she and her brother Elias, then president of the Congress, hosted a party at the mansion in their honor.

A few years later in 1788, Richard "the Duke," the son of Richard and Annis, inherited the property. This Richard, like his father was an attorney and very politically active. He served as a United States Congressman and Senator. Richard made several changes to the estate, including rebuilding the central portion of the mansion in 1790.

When "the Duke" died in 1828, the property passed to his son, Commodore Robert Field Stockton. Robert was a naval hero and the developer of the first screw-propelled warship. Like the rest of the family, Robert was also very politically active, winning elections to the United States Senate. In his time at *Morven*, Robert saw to the development of the Delaware and Raritan Canal and the Camden and Amboy Railway. During the 1850s, he had the mansion expanded, adding a washhouse and servants' quarters to the rear of the house and re-landscaped the property.

As successful as he was, at the time of his death in 1866, Robert's financial affairs were not in order. The estate was sold to a cousin, Samuel Witham Stockton. Unfortunately, Samuel did not have the same financial resources of earlier generations of the family. The estate was soon sold and continued to change several times throughout the years.

*Morven* was eventually rented to General Robert Wood Johnson, the son of one of the founders of the Johnson & Johnson pharmaceutical company. Johnson added such modern amenities as the swimming pool, pool house, and tennis courts.

In 1945, Governor Walter Edge purchased *Morven* and willed the property to the State of New Jersey upon condition that it be used as either the governor's mansion or a museum. For the next 27 years, this was the official governor's residence. Many celebrities and world leaders were entertained at this house including President John F. Kennedy, Fidel Castro, and Princess Grace of Monaco.

Today, the Governor of New Jersey resides in nearby Drumthwacket, which is just down the road. During the late 1980s, the estate came under the direction of the New Jersey State Museum. A major three-phased renovation started in 1999. The goal was to transform the historic building into a museum.

Today, tours are conducted of the mansion and the beautifully landscaped gardens out back.

**Nassau Hall**
Nassau Street
Princeton
Mercer County
609-258-3603
Open during tours of Princeton
      University
Free admission

Completed in 1756, Nassau Hall was the first building to be constructed specifically for use by Princeton University. It was named for King William II, Prince of Orange-Nassau. Through the years, the hall has served the university in various ways including as classrooms, administrative offices, and as a dormitory.

During the Revolutionary War, Nassau Hall occupied a key strategic point and was the scene of much fighting. As both sides fought to occupy the hall, there was a great deal of damage inflicted upon it. The library was plundered, the organ in the prayer hall was ruined, and furniture was broken down and used for fuel. During the Battle of Princeton alone, Nassau Hall changed hands three times. General Washington's troops finally drove the British out of the building for good by targeting the hall with cannons.

From July through October of 1783, Nassau Hall served as our nation's capital. The Continental Congress convened a special session here on August 26, 1783, to congratulate George Washington on the successful campaign and final victory. And it was here too, that the first foreign ambassador to the fledgling United States, the ambassador from the Netherlands, was welcomed.

A raging fire in 1802, nearly destroyed Nassau Hall, leaving only the outside walls standing. Architect Benjamin Henry Latrobe was commissioned to rebuild the structure along its original lines. He would later earn fame for his work on the restoration of the United States Capital after the British burned it to the ground during the War of 1812. Latrobe made several changes to the structure in order to make the building more resistant to fire. Wood floors were replaced with brick and the stairs were rebuilt with stone. Nassau Hall was also given an iron roof. Latrobe also raised the belfry on a large square base to accommodate a new clock. With this restoration complete, Nassau Hall was made over to a more Federal-style appearance rather then its original Colonial design.

Another disastrous fire in 1855 left only the walls standing once again. This time Philadelphia architect John Notman, who had previously designed three residences in Princeton including the Prospect House, was hired to restore the building. His modifications to the structure were far more extensive and the results altered the appearance once again, this time to an Italian Renaissance-style. Once again more fireproofing measures were performed. Stoves, which were believed to have been the cause of the fire, were removed and replaced with nine furnaces, which provided central heat to the building. Other structural changes included the removal of two of the three front entrances and replacing the doorway at the center of the building with a larger, arched doorway of Florentine style and with more massive steps.

Toward the end of the nineteenth century, Nassau Hall's use as a dormitory steadily declined as the university expanded and new buildings were erected on campus. Today, Nassau Hall houses the president's and other administrative offices. Visitors are welcome in the building only while participating in tours that are organized by Princeton University.

### Old Barracks of Trenton
Barrack Street
Trenton
Mercer County
609-396-1776
Open daily from 10 A.M. to 5 P.M.
$6 adults and free for seniors

From 1755 to 1763, war between England and France raged in Europe. The war expanded to the North American continent as each government sent troops to protect their colonial interests. In New Jersey, many of the British soldiers were quartered in the colonist's private homes. Over time, the colonists complained of this inconvenience and petitioned the government to construct permanent structures for the troops. A bill was passed and a total of five barracks were built. The barracks were located in the towns of Perth Amboy, Elizabeth, New Brunswick, Trenton, and Burlington.

In Trenton, an acre of land was purchased from Mrs. Sarah Cubb. Sarah's father, Joseph Peace, had originally purchased a 36-acre tract from James Trent, the son of the founder of Trenton. Construction of the barracks began in May of 1758. Even before the structure was complete, it was filled with soldiers. At the time, it was the biggest building in the town. The barracks could accommodate about 300 soldiers and in December of 1759, the officer's quarters were completed, increasing the building's size and capacity.

During the Revolutionary War, the barracks at Trenton were occupied at various times by both British and Hessian troops. Just prior to the battle of Trenton, the Hessian mercenaries occupied the barracks along with a number of Tory refugees from Monmouth and Burlington counties. After the battle, with General Washington and his Continental soldiers firmly in control of the area, the barracks were converted into a hospital under the direction of Dr. Bodo Otto.

A few years after the end of the Revolutionary War, the General Assembly of New Jersey directed the commissioner of the state to sell all five of the barracks and the adjoining lands. In February of 1787 William Odgen and William Paterson purchased the barracks at Trenton for 3,260 pounds.

Over the years the Trenton Barracks was used for a variety of things. In 1855, it was home to the Widows and Single Women Home Society. The Old Barracks Association purchased the south section of the building in 1902 and the north section in 1914. The barracks were restored to its 1758 appearance. Today, the Trenton Barracks is the only remaining barracks of the original five in the state.

## William Trent House

15 Market Street
Trenton
Mercer County
609-989-3027
Open daily from 12:30 P.M. to
    4 P.M.
Free admission

Born in Scotland, William Trent moved to Philadelphia in 1682. He established an export business in the city and soon became one of Philadelphia's most successful businessmen. He exported tobacco, flour, skins and furs, and imported luxuries such as fine wines.

In 1714, William purchased 800 acres of land on the New Jersey side of the Delaware River and established the first permanent settlement in the area. Construction for his house began in 1716 and continued until 1719. The house was used as a summer estate, while Trent continued to live in Philadelphia. Trent encouraged the growth of the area by laying out the lanes and streets of what would become today's downtown. He built mills and an iron works along the Assunpink Creek. The settlement,

**FACT:** *In December of 1825, trustees renamed Queens College in honor of Colonel Henry Rutgers, a Revolutionary War hero and wealthy landowner.*

originally called "The Falls" because of the rapid flow of the water from the Delaware River, soon became a depot for merchandise moving between the markets of New York City and Philadelphia. People began to refer to this settlement as "Trent's Town." The name was later shortened to Trenton.

Part of the reason for the success of Trenton in those early days, was Trent's activity in state politics. He later became the fifth Chief Justice of New Jersey. Trenton proved to be such a vital point, that for brief time it became the capital of the United States in 1784 and again in 1799.

Over the years, Lewis Morris, Philemon Dickerson, and Rodman Mac-Camley, who were all Governors of New Jersey, owned Trent's Georgian-style house in succession.

Today, the Trent House stands as the oldest building in the city of Trenton. Visitors may tour the house, which is now a museum and is furnished according to an inventory completed in 1726, shortly after William Trent's death. Though the furnishings are not original and did not belong to William, the pieces do reflect the lifestyle and tastes of the times.

**Edison Memorial Tower &
Museum**
37 Christie Street
Edison
Middlesex County
732-248-7298
Open Wednesdays through
Sundays from 10 A.M. to
4 P.M.
Free admission

The Thomas A. Edison Memorial Tower and Menlo Park Museum was dedicated on February 11, 1938, to commemorate Thomas Edison's 91st birthday. The tower, which is shaped like a large electric light with a bulb on top, is located on the exact spot where Edison's Menlo Park Laboratory once existed. Henry Ford, a personal friend of Edison, moved the original laboratory to his Americana Museum located in Dearborn, Michigan.

While at Menlo Park, Edison and his team of engineers were awarded over 400 patents on inventions such as the incandescent light bulb, the phonograph, and the electric railroad car. Edison made such drastic improvements to telegraph and telephone technology that he soon earned the nickname "The Wizard of Menlo Park."

The museum contains some of Edison's inventions and products including a 1929 Edison "Light-O-Matic" Radio. Thomas Edison once remarked that some of his greatest triumphs were made in his laboratory at Menlo Park.

## Guest House Museum

60 Livingston Avenue
New Brunswick
Middlesex County
732-745-5116
Tours by appointment only
Free admission

Local businessman and tanner, Henry Guest, built this historic, stone farmhouse in 1760. There is a local legend about the house, which tells that one day, during the Revolutionary War, Henry was hanging some hides outside on a line to dry in the sun just as British troops were entering town. From a distance the British mistook the brown hides for a group of American militia and began to open fire with their cannons. When the "militia" did not flee, the British, though impressed with their bravery, continued to fire. Eventually, their mistake was realized and, fortunately for Mr. Guest, the hides were not harmed.

The house was originally located on Carroll Place between Livingston Avenue and George Street. The structure was moved and today is now part of the public library. A museum inside contains a Civil War exhibit as well as history about the local area.

## Middlesex County Museum

1225 River Road
Piscataway
Middlesex County
732-745-4177
Open Tuesdays through Fridays
    from 1 P.M. to 4 P.M. Sundays
    1 P.M. to 4 P.M.
Free admission

Cornelius Low was born in New York City in 1700. Thirty years later, he and his wife moved to Raritan Landing, a prosperous community located on the banks of the Raritan River. The young couple lived in a modest house located on the flats of the river. Cornelius became involved with the building of docks and warehouses along the Raritan River and soon emerged as a leading citizen in the community. He established a business that shipped such products as grain, flour, lumber, and leather to colonies as far away as the West Indies.

In 1739, a flood destroyed the Low's home. Cornelius had a new house built and had it perched high upon a hill overlooking the community. It was completed in 1741 and is believed to have been one of the most expensive houses in the area. Over 350 tons of stone were used in its construction.

Cornelius lived in the house until his death in 1777. His son inherited the property but sold it in 1793. The community continued to prosper until the completion of the Delaware and Raritan Canal, which opened in 1834. The new canal made trade faster and cheaper rendering the port town obsolete.

Today, the house stands on almost two acres of land and has been converted into the Middlesex County Museum. The museum presents a series of rotating exhibits about state and local history. A major restoration of the Low House was completed in 1996, ensuring that the structure would last for generations to come.

**New Jersey Museum of Agriculture**
Rutgers University
College Farm Road
New Brunswick
Middlesex County
732-249-2077
Open Tuesdays to Saturdays from 10 A.M. to 5 P.M. and Sundays from 12 P.M. to 5 P.M.
$4 adults, $3 seniors, and $2 children

Located on the campus of Cook College at Rutgers University, the New Jersey Museum of Agriculture features exhibits of early farming techniques and equipment, from the early 1800s through the mid 1900s. The heart of the museum features the 8,000-piece Wabun C. Kreuger Collection, which contains artifacts that were donated by over 500 New Jersey families, individuals, and organizations.

Complementing the Kreuger Collection is the George H. Cook College Collection of Agricultural and Scientific Photographs. This collection contains an impressive 20,000 glass-negative and vintage prints that portray the saga of early farm life in the Garden State. Other collections and exhibits include wagons, farming tools, tractors, grain threshers, and kitchen tools. The museum also contains a small store, which sells many interesting and educational products related to agriculture.

## Proprietary House
149 Kearny Avenue
Perth Amboy
Middlesex County
732-826-5527
Open Wednesdays from 10 A.M.
    to 4 P.M. and Sundays from 1
    P.M. to 4 P.M.
Free admission

In 1651, a point of land that was referred to as "Ompoge," a Native American word meaning large and level land, was purchased by August Herman from the Lenni-Lenape Indians. This tract of land was renamed "Amboyle" and eventually came to be called Ambo Point. The first group of people to settle this area numbered approximately 200 oppressed Scottish Presbyterians, whom the Earl of Perth had given permission to leave their homeland. Soon after, the Quakers and Dutch followed. The settlement was permanently established in 1663 and christened Perth Amboy. As the town grew, it became the capital of the eastern division of New Jersey. Twelve leading businessmen of the community pooled their resources in the 1680s and began to layout 150 town lots in order to erect more buildings and encourage the community's growth. These men formed the local government, a proprietorship over the community. However, revolts and riots in the town forced the British royal government to replace this proprietary government in 1702. This did little to stem the development of the thriving village, which was charted as a city in 1718.

In February of 1763, New Jersey Royal Governor William Franklin visited the City of Perth Amboy and concluded that it would make a fine place for him to stay while presiding in East Jersey. The Proprietors of East Jersey commissioned English master builder John Edward Pryor to design and build a house suitable to serve as an official residence for the Royal Governor. This gesture was done mainly to ensure the continuing dominance of East Jersey in Colonial politics.

William Franklin was the son of one of the nation's founding fathers, Benjamin Franklin. William was a popular and well-respected governor. He accomplished many tasks including starting a lottery that provided the funding to found Queens College, now Rutgers University. He also introduced a welfare plan to aid farmers, established the nations first Indian reservation, and built roads and bridges.

At the onset of the Revolutionary War, Benjamin Franklin came to Perth Amboy to visit with his son William. Benjamin's goal was to try and persuade his son to switch allegiances, to renounce the King of England and support the rebel cause. Unfortunately, he was unsuccessful and William Franklin, the last Royal Governor of New Jersey, was arrested and taken prisoner by the Continental Army in 1776.

The Proprietary House suffered heavy damage during the war. At one point it was the headquarters for the British forces massing in New York City and the harbor. Perth Amboy's strategic location made control a vital necessity. As a result, much fighting occurred and military control of the city switched hands several times during the war.

In 1794, the house was sold to John Rattoon, a local merchant who had served as a spy during the Revolution. Rattoon, who would later become mayor of the city, had the house fully restored and used it as his residence.

Richard M. Woodhull purchased the building in 1808. He added a third floor and a south wing, transforming the house into one of America's first resort hotels. It was named *The Brighton* and had stables that could accommodate up to 60 horses. The hotel closed its doors during the War of 1812.

Shortly after that war, the house was sold to millionaire businessman Matthias Bruen who lived in it until his death in 1846. His heirs had plans to convert the mansion into a resort once again. However, after a series of economic depressions and the Civil War, they were forced to abandon those plans. In 1883, the family no longer wanted to be responsible for the upkeep of the house and decided to sell it. The mansion was eventually purchased and used as a rest home for retired Presbyterian ministers.

Twenty years later, the Bruen family repurchased the house but once again put it back on the market. It was sold in 1904 and the lands were subdivided. The State of New Jersey finally acquired the dilapidated structure in 1967. However, little restoration was done to the building for the first few years.

Today, visitors may tour the Proprietary House, which is the only official royal governor's residence still standing in the former Thirteen Colonies. The ground floor of the mansion contains the kitchen, servant's hall, and a beautiful, highly valued, wine cellar made of brick. The main floor has a grand hall that includes a fireplace, dining room, and a study. The upper level has the governor's bedroom and guest chambers. There are a total of 16 fireplaces throughout the mansion.

### Rutgers Geology Museum

Rutgers University
Hamilton St. and College Avenue
New Brunswick
Middlesex County
732-932-7243
Open Mondays from 1 P.M. to 4 P.M. and Tuesdays through Fridays from 9 A.M. to Noon
Free admission

The Rutgers University Geology Museum features many exhibits on the geology and anthropology of New Jersey. The museum, which is located on the second floor of the campus's Geology Hall, includes a huge room that is ringed by a balcony. Exhibits include a mastodon from Salem County, New

Jersey and a collection of unique minerals from the Franklin Mines. A small gift shop is located in the museum and has a variety of rocks and minerals for sale.

## Zimmerli Art Museum

71 Hamilton Street
New Brunswick
Middlesex County
732-932-7273
Open Tuesdays to Fridays from
10 A.M. to 4:30 P.M. and
weekends from 12 P.M. to 5
P.M. Closed Tuesdays in July
and August
$3 per person

The Zimmerli Art Museum features works of art from the late eighteenth century to the present day. The collection includes over 4,000 pieces and illustrations from many sources including children's literature. The Gordon Henderson Collection of American Stained Glass Design contains excellent examples of New Jersey-made stained glass windows. There is also a collection of European paintings from the fifteenth through the nineteenth centuries.

The Norton and Nancy Dodge Collection of Nonconformist Art displays works from the former Soviet Union and is the largest and most comprehensive collection of its kind in the world. It features well over 17,000 pieces created during the Cold War period.

The Zimmerli Art Museum also contains a small café and gift shop, which sells posters, tote bags, mugs, and t-shirts as well as books on art, its history and appreciation. The museum has recently undergone a five million dollar renovation and reopened in November 2000.

## Allen House

Route 35 and Sycamore Avenue
Shrewsbury
Monmouth County
732-462-1466
Open May through September,
Tuesdays, Thursdays, and
Sundays from 1 P.M. to 4 P.M.
and Saturdays from 10 A.M. to
4 P.M.
$2 adults, $1.50 seniors, and $1
children

Located at Shrewsbury's historic "Four Corners," the Allen House was built in 1688, by Quaker settler, Judah Allen. In 1764, the house was sold to Josiah Halstead, who enlarged the building and turned it into a tavern called the *Blue Bell*. The tavern was located along a popular carriage stop and quickly became a favorite gathering place for local residents and weary travelers.

Today, the Monmouth County Historical Association maintains the Allen House as a museum. Two rooms in the house are still furnished in the decor of the former tavern. The upper level features exhibits that change on a regular basis.

**Covenhoven House**
150 West Main Street
Freehold
Monmouth County
732-462-1466
Open May through September,
    Tuesdays, Thursdays, and
    Sundays from 1 P.M. to 4 P.M.
    and Saturdays from 10 A.M. to
    4 P.M.
$2 adults, $1.50 seniors, and $1
    children

William Covenhoven completed this Georgian-style home, located on the outskirts of Freehold, in 1753. At the time, it was considered to be one of the finer homes in Monmouth County. William and his wife, Elizabeth, prospered on their large farm until the outbreak of the revolution. On June 26, 1778, just days before the Battle of Monmouth took place, British General Henry Clinton entered Freehold and commandeered the Covenhoven House for use as his headquarters. During the occupation, his soldiers plundered the house of the now widowed, 74-year-old Elizabeth, taking personal belongings and even her cows and chickens.

Today, the Covenhoven House is one of five houses that are maintained by the Monmouth County Historical Association. The house has been carefully refurnished with authentic pieces that were listed in the 1790 records of the estate. There are also many colonial-era artifacts on display and demonstrations of open-hearth cooking are routinely held in the kitchen.

**FACT:** *In 1883, the town of Roselle, Union County, became the first town in the United States to be lighted by electricity.*

## Metz Bicycle Museum

54 West Main Street (rear
    building)
Freehold
Monmouth County
732-462-7363
Open Wednesdays and Saturdays
    from 12 P.M. to 4:30 P.M.
$5 adults, $4 seniors, and $3
    students

Inside the Metz Bicycle Museum, there is an impressive collection of antique bicycles built from the 1850s through the 1950s. There are hundreds of pieces on display including a rare bike called the "Zimmy." Freehold businessman Authur Zimmerman, who became the world's first bicycle racing champion in the 1880s, designed this bicycle. The museum has several other displays besides bicycles. It features a number of antique cars and a variety of household gadgets.

## Monmouth County Historical
## Association

70 Court Street
Freehold
Monmouth County
732-462-1466
Open Tuesdays to Saturdays
    from 10 A.M. to 4 P.M. and
    Sundays from 1 P.M. to 4 P.M.
$2 adults, $1.50 seniors, and $1
    children

This three-story, Georgian-style home, was built for the Monmouth County Historical Association in 1931. Inside is a museum that contains mahogany furniture, rare pieces of china, and paintings. There is also a room that features several hands-on exhibits for children. The historical association's research library contains over 5,000 books and over 4,000 photographs making it one of the largest collections of printed and original materials on local history in the state. The library and its archives are open Wednesdays through Saturdays from 10 A.M. to 4 P.M.

**Monmouth Museum**
Brookdale Community College
Newman Springs Road
Lincroft
Monmouth County
732-747-2266
Open Tuesdays to Saturdays
   from 10 A.M. to 4:30 P.M. and
   Sundays from 1 P.M. to 5 P.M.
$4 per person

The Monmouth Museum contains three separate galleries. One gallery is devoted to various works of art and rotates its exhibits from time to time. The Becker Junior Gallery is geared toward children seven to 12 years old and has displays that focus on particular themes. The Wonder Wind Gallery, which features a tree house and a waterfall, has hands-on exhibits for children three to six years old.

**National Guard Militia Museum**
Camp Drive
Sea Girt
Monmouth County
732-974-5966
Open Tuesdays and Thursdays,
   Memorial Day through Labor
   Day, 10 A.M. to 3 P.M., and
   Weekends, 10 A.M. to 3 P.M.
Free admission

The mission of this museum is to preserve and display the military heritage of New Jersey. Visitors will come to understand how wars have shaped the state and learn about the sacrifices of New Jersey's citizen-soldiers. The exhibits feature artifacts and memorabilia, which are specific in their historical significance to the Army National Guard, the Air National Guard, and the Naval Militia of New Jersey.

**FACT:** *The first "condensed" soup was cooked and canned in the City of Camden in 1897. This would later become the famous Campbell's Soup.*

**Steamboat Dock Museum**
American Legion Drive
Keyport
Monmouth County
732-739-6390
Open April, May, October, and
    November, Mondays from
    10 A.M. to 1 P.M., June
    through September, Mondays
    from 10 A.M. to 1 P.M. and
    Sundays from 1 P.M. to 4 P.M.
Free admission

Throughout the 1800s, the town of Keyport was a major center for steamship building. About 50 steamboats were built in this town including the *River Queen,* which was used by General Ulysses S. Grant as a dispatch boat on the Potomac River during the Civil War. Keyport continued to be a busy docking facility for steamboats until 1950, when a devastating hurricane battered the coast and demolished the docks and ships.

The Steamboat Dock Museum contains a number of photographs and exhibits of Keyport's history, focusing on its ship building days. William Gehlhaus, who is known for building New Jersey's first amusement park located nearby at Keansburg, once owned the building. William used the building as a machine shop and ticket booth, for when his boats made their runs between Keansburg and New York City.

**Vietnam Era Educational
    Center**
PNC Bank Arts Center
Exit 116 on Parkway
1 Memorial Lane
Holmdel
Monmouth County
732-335-0033
Open Tuesdays to Saturdays
    from 10 A.M. to 4 P.M.
$4 adults, $2 seniors and students

Located on the grounds of the PNC Bank Arts Center, this museum along with the adjoining, open-air memorial, is not only dedicated to those who served during Vietnam War but to the whole era that marks the trials and tribulations surrounding the war. The same architectural firm that created the Holocaust Museum, located in our nation's capital, designed the building. The museum contains many exhibits such as the history of Vietnam and the impact of the war on the United States and New Jersey in particular. One section features letters handwritten by soldiers who were stationed in Southeast Asia. The adjacent memorial is dedicated to the men and women who lost their lives fighting in the Vietnam War. The names of 1,556 soldiers from New Jersey are inscribed on a circular, black marble wall surrounding a hillside amphitheater. Inside the amphitheater is a statue dedicated to the nurses who risked their lives to care for the wounded.

### Whitlock-Seabrook Homestead
119 Port Monmouth Road
Middletown
Monmouth County
732-787-1807
Open by appointment
Free admission

Thomas Whitlock established the Shoal Harbor estate in 1663. The estate was later sold to Daniel Seabrook who developed the land for farming, growing an orchard, and raising livestock. Through Seabrook's efforts, Shoal harbor grew into one of the largest plantations in the area.

During the Revolutionary War, Seabrook's widow converted her private home into an inn that catered to British seaman whose ships had sailed into the harbor. This was done in order to dissuade the British from destroying the house. It was as a result of this action that the house at Shoal Harbor received its nickname, "The Spy House," from a British officer, who noted that every time a British vessel would dock in the harbor, patriots in whaleboats would attack the ship. The inn was, of course, a front where American spies could monitor enemy ship movements into and out of the harbor.

During the 1960s, the house at Shoal Harbor came close to being destroyed once again, though this time, by developers. Local resident, Gertrude Neidlinger, came to its rescue, promoting its historical significance and establishing a museum. An odd curiosity arose during museum visits, however. Visitors to the museum would often report strange noises and sightings of spirits.

In 1990, ghost tours began at Shoal Harbor as the house became a more popular destination to visit. There have been numerous accounts of a young English boy, who the locals have named Peter, who's spirit is known to interfere with cameras. Both amateur and professional photographers reported that their camera equipment would function properly outside the house, but whenever they tried to take a photograph inside, the camera seemed to malfunction. The problem would go away only after the photographer would acknowledge the presence of the spirit.

The spirit of Penelope Stout has also been reported many times. She was once a resident of the Whitlock-Seabrook house and has been sighted in the front bedroom holding a baby in her arms, though she reportedly died childless. Once, during a guided tour of the house, a member of the tour group was holding her baby tightly in her arms. All of the sudden, she felt the infant being lifted out of her arms and began to scream. The lady described the encounter as if a ghost grabbed hold of the baby and held it aloft, although reportedly the baby never left her arms.

During tours of the house it was common to hear banging noises around the potbelly stove that could not be accounted for. This noise is believed to come from the spirit of Thomas Whitlock, the first owner of the house. One time, a visiting skeptic jokingly invited Thomas to come home with him. The next morning the museum curator received a phone call from the skeptical tour participant. The man was scared, tired, and begging for help as to how to release the spirit from his house.

Of course, the reports of ghost-like visions have not all come from people inside the house. Many people have claimed to see the spirit of a woman, named Abigail, looking out the upstairs window staring out to sea. She reportedly waits for her husband, a sea captain who was lost at sea, to return. At times, loud sobs have been heard coming from the bedroom.

All tours of the Shoal Harbor Plantation were stopped a few years after the ghost stories gained notoriety. The board of trustees evicted the curator and founder of the museum, Gertrude Neidlinger. This was done, they said, because the tours had started to focus too much on the legend of the place and not its factual significance.

Today, the museum functions in a more straightforward manner. But even though it has undergone a lot of changes, the legends and fascinating stories still remain.

**Craftsman Farms**
Manor Lane off Route 10
Parsippany-Troy Hills
Morris County
973-540-1165
Grounds are open daily from
    sunrise to sunset
$5 adults, $4 seniors and
    students, and $3 children for
    museums tours only

Gustav Stickley, a well-known furniture designer during the early 1900s, made his home at Craftsman Farms. Stickley built this log cabin-style house in 1911. He was an outspoken leader for the Arts and Crafts movement and also the publisher of a journal called *The Craftsman*. His paper featured simple-yet-sturdy house and furniture designs that any local builder could use. At the time a sensational idea, his designs became very popular and came to be called "Craftsman-style Houses." However, when tastes changed and his styles were no longer popular, he was forced into bankruptcy. Stickley is best remembered today for his straightforward furniture, sometimes reffered to as "mission" or "Stickley Furniture." Stickley and his family lived at Craftsman Farms until 1915.

In 1917, Major George and Sylvia Wurlitzer Farny purchased the property and their decendants lived in the house until 1989. When the property was threatened by the possible creation of a housing development, both local citizens and the town government stepped in to purchase and preseve this beloved historic site.

Today the cabin has been restored to its original, early 1900s appearance. The house features many pieces of Stickley Furniture and also a museum shop, which sells books on art, pottery, and glassware.

Tours of Stickley's cabin are conducted from April 1 through November 15, Wednesdays through Fridays from Noon to 3 P.M., with the last tour starting at 2:20 P.M. On Saturdays, tours are given from 10 A.M. to 4 P.M. and on Sundays from 11 A.M. to 4 P.M. with the last tour starting at 3:20 P.M. for both days.

## Museum of Early Trades and Crafts
Main Street and Green Village Road
Madison
Morris County
973-377-2982
Open Tuesdays through Saturdays from 10 A.M. to 4 P.M. and Sundays from noon to 5 P.M.
$3.50 adults and $2 seniors and children

The Museum of Early Trades and Crafts is dedicated to the lives and tools of nineteenth century craftsman from around the country. The

> **FACT:** *Frank Sinatra, widely believed to be the most famous entertainer in the history of popular music, was born on December 12, 1915 in Hoboken, Hudson County. Sinatra is known mostly for his talented voice and won nine Grammys. However, he also appeared in over 50 motion pictures. Sinatra, known as "Ol' Blue Eyes", won an Oscar for best supporting actor in the 1953 motion picture, "From Here to Eternity." Singing well into his 70s, Sinatra passed away May 14, 1998, in Los Angeles, California.*

museum contains over 8,000 artifacts related to 21 different trades. It explores the methods and products of skilled craftspeople working with both traditional and modern materials.

The building, which is a work of art in and of itself, was built in 1900 to originally serve as the town's public library. Inside there are vaulted ceilings, stained glass windows, and elaborate fireplaces, all of which add to the detail and ornateness of this landmark. The museum also has a gift shop, which contains a number of handcrafted glass and pottery items that are for sale.

## New Jersey Fireman's Museum

565 Lathrop Avenue
Boonton
Morris County
973-334-0024
Open Mondays to Fridays from
    1 P.M. to 4 P.M. and weekends
    from 1 P.M. to 3:30 P.M.
Free admission

From 1850 to 1852, William G. Lathrop served as the general manager of the Fuller, Lord & Company Iron Works, located in Boonton. Under his leadership the iron works flourished. Lathrop expanded his company's markets into places as far away as Japan and South America. Lathrop used his wealth to construct a lavish, 25-room mansion. It would not be until 1873, that construction would be complete.

In 1898, the 60-acre estate became New Jersey's first retirement facility for fireman. Today, part of the building has been converted into a museum that features many exhibits relating to the history of fire fighting and the professionals and volunteers who joined the ranks.

## Ocean County Historical Museum

26 Hadley Avenue
Toms River
Ocean County
732-341-1800
Open Tuesday and Thursdays
    from 1 P.M. to 3 P.M. and
    Saturdays from 10 A.M. to
    4 P.M.
$2 per person

Housed in a beautiful, nineteenth century, Victorian-style home, the Ocean County Historical Museum features permanent displays and changing exhibits that depict the lifestyle of the early settlers of Ocean County. Exhibits include a history of lighter-than-air aviation at Lakehurst Naval Air Station, local Revolutionary and Civil War artifacts, and Native American artifacts. The house contains a nineteenth century, Victorian-style kitchen and a one-room schoolhouse. There is a diorama of the Toms River Block-house Fight, which occurred on March 20, 1782. During the skirmish the British set fire to the entire town of Toms River.

The museum also contains a research library and archives, which have over 8,000 volumes of books related to the history and genealogy of Ocean County. These facilities are open Tuesdays to Thursdays from 1 P.M. to 4 P.M. and Saturdays from 10 A.M. to 1 P.M.

**Toms River Seaport Museum**
Corner of Hooper Avenue and
    Water Street
Toms River
Ocean County
732-349-9209
Open Tuesdays, Thursdays, and
    Saturdays from 10 A.M. to
    2 P.M.
Free admission

The Toms River Seaport Museum is housed in an 1868 carriage house, which once served the estate of Joseph Francis, the developer of the "Life-car." The museum is dedicated to the preservation of the rich maritime heritage of the Toms River and Barnegat Bay areas. On display are boats and artifacts associated with the marine history and development of the area. A workshop is located on the grounds and is the center for boat restoration, educational programs, and seminars in such areas as navigation and marine carpentry.

A small museum store is located on the premises and sells such items as post cards, hats, tee shirts, and books.

**American Labor Museum**
83 Norwood Street
Haledon
Passaic County
973-595-7953
Open Wednesdays to Saturdays
    from 1 P.M. to 4 P.M.
$1.50 adults, children are free

Also known as the Botto House, this museum was once the home of an Italian immigrant worker, Pietro Botto, and his wife, Maria. During the famous 1913 Paterson Silk Strike, Pietro, a skilled weaver who worked in the Paterson mills, invited the striking workers to use his house as a gathering place and meeting hall. The striking workers were safe at Botto's house because it was located outside city limits. At the time, the Paterson City government banned all group assemblies for workers. This suburb of Paterson soon became a rallying point for striking union members, with the Botto House at the center. The second floor balcony of the house served as a podium for influential speakers such as Upton Sinclair, John Reed, Big Bill Hayward, and Elizabeth Gurley Flynn. During these speeches there would be thousands of strikers on the property.

The house has been restored to resemble how it appeared from 1903-1913. The museum features video displays and static exhibits about the early American labor movement. There are many photographs depicting the history of the 1913 strike and the unsafe working conditions common throughout many factories of the time, which sparked the strike. Several rooms of the house are still furnished in the manor of the time when the Botto family lived at the house.

## Dey Mansion

199 Totowa Road
Wayne
Passaic County
973-696-1776
Open Wednesdays through
    Fridays from 1 P.M. to 4 P.M.
    and weekends from 10 A.M.
    to 4 P.M.
$1 adults, children are free

Dirk Dey, a Dutch born planter, constructed this fine example of Georgian-style architecture between the years of 1740 and 1750. During the Revolutionary War, Colonel Theunis Dey, the son of Dirk and the commander of the Bergen County Militia, offered this house and land to be used as a headquarters for General George Washington. Washington and thousands of his soldiers camped here from July through November of 1780.

Members of the Dey family continued to live in the mansion until 1801, when it was sold to a private owner. In 1930, the house was purchased by the State of New Jersey to be used as a museum. The house sits on two acres of land, which is all that remains of the once large estate. Tours of the grounds include visits to the formal garden, picnic area, blacksmith shop, and plantation house. The estate has been restored to its 1780 appearance.

**Hancock House**
454 Fort Mott Road
Pennsville
Salem County
856-935-4373
Open Wednesdays through
    Saturdays from 10 A.M. to
    12 P.M. and 1 P.M. to 4 P.M.,
    Sundays 1 P.M. to 4 P.M.
Free admission

During the frigid winter of 1778, the defeated and demoralized Continental Army was encamped at Valley Forge, Pennsylvania. In February, General Washington sent General "Mad" Anthony Wayne to Salem County with orders to forage for food and gather supplies for the starving army. With the help of sympathetic local farmers, Wayne was able to complete his task and return to camp with enough provisions to supply the army until spring.

A month later, on March 17, the British, who were camped in Philadelphia, sent General Charles Mawhood and 1,500 troops into southern New Jersey to confiscate supplies and to punish the people for helping Wayne. Major John Graves Simcoe was sent with a force of 300 soldiers to attack the Hancock House. Mistakenly, British intelligence indicated that there was a large force of Americans stationed at the house. Simcoe's force attacked at 5 A.M. on the morning of March 21$^{st}$. The fight was a slaughter, a total of eight civilians and American militiamen were bayoneted to death. Not a single shot was fired during the massacre. Ironically, among the casualties was Judge William Hancock, Royal Magistrate for Salem County, whom the King had appointed.

The four remaining American soldiers were taken prisoner, though there is a story that another soldier escaped. It is said that during the commotion he remained quiet, safely hidden behind a door. He then mingled with the British soldiers in the dark and ran for the American lines. Legend also says that an expectant wife of one of the soldiers, managed to jump out of a second story window and escape.

In 1930, the house was going to be sold to a Baltimore firm to be converted for use as a fertilizer warehouse. Local citizens rallied and petitioned the state to buy it. In 1931, the State of New Jersey formally purchased the house and preserved it as a historical site. The Hancock House was forced to close in 1991, due to lack of funds, but in 1995, the Friends of the Hancock House formed and organized efforts to reopen it. In 1996, the state approved funding for a comprehensive restoration and the house reopened on March 21, 1998, the 220$^{th}$ anniversary of the Hancock Massacre.

**Golf House**
Route 512
Far Hills
Somerset County
908-234-2300
Open Mondays to Fridays from
    9 A.M. to 5 P.M. and weekends
    from 10 A.M. to 4 P.M.
Free admission

   Originally, this beautiful, Georgian-Colonial-style house was built in
1919, to serve as a private residence. In 1934, the United States Golf Association purchased the estate and renovated it for use as a museum. The
museum contains a number of exhibits about the history of the game as
well as the evolution of its equipment. There is also a large exhibit on the
history of women in the sport and several rare artifacts such as the golf
clubs of Presidents Franklin Roosevelt and Dwight Eisenhower, and the
club Allen Shepard used on the moon during his Apollo XIV mission.
   A small theater shows vintage golf footage and highlights throughout the
day. The association has also created a library that contains over 8,000 volumes of books, manuscripts, and periodicals about the game and is
regarded as the most complete public collection dedicated to golf in the
world. The museum's archives contain many personal items from some of
golf's greatest heroes including Bobby Jones, Ben Hogan, Arnold Palmer,
and Jack Nicklaus. While at the museum, be sure to check out the research
and testing center and get a greater understanding for how golfing equipment is rated and tested.

**Millstone Forge Museum**
North River Street
Millstone
Somerset County
732-873-2803
Open April through June on
    Sundays from 1 P.M. to 4 P.M.
    and October through
    November on Sunday from
    1 P.M. to 4 P.M.
Free admission

   The Millstone Forge Museum is housed in a historic forge that was built
in 1740. The museum displays many tools and handmade implements from
the eighteenth century depicting the hard work and skill that went into
building the early American settlements. There are also several amateur
blacksmiths on hand to demonstrate the trade and explain its history.

**Old Dutch Parsonage**
Washington Place
Somerville
Somerset County
908-725-1015
Open Wednesdays to Saturdays
 from 10 A.M. to noon and
 from 1 P.M. to 4 P.M. and
 Sundays from 1 P.M. to 4 P.M.
Free admission

The Old Dutch Parsonage was once the home of Pastor Frelinghuysen, the minister of the Dutch Reformed Church, whose son Frederick is credited with firing the shot that killed the Hessian Commander Johann Rall during the battle of Trenton. The parsonage was later home to the Revered Jacob Hardenburg, who married the widowed Mrs. Frelinghuysen. Reverend Hardenburg was known as one of the fighting parsons who condemned the British from the pulpit.

The Reverend Jacob Hardenburg taught theological classes at the house. The classes soon grew in size and scope. To accommodate the growing student body, Reverend Hardenburg, together with other learned men founded Queens College, now Rutgers University, with Reverend Hardenburg serving as its first president in 1785.

In 1913, the house was to set be demolished by the Jersey Central Railroad, but through the work of local townspeople, it was moved to its present location. The house, originally built in 1751, was restored to reflect the life and times of these pastors.

**Rockingham**
Lauren Road (Route 603)
Rocky Hill
Somerset County
609-921-8853
Open Wednesdays to Saturdays
 from 10 A.M. to noon and
 from 1 P.M. to 4 P.M. and
 Sundays from 1 P.M. to 4 P.M.
Free admission

John Berrien, a New Jersey Superior Court Justice, built this house in 1734. It was originally located closer to the Millstone River than it is today, but it was moved because the mountain it stood on began to erode. Originally, plans were made to simply knock it down. In an effort to preserve the house, the Washington Headquarters Association was formed and the necessary funding was raised to move the house a quarter-mile up the hill.

It was fully restored and opened to the public in 1897. However, the house was moved again in 1959 and once again in early 2001, to its present location on property owned by the Delaware and Raritan Canal State Park.

The historical significance of Rockingham lies in the events that took place at the end of the American Revolution. After the surrender of the British at Yorktown, Congress, at the time meeting at Nassau Hall in Princeton, was embroiled in a constitutional crisis over the functions and organization of the government. They relied on General Washington for his input on several important matters and called upon him to aid the country again. He traveled to the area and found no other place in town that could accommodate him and his staff of over 100. On August 23, 1783 he arrived and settled in at Rockingham. It was while staying at this house that General Washington wrote his "Farewell Orders to the Armies of the New United States" and officially retired from its command. Today, copies of the letter hang in the entrance hall of the house.

## Somerset County Historical Society

Van Veghten Road, off Finderne
    Avenue
Bridgewater
Somerset County
908-218-1281
Open by appointment only
Free admission

In 1694, Michael Van Veghten purchased over 800 acres of land on the north side of the Raritan River and constructed a house for his family. His son, Derrick, later inherited the estate and, during the Revolutionary War, offered his property to Quartermaster General Nathaniel Green for use as his headquarters. Several Continental Army commanders visited here including General Washington and General Anthony Wayne who's Pennsylvanian troops camped on the grounds.

When Derrick died in 1781, the estate passed through several owners and the house was renovated several times. The estate was finally donated to the Somerset County Historical Association in 1971. The association is dedicated to preserving the history of Somerset County. Inside the house, the association established a library that contains a substantial collection of maps, photographs, and newspapers. Researchers and local historians are very appreciative of the association's collection of archival materials. The library is open December through March, on every second and fourth Tuesday from 12 P.M. to 3 P.M.

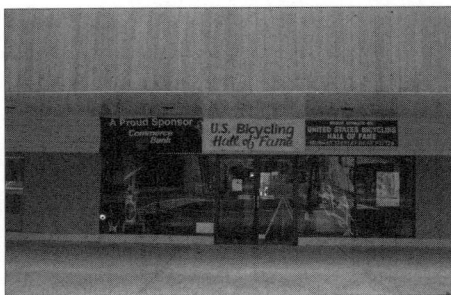

**U.S. Bicycling Hall of Fame**
135 West Main Street
Somerville
Somerset County
908-722-3620
Open Wednesdays from Noon to
3 P.M.
Free admission

The U.S. Bicycling Hall of Fame features jerseys, photographs, and memorabilia from famous cyclists and events. The town of Somerville is well known to cyclists and fans for its annual bicycle tour, the Tour of Somerville, America's oldest, continuously run race. The tour is held every Memorial Day. The museum is dedicated to promoting and preserving the history of cycling. The Hall of Fame has inducted 50 of cycling's most significant people including Marshall "Major" Taylor, Frank Kramer, and Jackie Simes III.

**Wallace House**
38 Washington Place
Somerville
Somerset County
908-725-1015
Open Wednesdays to Saturdays
from 10 A.M. to Noon and
from 1 P.M. to 4 P.M. and
Sundays from 1 P.M. to 4 P.M.
Free admission

John Wallace, a wealthy merchant from Philadelphia, built this house in 1776. At the time, it was the largest house ever built in town. During the 1778-1779 winter encampment at Middlebrook, General Washington established his headquarters in this house. He stayed here for six months and entertained such visitors as the Marquis de Lafayette, Alexander Hamilton, and Benedict Arnold.

Today, guided tours are offered in this historic house. Rooms are decorated with period furnishings that depict the tastes and sensibilities of the Revolutionary War era population.

## Dar Van Bunschooten Museum
1097 Route 23
Wantage
Sussex County
973-875-5335
Open May 15 to October 15,
    Thursdays and Saturdays
    from 1 P.M. to 4 P.M.
$2 adults and $1 children

This handsome, Dutch-Colonial-style house, built in 1787, was the home of the Reverend Elias Van Bunschooten, appointee of the Synod of the Dutch Reformed Church. The Reverend Van Bunschooten was 37 years old when he arrived in this town in 1785, and provided for the spiritual well being of the area until his death, 40 years later.

Van Bunschooten bequeathed the original 1,000-acre property to his nephew, Elias Cooper. Cooper continued to expand the estate, adding a small section to the east. In 1870, the family struck oil in Pennsylvania and, with their newfound wealth, began to modernize the house. When Elias Cooper died, the property was divided equally among his five sons. The home remained in the family until the late 1920s.

The eight-room house has been restored to a mid 1800s style and is now used as a museum, operated by the Daughters of the American Revolution. The grounds include a barn, an icehouse, and a wagon house that features a vintage carriage and has a variety of farming implements on display. The museum contains collections of period china, cookware, paintings, and Revolutionary War artifacts. The inside of the house is fully furnished and contains an extensive collection of clothing from the 1830s to the 1930s.

## Belcher-Ogden Mansion
1046 East Jersey Avenue
Elizabeth
Union County
908-351-2500
Open by appointment only
Free admission

This mansion was constructed in 1680 and had several owners including New Jersey Royal Governor Jonathon Belcher, who resided in the house for 10 years, until his death in 1757. Belcher was an avid supporter of higher education and laid the groundwork for the College of

New Jersey, which is now Princeton University. In 1778, an independence supporter entertained George Washington and Alexander Hamilton at the house. In later years, New Jersey Governor Aaron Ogden also lived here.

**Boxwood Hall**
1073 East Jersey Avenue
Elizabeth
Union County
973-648-4540
Open Mondays to Saturdays from 9 A.M. to noon and from 1 P.M. to 5 P.M.
Free admission

Constructed in 1750, Boxwood Hall originally had a wing on either side of the main building and an avenue lined with boxwood trees that ran from the front door to the river. In 1722, the house was purchased by Elias Boudinot and his wife, Hanna, who was the sister of Richard Stockton, a signatory of the Declaration of Independence. Elias, who was the president of the Continental Congress, lived with his wife in the house until 1795. George Washington stopped here for lunch on the way to New York for his inauguration as the first President of the United States, on April 23, 1789.

Today, guided tours are conducted of Boxwood Hall. Inside visitors will find many colonial and pre-colonial furnishings and various artifacts from those times. There is also a display dedicated to General Jonathon Dayton, which contains his military uniform, among other important items

**Drake House Museum**
602 West Front Street
Plainfield
Union County
908-755-5831
Open Sundays from 2 P.M. to 4 P.M.
$3 adults and $1 children

This house was built in 1746 by Isaac Drake and used as a home for his son and daughter-in-law, Nathaniel and Dorothy. During the Battle of Short

Hills, General Washington used the Drake house to consult with his officers. He continued to keep his headquarters at the house for several days
after the battle as well.

John S. Harberger of New York City, president of The Manhattan Banking Company, which later became The Chase Manhattan Bank, purchased
the house in 1864 from the Drake family. Harberger made many improvements to the structure, including extending the downstairs hall, adding a
library, and raising the roof. He also made the loft into a music room and
built the towers that complete the architecture we see today.

The Drake House, as seen on tours today, has a first-floor kitchen, bedroom, and dining room, which are typical of those found in homes of the
eighteenth century. The Historical Society of Plainfield operates this city-
owned public museum.

**Liberty Hall Museum**
1003 Morris Avenue
Union
Union County
908-527-0400
Open April through December,
    Wednesdays through
    Sundays from 1 P.M. to 4 P.M.
$6 adults, $5 seniors, and $4
    children

This beautiful mansion was once the country estate of William Livingston, the first governor of New Jersey. The house was originally built in
1772. Livingston was a member of both the first and second Continental
Congress, a Brigadier General in command of the New Jersey Militia, and
the son-in-law of John Hay, the first Chief Justice of the United States.

In 1811, Livingston's niece, Susan Livingston Kean Niemcewicz, purchased the estate. This house and property remained in the Kean family for
the next 185 years. When Mary Alice Barney Kean died in 1995, her son
John donated the house to the Liberty Hall Foundation, which had been
established by Mary and her children.

Today, tours are conducted in this 50-room mansion, which is set on 26-
acres of beautifully landscaped property. Before touring the house, a short
10-minute film is shown to visitors about the history of the estate. Liberty
Hall contains an impressive collection of American furniture and other
works of art. There are also many collections of silver, glass, ceramics, and
paintings located throughout the rooms.

**Shippen Manor Museum**
8 Belvidere Avenue
Oxford
Warren County
908-453-4381
Open the first and second
  Sunday of every month from
  1 P.M. to 4 P.M.
$3 per person

This beautiful, three-story, Georgian-style mansion was built by the Shippen family, to be used as a home for the manager of the nearby Oxford Furnace, from the years 1754 to 1870. The Shippen family, owners of the iron works, were socially prominent citizens of Philadelphia. Oxford Furnace Number One was constructed in 1741 and retired in 1884, making it the longest running furnace in the history of the United States.

The State of New Jersey purchased the house and grounds in 1974. Confronted with a lack of funding, the building went unused and began to deteriorate. Finally, in 1984, the Warren County Cultural Heritage Commission transferred operative control of both the mansion and the remains of the iron works to the county. Today, the restored Shippen Manor contains a number of colonial artifacts and period furnishings.

**Warren County Historical Museum**
313 Mansfield Street
Belvidere
Warren County
908-475-4246
Open Sundays from 2 P.M. to 4
  P.M.
Free admission

The Warren County Historical Museum is dedicated to preserving the history of Warren County and protecting its treasured historical sites. The museum features many exhibits focused on the history of the county and contains displays of local artifacts, including many from the Lenni-Lenape Indians. Its research library includes many books and manuscripts documenting the history of Warren County.

# Amusement Parks

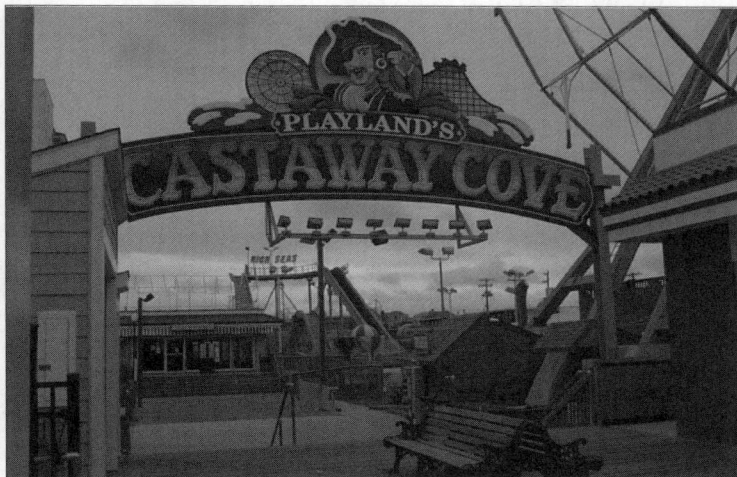

*Playland's Castaway Cove*

**Blackbeard's Cave:** Blackbeard's Cave features an adrenaline-pumping go-cart track complete with narrow bridges and darkened tunnels. There are batting cages, a miniature golf course, and a driving range for the sports enthusiast. Some of the unique activities in this park include an archery range, remote control boats, pony rides, and a huge arcade. *Location:* 136 Route 9, Bayville, Ocean County. *Phone:* 732-286-4414.

**Bowcraft Amusement Park:** Bowcraft Amusement Park features 19 rides, with separate attractions for adults, teens, and younger children. There are a number of roller coasters, a miniature train ride, and an 18-hole miniature golf course. Bowcraft also features an indoor arcade and food court. Party rooms are available for birthdays and other special events. *Location:* Route 22 West, Scotch Plains, Union County. *Phone:* 908-233-0675.

**Casino Pier and Water Works:** This entertainment complex contains both an amusement park and a water park. There are roller coasters to ride, water slides to splash down, games of chance to play, an arcade, a miniature golf course, and more food stands than you can try in a day. Located on the boardwalk, the pier is the home of one of the two surviving, American-crafted carousels in the State of New Jersey. This fun center features over 35 rides and 20 water attractions, including a 54-foot tall, free-fall side, a 400-foot long, tidal wave tube-ride, and a quarter-mile long, lazy river ride. *Location:* 800 Ocean Terrace, Seaside Heights, Ocean County. *Phone:* 732-793-6488.

**Clementon Amusement Park and Splash World:** Clementon Amusement Park was established in 1907 and includes a giant Ferris wheel, which features a view 10-stories high and the exhilarating Yo-Yo, which swings you through the air as if you were weightless. There is also a brand new, fully enclosed Kiddie Land, which has gentle rides for children. Splash World features over 700 feet of enclosed chutes for rides including The Black Viper and Sky River Rapids, where visitors glide through three sets of waterslides and three splash pools. Another popular feature of Splash World is Caribbean Cove, which is a 5,000 square foot activity area for children of all ages. There is something fun for everyone. Two of the main attractions are a pirate ship, anchored in the midst of its own 10,000 square foot kiddy pool, which delights visitors with is stunning realism and a 1,200-foot Endless River, which is a tube ride through scenic waterfalls and beautifully landscaped rock formations. The park also includes the Big Cat Encounter, which provides African Lions and endangered Bengal Tigers for close-up encounters. In addition to the fun, there are also a variety of educating and entertaining shows available. *Location:* 114 Berlin Road, Clementon, Camden County. *Phone:* 856-783-0263.

**Fantasy Island Amusement Park:** Fantasy Island is a unique, Victorian-style amusement park, which includes brick walkways, oak benches, and ornate lampposts. Among its many attractions are an arcade, a giant Ferris wheel, and a variety of rides and entertaining shows. *Location:* 320 West 7th Avenue, Beach Haven, Ocean County. *Phone:* 609-492-4000.

**Gillian's Island Water Theme Park:** Located just a few streets from Gillian's Wonderland Pier is their Island Water Theme Park. This water park includes Shotgun Falls, which is a six-foot drop into a 10-foot pool, tubes slides, and a skypond, which is a pool that is elevated 15-feet in the air. For children, there is Li'l Bucs Bay, an 18,000 square foot water spraying children's playground. There is also a miniature golf course that contains waterfalls and scenic landscaping. *Location:* Plymouth Place & Boardwalk, Ocean City, Cape May County. *Phone:* 609-399-0483.

**Gillian's Wonderland Pier:** Gillian's Wonderland Pier features over 38 family-fun rides including the popular, 138-foot high, giant Ferris wheel. The amusement park also includes a monorail that circumnavigates the park, giving visitors a full 360-degree tour of the park. Special attractions including an antique carousel and a go-cart speedway are highlights of everyone's visit. *Location:* 6th Street and Boardwalk, Ocean City, Cape May County. *Phone:* 609-399-7082.

**Hot Diggity's at Fairy Tale Forest:** Established in 1957, Fairy Tale Forest features 20 life-sized displays from classic fairytales complete with story-book cottages and a picturesque forest setting. Original creator, Paul Woehle Sr., started Fairy Tale Forest in 1955. He spent three years developing the main facade, which makes up the castle, surrounding walls, and the famous shoe. All of the storybook cottages were designed and handcrafted by Paul and his two sons. Exhibits of children's nursery rhymes include such favorites as *Pinocchio, Goldilocks and the Three Bears,* and *Cinderella.* During Christmas, the park is transformed into a winter wonderland with thousands of lights, holiday exhibits, and yes, a visit by that jolly, old elf, Santa Claus. *Location:* 140 Oak Ridge Road off Route 23, Oak Ridge, Sussex County. *Phone:* 973-697-5656.

**Jenkinson's:** Jenkinson's features 27 rides including many that are designed specifically for young children. A funhouse provides hours of entertainment for the whole family. Inside, there is a hall of mirrors, a maze, and an echo room that produces an echo for every sound emitted. To exit the funhouse, visitors must slide down the "Mysterious Forest" black tunnel slide. The park's location significantly adds to its allure, sitting on the white sandy beaches. There is a Victorian-style, sweet shop that features homemade fudge and chocolate. An aquarium with many varieties of marine life and a shark touch tank are highlights for all of the people to enjoy. There is also a wide variety of food on-hand, for every appetite. Jenkinson's also includes batting cages and a total of three miniature golf courses. *Location:* 300 Ocean Avenue, Point Pleasant Beach, Ocean County. *Phone:* 732-892-0600.

**Keansburg Amusement Park and Runaway Rapids:** Keansburg Amusement Park as been around for decades. This park's star attraction is the brand new, Double Shot, which blasts riders 100 feet in to the air, then propels them back to earth at ever-increasing speeds. There are also many other exhilarating roller coasters, a go-cart track, bumper cars, an antique carousel, games of chance, and batting cages. Next to the amusement park is Runaway Rapids, a brand new, five million-dollar water park. It features the only uphill waterslide on the East Coast. The park is a special favorite for children and the young-at-heart and includes a 10,000 square foot play area with rope swings, speed slides, the lazy river water-ride, and New Jersey's biggest hot tub. *Location:* 275 Beachway, Keansburg, Monmouth County. *Phone:* 800-805-4386.

**Land of Make Believe:** The Land of Make Believe is a 30-acre amusement and water park. There is hayride drawn by a rustic, farm tractor and a Civil War Locomotive, which traverses around the park. A unique feature of this park is its richness in local flavor. Within the grounds of the park is the preserved Jump House. Inside the house is an informative display on the legend of Jenny Jump, a one-time occupant of the house. Also available for hands-on exploration is a vintage WW II plane's cockpit, an enchanted Christmas village, a pirate ship with life-size nets and waterslides, and live animals at Old MacDonald's Farm. *Location:* Great Meadows Road (Route 611), Hope, Warren County. *Phone:* 908-459-9000.

**Morey's Piers and Raging Waters:** Morey's operates three successful amusement piers and two oceanfront water parks. Its piers feature over 150 rides and attractions. One of the more popular attractions is the boomerang coaster, which begins 12 stories above the piers and plunges into a free fall at 45 miles per hour. It then takes riders through a series of loops and corkscrews before hurtling to a stop. The water parks feature magnificent ocean views and include over 50 water slides and other attractions. There is a slide for everyone at Morey's; from high-speed slides for the adventurous to gentle tube rides for the pleasure seekers. *Location:* Wildwood Pier, Wildwood, Cape May County. *Phone:* 609-522-3900.

**Mountain Creek:** Mountain Creek operates the former Action Park site, after assuming ownership in 1999. This water park features over 25 unique rides, slides, and other attractions. For action, there is the Colorado River Ride, with 1,600 feet of whitewater rapids to get the blood flowing. Or for the more adventurous, you can dive from the 18-foot high Canyon Cliff and splash into a pool of blue water below. Mountain Creek also features Vertigo and Vortex, twin speed tubes that drop 40 feet into the dark. There is also the Hightide Wavepool, which is one of the largest pools of its kind, for those looking for a little virtual-ocean swim. It contains 450,000-gallons of water and randomly generates waves of alternating height and frequency. For children, there is never a dull moment with the interactive water-play fort complete with water slides and spray cannons. There is also a theater for the children to watch clowns and other performers. The park just recently opened the 20,000 square foot Gravity Park, which is devoted to satiating the most extreme stunt-enthusiast, whether they ride skateboards, or stunt bikes, or rollerblades. There are mini ramps and launch ramps for all skill levels. *Location:* Route 94, Vernon, Sussex County. *Phone:* 973-827-2000.

**Playland's Castaway Cove:** Established in 1959, this amusement park features over 30 rides including Ocean City's only looping coaster, the Python. Other attractions include bumper cars, a Tilt-A-Whirl, and an old fashioned locomotive with rail cars. *Location:* 10th Avenue and Boardwalk, Ocean City, Cape May County. *Phone:* 609-399-4751.

**Six Flags Great Adventure:** This is the largest theme park in all of New Jersey and features among its countless rides and attractions, the cutting-edge in coaster technology. There is the all-new Nitro roller coaster, which approaches the blistering speed of 80 miles per hour as it hurtles riders along its precariously winding track. Then there is the world's first floorless coaster, Batman and Robin the Chiller, which blasts off from zero to 70 miles per hour in less then four seconds. And there is Stuntman's Freefall, which features a 130-foot drop at 55 miles per hour. Along with the rides, there are many shops and restaurants to please every visitor and special shows, which include concerts and fireworks extravaganzas throughout the year. During Halloween, the park transforms into the scariest, haunted theme park ever known to exist. Park employees become ghosts, goblins, and zombies. Laser lights flicker throughout the night, strange howls and shrieks punctuate the crowd noise, and eerie fog rolls along the grounds. Starting in 2001, in order to better accommodate all of its guests, the park is implementing a program called Fast Lane, which gives guests the opportunity to make reservations on some of the parks most popular rides in order to avoid the dreaded long waits. *Location:* Route 527, Jackson Township, Ocean County. *Phone:* 732-928-2000.

**Six Flags Hurricane Harbor:** Hurricane Harbor is adjacent to the amusement park and safari, but has a separate entrance and parking area. Combination passes are available for guests to visit all three. This water park opened to packed crowds and rave reviews on Memorial Day, 2001. It encompasses 45 acres of land and features over 25 major water rides and other attractions. Its most popular attraction, Hurricane Harbor, features a 42,000 square foot wave pool that contains almost a million gallons of water. It generates a series of waves up to five feet in height every 15 minutes. There are a number of speed slides, including one that hurtles sliders over 40 miles per hour through dark tunnels. Younger children can have fun also, with the interactive Family Water Lagoon that features over 70 unique activities. For the thrill-seeker in all of us, there is the massive, one-of-a-kind, Hurricane Mountain with its 50-foot tower and six separate slides. *Location:* Route 527, Jackson Township, Ocean County. *Phone:* 732-928-2000.

**Storybook Land:** Storybook Land is a nursery rhyme-theme park with rides and attractions geared for the entire family. There are live animals to touch, food stands to try and picnic areas to enjoy. The park offers the opportunity for the entire family to literally walk through their all-time favorite stories and nursery rhymes. *Location:* 6415 Black Horse Pike, Egg Harbor Township, Ocean County. *Phone:* 609-641-7847.

# Zoos, Aquariums, and Planetariums

*Prarie Dogs at Space Farms Zoo*

# Zoos

**Bergen County Zoo:** Located in Van Saun County Park, the Bergen County Zoo features many different species of birds, reptiles, and mammals. Visitors will have the opportunity to see over 200 animals including the Arctic Fox, the American Bison, and the ferocious Mountain Lion. A farmyard, modeled on typical farmyards of the 1890s, invites both children and adults to get close to many types of animals that live on a typical farm. There are also various programs for children and special events held from time to time. A special feature of the zoo is the miniature train, which takes children on a tour of the zoo. *Location:* 216 Forest Avenue, River Edge, Bergen County. *Hours:* Daily from 10:30 A.M. to 4:30 P.M. Hours extended April through September on weekends from 9:30 A.M. to 5 P.M. *Phone:* 201-262-3771. *Admission Fee:* $2 adults and $1 children only on Fridays, Saturdays, and Sundays from May through October.

**Cape May County Zoo:** Housed in a beautiful, park-like setting, the Cape May County Zoo is home to over 100 species of wildlife including bears, tigers, buffalos, and giraffes. The zoo's Reptile House is a very popular attraction, as are the avian section with its many colorful varieties of birds. There is also a section of the zoo set aside for monkeys, so visitors can really enjoy their childlike antics. A children's zoo allows the young ones to get up close to pet and feed the animals. The zoo has a snack bar and picnic tables with nearby trails that wind through this beautiful county zoo. *Location:* Route 9 and Crest Haven Road, Cape May Courthouse, Cape May County. *Hours:* Daily from 9 A.M. to 5 P.M. *Phone:* 609-465-5271. *Admission Fee:* Free.

**Cohanzick Zoo:** The Cohanzick Zoo is housed inside the 1,110-acre Bridgeton City Park. The zoo contains over 200 animals and is famous not only for being the first zoo ever established in New Jersey, but also for its beautiful white tigers. There are picnic tables and nature trails nearby. *Location:* Mayor Aiken Drive, Bridgeton City Park, Bridgeton, Cumberland County. *Hours:* Spring and Summer, daily from 10 A.M. to 6 P.M., Winter, daily from 9 A.M. to 4 P.M. *Phone:* 856-455-3230, ext. 242. *Admission Fee:* Free.

**Johnson Park Zoo:** This small zoo, located within picturesque Johnson Park, contains a mixture of both farm and wild animals. Located on the bank of the Raritan River, this is a great place to relax and get in touch with nature. The park has many facilities including picnic tables, tennis courts, and fishing ponds. *Location:* River Road, Piscataway, Middlesex County. *Hours:* Daily from sunrise to sunset. *Phone:* 732-745-3900. *Admission Fee:* Free.

**Lakota Wolf Preserve:** Visitors to this preserve will be able to observe wolves in their natural habitat and learn about the social structure of wolf packs, their eating habits, how they interact with man, and many other interesting facts. A guided tour will take you to a scenic observation area were you will be able to watch the wolves play and interact with each other, and you may even hear one of them howl. *Location:* Camp Taylor Campground, 85 Mount Pleasant Road, Knowlton Township, Warren County. *Hours:* Summer: Daily from 10:00 A.M. to 3 P.M. Fall and Winter: Daily from 10:30 A.M. to 3 P.M. *Phone:* 877-733-9653. *Admission Fee:* $15 adults and $7 children.

**Popcorn Park:** Established in 1977, Popcorn Park exists for the purpose of providing a safe refuge for wildlife that are either injured, elderly, or abandoned. The Associated Human Society maintains this facility, which is located on seven acres of land and includes around 200 animals. *Location:* Humane Way and Lacey Road, Forked River, Ocean County. *Hours:* Daily from 11 A.M. to 5 P.M. *Phone:* 609-693-1900. *Admission Fee:* $3.50 adults, $2.50 seniors and children.

**Six Flags Great Adventure Safari:** Six Flags owns the largest drive-through safari outside of Africa. The safari is situated on 350 acres of land and features over 1,000 animals from six continents. Visitors are allowed to drive their own cars on the four and a half mile, three-lane road, to get a first hand glimpse of many of the animals, including elephants, giraffes, kangaroos, and tigers. If you prefer not to have the pesky baboons jump on your car towards the end of the safari, you can either skip that section or for a minimal fee hop in one of the comfortable tour buses instead. *Location:* Route 537, Jackson, Ocean County. *Hours:* Open when theme park is operating; April through October, daily from 9 A.M. to 4 P.M. In October, the safari opens at 10 A.M. on weekends. *Phone:* 732-928-1821. *Admission Fee:* $17.50 per car.

**Space Farms Zoo:** Located on more than 100 acres of land, this large, privately run zoo features over 500 animals, including those infamous lions, tigers, and bears, though it is guaranteed that no cowardly lion will jump out at you. Inside the main building stands Goliath, mounted in a fearsome pose. This 12-foot tall bear once lived at the zoo from 1967 to 1991. Goliath is considered to have been the largest bear in the world. A restaurant and a gift shop are also located inside the main building. The grounds also include an American History Museum, antique cars, motorcycles, old-fashioned carriages and wagons, and weapons from both the Revolutionary and Civil Wars. *Location:* 218 Route 519, Sussex, Sussex County. *Hours:* May 1 to October 31, daily from 9 A.M. to 5 P.M. *Phone:* 973-875-5800. *Admission Fee:* $9.95 adults, $8.95 seniors, and $5.50 children.

**Thompson Park Zoo:** A featured attraction of Thompson Park Zoo includes a number of farm animals. Walking trails and picnic areas are also located in the park. *Location:* Forsgate Drive, Monroe, Middlesex County. *Hours:* Daily from sunrise to sunset. *Phone:* 732-745-3900. *Admission Fee:* Free.

**Turtle Back Zoo:** Located behind the South Mountain Arena in beautiful South Mountain Reservation, Turtle Back Zoo features over 500 animals from over 200 types of species. The zoo focuses on native New Jersey wildlife with animals like cougars, bison, eagles, and wolves. Other animals include elk, llamas, and white-tailed deer as well as domesticated animals that children can feed. A pony ride and miniature train ride are also popular attractions for the young ones. *Location:* 560 Northfield Avenue, West Orange, Essex County. *Hours:* Summer: Mondays to Saturdays from 10 A.M. to 5 P.M. and Sundays from 10:30 A.M. to 6 P.M. Winter: Daily from 10 A.M. to 4:00 P.M. *Phone:* 973-731-5800. *Admission Fee:* $5 adults, $2 seniors and children.

# Aquariums

**Jenkinson's Aquarium:** Located on the boardwalk at popular Point Pleasant, Jenkinson's is home to numerous species of marine life including seals, sharks, and tropical fish. The aquarium also features an alligator pit and a touch tank, which allows visitors to get up close and feel many varieties of fish. Jenkinson's is also home to the *Bounty,* the original boat used in the movie *Mutiny on the Bounty. Location:* Ocean Avenue and Parkway, Point Pleasant Beach, Ocean County. *Hours:* Summer: Daily from 10 A.M. to 10 P.M., Winter: Daily from 10 A.M. to 5 P.M. *Phone:* 732-899-1212. *Admission Fee:* $7 adults, $4.50 seniors and children.

**Marine Mammal Stranding Center:** The Marine Mammal Stranding Center is the only organization in the State of New Jersey authorized to rescue and rehabilitate stranded marine animals. Founded in 1978, this organization has responded to over 2,000 calls for stranded whales, dolphins, seals, and sea turtles that have washed ashore on the beaches of New Jersey. The inside of the building contains a sea life education center, a gift shop, and photographs of the numerous rescues that have been performed. The center also features 25 life size replicas of marine mammals, fowl, lizards, and fish that are found in the New Jersey waters. A 1,000-gallon fish tank is located in the property. *Location:* 3625 Brigantine Boulevard, Brigantine, Atlantic County. *Hours:* Memorial Day through Labor Day, daily from 11 A.M. to 5 P.M. Off-season, weekends from 12 P.M. to 4 P.M. *Phone:* 609-266-0538. *Admission Fee:* Free.

**New Jersey State Aquarium:** Located on the banks of the Delaware River, the New Jersey State Aquarium is a state-of-the-art facility that features over 80 exhibits and includes more than 5,000 fish and other aquatic animals. The Open Ocean Tank, the main tank in the aquarium, is considered to be one of the largest in North America holding over 760,000 gallons of water. If you are a shark lover, then you will appreciate the shark touch tank, which is designed for visitors to get up close and personal with a wide range of sharks. A unique feature of the aquarium is the 120-seat theater, which includes a scuba phone that allows divers to talk directly to the audience. If you get hungry, you can always relax and eat lunch at the Riverview Café, complete with impressive panoramic views of the Delaware River and Philadelphia skyline. *Location:* 1 Riverside Drive, Camden, Camden County. *Hours:* September 16 to April 15, weekdays from 9:30 A.M. to 4:30 P.M. and weekends from 10 A.M. to 5 P.M. April 16 to September 15, daily from 9:30 A.M. to 5:30 P.M. *Phone:* 856-365-3300. *Admission Fee:* $12.95 adults, $9.95 children aged 3 to 11, and $11.45 seniors and students with ID. Children aged 2 and under are free.

**Ocean Life Center:** This 4.5 million dollar facility opened in May of 1999. Its three floors contain over 14,000 square feet of space and feature eight tanks totaling 29,800 gallons. At the Ocean Life Center, visitors will get a chance to see over 100 varieties of fish and other marine animals. Computer stations are set up throughout the building and feature additional information about the nearby exhibits. The aquarium's Mullica River exhibit provides both a bird's eye and a cross section view of the river and allows visitors to touch and feel various objects that are found along the riverbed. A 750-gallon touch tank brings humans up close to many kinds of marine life. Don't forget to go up to the third floor where the observation deck provides spectacular views of the Absecon Inlet, the Atlantic Ocean, and neighboring Brigantine Island. *Location:* 800 North New Hampshire Avenue, Atlantic City, Atlantic County. *Hours:* Daily from 10 A.M. to 5 P.M. *Phone:* 609-348-2880. *Admission Fee:* $7 adults, $5 seniors, and $4 students and children.

# Planetariums

**Carl Sandburg Middle School Planetarium:** Seats 65 people. *Location:* Route 516, Matawan, Monmouth County. *Phone:* 732-290-3985.

**College of New Jersey Planetarium:** Seats 48 people. *Location:* Department of Physics, Pennington Road, Trenton, Mercer County. *Phone:* 609-771-2569.

**Dreyfuss Planetarium:** Seats 50 people. *Location:* Newark Museum, 49 Washington Street, Newark, Essex County. *Phone:* 973-596-6529.

**Fair Lawn Planetarium:** Seats 30 people. *Location:* Fair Lawn High School, Berdan Street and Burbank Street, Fair Lawn, Bergen County. *Phone:* 201-794-5464.

**Jonas Salk Middle School Planetarium:** Seats 65 people. *Location:* West Greystone Road, Old Bridge, Middlesex County. *Phone:* 732-360-4536.

**Liberty Science Center:** Seats 400 people. *Location:* Liberty State Park, 251 Phillip Street, Jersey City, Hudson County. *Phone:* 201-200-1000.

**New Jersey State Museum:** Seats 150 people. *Location:* 205 West State Street, Trenton, Mercer County. *Phone:* 609-292-6303.

**Northern Highlands Planetarium:** Seats 60 people. *Location:* Hillside Avenue, Allendale, Bergen County. *Phone:* 201-327-8700, ext. 259.

**Planetarium of the County College of Morris:** Seats 80 people. *Location:* 214 Center Grove Road, Randolph, Morris County. *Phone:* 201-328-5755.

**Planetarium of Trailside Nature and Science Center:** Seats 42 people. *Location:* 452 New Providence Road, Mountainside, Union County. *Phone:* 908-789-3670.

**Raritan Valley Community College Planetarium:** Seats 100 people. *Location:* Route 28 and Lamington Road, North Branch, Somerset County. *Phone:* 908-231-8805.

**Robert J. Novins Planetarium:** Seats 119 people. *Location:* Ocean County College, Toms River, Ocean County. *Phone:* 732-255-0342.

# Lighthouses

*Sandy Hook Lighthouse*

Long before radio and global positioning systems, lighthouses guided mariners safely along the coastal waters of New Jersey. At night, their bright lights were beacons, warning vessels of dangerous shoals. During the day, these tall structures, each unique with distinctive stripes and colors, served as landmarks along the coast. To ease the danger inherent in fog and poor visibility, many lighthouses were equipped with loud horns to alert incoming vessels of the nearby shore.

With the passage of time and the development of more modern navigational aids, lighthouses lost their purpose. Many were left to the elements, battered by ocean waves and neglect. Many more were destroyed to make way for new beachfront dwellings. Fortunately, the people of New Jersey have worked hard to preserve many of the state's lighthouses and save them from destruction. They stand today as a reminder of our past and for all to enjoy and visit.

### Absecon Lighthouse
Rhode Island and Pacific
    Avenues
Atlantic City
Atlantic County
609-449-1360
Open Memorial Day through
    Labor Day, Thursdays to
    Mondays 11 A.M. to 4 P.M.,
    open daily during July and
    August
$4 adults and $1 children

When Doctor Jonathan Pitney visited the village of Absecon, nestled on the New Jersey shore, during the 1830s, he was intrigued by the medicinal qualities of the coastal area. He encouraged his patients and friends to take lengthy excursions to the area. His dream was to turn this tiny town on the Atlantic Coast, into a health spa and resort city. He worked with local people to bring the Camden and Atlantic Railroad to the island in 1852. This was the first step in making his dream come true. Today, Dr. Pitney is referred to as the father of Atlantic City.

Doctor Pitney also worked to establish a lighthouse and lifesaving station in the village of Absecon, as the area had always posed a threat to ships. The waters were once ominously known as "Graveyard Inlet." He wrote many letters to Congress asking that a lighthouse be erected, but they went ignored until 1856 when, after years of his continuing efforts, Congress approved the money to build a lighthouse. Lieutenant George Gordon Meade, an Army engineer who also designed the Barnegat and Cape May lighthouses, was placed in charge of construction. Lieutenant Meade would go on to gain a greater place in history as a Union General during the Civil War.

When complete, the Absecon Light would rival the most advanced lighthouses of the day. Over half a million bricks were used during its construction. The tower had a sophisticated, first-order Fresnel lens, direct from Paris, installed. These lenses were considered the best and brightest of the time. The first lighthouse keeper, Daniel Scull, was appointed on November 25, 1856.

The lighthouse was in service daily until 1933, when it was decommissioned. Fortunately, opposition to tearing it down was strong enough that the lighthouse remains today for all to see. The lighthouse stands 169 feet tall and has recently been restored. Visitors may climb the 228 steps to the top for panoramic views of Atlantic City and the surrounding waters, which were once referred to as "Graveyard Inlet."

**Barnegat Lighthouse**
Broadway Avenue
Barnegat Light
Ocean County
609-494-2015
Open daily Memorial Day
    through Labor Day and on
    weekends from November
    through April
$4 adults and $1 children

Barnegat Lighthouse stands on the south side of the Barnegat Inlet. Owing to the large cresting waves, which made navigation difficult, the Dutch named it "Barendegat" or "Breakers Inlet." Shipwrecks were all too common in this area.

In 1834, because of the location's importance as a navigational point for transatlantic travel and shipping, Congress approved the money for construction of a lighthouse. Lieutenant George Meade, a West Point graduate and an engineer who also designed the Cape May Lighthouse, oversaw the construction. It was completed a year later, but many ship captains complained that the 40-foot structure was not tall enough and that the lighting apparatus was inadequate. When visibility was poor, they would often mistake the lighthouse beacon for the lights of other ships and come dangerously close to the shore.

It also soon became apparent that the sand that supported the lighthouse was eroding and a new lighthouse was desperately needed. In 1856, Lt. Meade was once again called upon for his expertise. He surveyed the area and reported as many as 6,000 ships would pass through the area each year. Meade concluded that nothing but a first-order Fresnel lens would do. The site chosen for the new lighthouse was 100-feet south of the original tower. Additionally, a two and one-half story home was constructed at the base of the tower. This house was designed for the people who would staff the lighthouse and had three separate living quarters, one for the lighthouse keeper and the other two for his assistants. The original tower was abandoned and collapsed into the sea.

The new lighthouse stood 170 feet tall and was equipped with a powerful first-order Fresnel lens. The lens, designed by Augustine Fresnel and manufactured by Henri LePaute of Paris, France, was six feet in diameter and 12-feet tall. Its unique shape formed over 1,000 separate glass prisms. Today, the lens is on display at the Barnegat Light Museum, on Central Avenue and 5th Street in the town of Barnegat Light.

During the early 1900s, under the threat of erosion, the Lighthouse Board considered abandoning the Barnegat Lighthouse in favor of a small lightship to be located just off the shore. When the townspeople learned about this, they were outraged. They forced the council to reconsider its decision and save this local landmark, which had become the most familiar feature along the Jersey Shore. Money was then raised to construct a sea wall to defend the lighthouse against future erosion.

Barnegat Lighthouse was in service until 1926, when it was decommissioned. During World War II, it served as a lookout tower for enemy U-Boats. After the war, the lighthouse was transferred to the State of New Jersey and reopened as a state park in 1957. A bust of Lt. George Meade stands next to Barnegat in honor of his bravery at Gettysburg as the Commanding General of Federal forces and for his local connection to many of the lighthouses that dot the New Jersey coastline.

The lighthouse underwent a lengthy renovation process in 1988 and reopened to the public in 1991. Visitors may now climb the 217 steps to the top of the lighthouse to feel cool breezes and enjoy a spectacular view of the Barnegat Inlet.

**Cape May Lighthouse**
Cape May Point State Park
Lighthouse Avenue
Cape May Point
Cape May County
609-884-5404
Open daily April through
    November and on weekends
    December through March
$4 adults and $1 children

This is the location of the first lighthouse to ever have been established in Cape May County. It was built in 1823 and stood 68 feet tall. By 1847, however, the tower was endangered due to an increasing rate of erosion. A new tower was needed and built 400 yards northeast of the original.

The second tower, in service for only a short time, began to leak because of poor workmanship. Therefore, a third lighthouse was needed and a young Army engineer by the name of Lt. George Meade was placed in charge of its construction. He immediately determined that since the tower would have to mark the entrance to the Delaware Bay, the lighthouse should be no less that 150-feet tall and be fitted with a first-order Fresnel lens. Construction was completed in 1859 and the lighthouse remains operational to this day.

In 1933, the lighthouse was renovated and made fully automated. A few years later the original lens was removed and put on display at the Cape May County Historical Museum, located in the town of Cape May Courthouse. The lighthouse was extensively modernized during the 1990s and currently contains a reflector lens and a 1,000-watt light that can be seen 24 miles out to sea.

The 199-step climb to the observation deck reveals the fantastic views of the Jersey Cape and the Delaware Bay. You will not see the first two lighthouses since they now lie beneath the waves. The former oil house, built in 1893, is located at the base of the lighthouse and now serves as a visitor's center and museum. The museum is open daily Memorial Day through Labor Day from 8 A.M. to 8 P.M. and on Mondays and Tuesdays 8 A.M. to 3:15 P.M. the rest of year.

### East Point Lighthouse
Lighthouse Road
Maurice River
Cumberland County
856-691-5934
Open only on the first Saturday
    in August and by
    appointment throughout the
    year
$4 adults and $1 children

Built in 1849, this is the second oldest lighthouse in New Jersey. It was constructed to mark the eastern shore of the Maurice River. The United States Coast Guard assumed control and began operating the East Point Lighthouse from 1938 until the start of World War II. Throughout the war, the lighthouse was blacked out to prevent its use as a navigational aid for German U-boats.

In 1956, the lighthouse and its property where deeded to the State of New Jersey. Years of vandalism and abuse from the weather had taken its toll on the antiquated structure and the lighthouse had deteriorated.

During the 1970s, concerned local citizens formed the Maurice River Historical Society with the primary goal of restoring the dilapidated building. Funded by local donations and fundraising efforts, they restored the lighthouse, including rebuilding the roof and lantern room that had been destroyed by fire.

A unique feature of this lighthouse is that the 40-foot tower is built into the keeper's residence. When open, visitors may climb to the top for panoramic views of the surrounding bay area. Over the years, East Point Lighthouse has become a popular subject for photographers and artists.

### Finn's Point Range Rear Light
Fort Mott and Lighthouse Roads
Pennsville
Salem County
609-935-1487
Open on the third Sunday of
  each month April through
  October from 12 P.M. to 4 P.M.
$4 adults and $1 children

Finn's Point Range Rear Light, constructed in 1877, stands 115 feet tall, and once worked in conjunction with Finn's Point Range Front Light (a building much like the East Point Lighthouse). These lights stood along the Delaware River to mark a nearby channel. During the 1950s, the channel was altered and the system became obsolete.

A spiral, cast iron staircase, allows visitors to climb to the top of the lighthouse. The tower was restored in 1983, however the original keeper's quarters have long been destroyed. The tower is now part of the Supawna Meadows National Wildlife Refuge.

### Hereford Inlet Lighthouse
Central Avenue
North Wildwood
Cape May County
609-522-4520
Open Memorial Day through
  Labor Day, daily from 9 A.M.
  to 4:45 P.M. Hours vary the
  rest of the year
$4 adults and $1.50 children

Unlike most lighthouses in the United States, the light at Hereford Inlet is actually a part of a Victorian-style home. It was built in 1874 by the United States Lighthouse Service to provide a navigational aide to mariners navigating the treacherous waters of the inlet. The Victorian design was chosen for the lighthouse because it was considered more sophisticated than the standard tower design. The picturesque structure contains five fireplaces and many other amenities that made it a comfortable residence for the keeper and his family. Hereford's first keeper, John March, served less than three months. Tragically, while returning to the mainland his boat capsized and he drowned.

For nearly 40 years the lighthouse stood its ground against the onslaught of fierce winds, heavy downpours, and rough tides. However, a severe storm in 1913 badly damaged the foundation. This resulted in the entire structure having to be moved westward by almost 150-feet. The lighthouse remained in service until 1964 when the Coast Guard darkened the light and built an automated tower adjacent to the lighthouse.

For years, the once beautiful Victorian lighthouse was left dormant and decaying. It wasn't until 1982 that concerned citizens banded together and started the restoration process. By popular demand, the automated steel tower was taken down and its optical system was placed in the tower of the original lighthouse. This fourth-order Fresnel lens is now on display.

Today the Hereford Inlet Lighthouse Commission maintains the lighthouse and its grounds. The once vacant sand lots were transformed into beautiful gardens, which feature a gazebo surrounded by many roses. This garden has become a popular spot for weddings and concerts.

### Navesink Twin Lights
Lighthouse Road
Highlands
Monmouth County
732-872-1814
Open daily Memorial Day
    through Labor Day from 10
    A.M. to 5 P.M. and on
    Wednesdays to Sundays from
    10 A.M. to 5 P.M. the rest of
    the year
Free admission

Colonists established the earliest beacon set atop the high cliffs of the Navesink in 1746. Poles over 100 feet in length were erected and topped with pots that burned whale oil by night. It was designed to be an early warning system against approaching enemy vessels. Raising or lowering the poles was a way of producing signals that lookouts with telescopes from Staten Island could interpret. The information was then passed on to New York City. This system was used to warn the British of enemy French ships in the War of Austrian Succession. The Americans also used it during the Revolutionary War and the War of 1812.

In 1828, a more permanent system was put in place. Two towers were built on the site, 320 feet apart. However, poor workmanship and problems in the masonry eventually necessitated the replacement of the towers in 1840. One year after the towers were rebuilt, a Fresnel lens, designed by Augustine Fresnel, was installed in the South Tower under the direction of Commodore Perry. It was the first lens of its kind to be used in the United States.

The lighthouse and towers that stand today were built in 1862. They were constructed of red sandstone, which was brought in by barge and carried up the 248-foot hill. The towers stand 64 feet in height, are 280 feet apart, and are connected by an 18-room lighthouse keeper's dwelling. The dwelling housed one head keeper, four assistants, and their families.

Twin Lights was at the time, the only two-tower lighthouse in the world. However, the name "twin" is misleading. One tower is octagonal and the other is square. The reason that the towers are referred to as twins obviously is not because of their structural design but rather due to the identical design of their original lights. The lights were fixed, white, and first-order Fresnel lenses. Each lens had the equivalent illumination of 60,000 candlepower, giving them a range of 22-miles out to sea.

In 1898, the Twin Lights became the first lighthouse in the United States to receive its own electrical power plant. A bivalve lens was installed in the South Tower in place of the Fresnel and provided the illumination equivalent to 195,000,000-candlepower. The North Tower, with its Fresnel still functioning, was then closed and used only during emergencies.

Today, the Twin Lights Society, which formed in 1956, operates a museum in the lighthouse that displays various artifacts including ship's logs, navigational equipment, photos, books, and the South Tower's Fresnel lens that was previously donated to the Boston Museum.

**Sandy Hook Lighthouse**
Gateway National Recreation
   Area
Sandy Hook Unit
Off State Highway 36
Atlantic Highlands
Monmouth County
732-872-5970
Open weekends from Memorial
   Day through Labor Day
Free admission

Explorer Giovanni de Verrazano first discovered Sandy Hook in 1524. However, Estevan Gomez, who sailed from Spain the following year, is credited with naming the hook. He called it "Cabo de Arenas," or "Cape of Sand."

Sandy Hook Light is the oldest currently standing lighthouse in the United States. Since the 1700s, it has shined its guiding light for thousands of ships that have traveled in and out of New York's great harbor.

Due to the many risks to commercial vessels that were traveling in the treacherous waters around the hook, merchants in New York City pressed the colony's government to create a lighthouse on Sandy Hook. In 1761, the assembly passed an act that authorized a lottery to raise funds for the construction of the lighthouse. However, the money raised was not enough to complete the lighthouse, so a second lottery was held in 1763. On June

11, 1764, the lighthouse lamps were lit for the first time. New York City collected a tonnage tax on incoming vessels to help pay for its maintenance.

Sandy Hook Light, originally called "New York Lighthouse," has served the shipping community with relatively few interruptions since it was built. One of the few occasions the light remained dark happened during the Revolutionary War when it was under British control. In June of 1776, colonists in small boats managed to elude patrolling British warships and fired their cannons at the lighthouse. Fortunately, the structure suffered only slight damage.

After America won its independence, President Washington wrote a letter to the lighthouse keeper and asked him to personally keep the light burning until Congress could provide for its maintenance. Shortly thereafter in 1789, Congress passed their 9th Act, which established the United States Lighthouse Service. The following year the service took control of the lighthouse and the keeper's yearly salary was set at $266.66 per year.

Today, the original, octagonal tower at Sandy Hook is under the control of the United States Coast Guard. The tower stands 85 feet in height, and when first built it stood about 500 feet from the northern end of the hook. Due to tidal action and sand being continuously eroded and deposited from the ocean year after year, the light is now over a mile from the tip. A lightship, stationed eight miles east off the coast, has lessened the importance of Sandy Hook Light, but it is still in operation today.

## Sea Girt Lighthouse

Beacon Boulevard and Ocean
    Road
Sea Girt
Monmouth County
732-974-0514
Open April through November on
    Sundays from 1 P.M. to 4 P.M.
Free admission

The lighthouse at Sea Girt was first lit on December 10, 1896. This location along the coast was chosen to mark the local inlet and light the area between the Navesink and Barnegat Lights. This lighthouse was fitted with a fourth-order Fresnel lens.

In 1921, Sea Girt was one of three area lights to begin emitting radio signals, pioneering the use of the radio compass as a navigational aide. During World War II, the light was put in blackout condition and the Coast Guard used the building as a lookout tower for German U-boats.

Sea Girt Light was decommissioned in 1945 and then sat idle for over a decade. Then, in 1956, the town purchased the structure and funded a full restoration. Today, this Victorian-style, two-story brick building is used as a private aid to navigation.

## Tinicum Island Rear Range Light

Billingport Recreation Area
Second Street
Paulsboro
Gloucester County
609-423-2545
The tower is open only on the third full weekend of each month from April through October on Saturdays from 12 P.M. to 4 P.M. and Sundays from 1 P.M. to 4 P.M.
$4 adults and $1 children

First lit on December 31, 1880, Tinicum Island Rear Range Light stands 80 feet in height and was used in conjunction with two Front Range lights to form a triangulated range. An interesting engineering feature of this tower is that it has only one window in the lens house, meaning the beam is intended to shine in only one direction. The original lens was removed sometime in the early 1940's. An oil house and the original two-story structure, built in the style of a farmhouse to serve as keeper's quarters, have since been demolished. Today, the tower sits in the middle of several surrounding baseball fields.

# Wineries and Breweries

*Amalthea Cellars*

**Alba Vineyard:** *Location:* 269 Route 627, Milford, Hunterdon County. *Hours:* Sundays, Wednesdays and Thursdays from 12 p.m. to 5 p.m., Fridays 12 p.m. to 7 p.m., and Saturdays 11 a.m. to 6 p.m. *Phone:* 908-995-7900

**Amalthea Cellars:** *Location:* 209 Vineyard Road, Atco, Camden. *Hours:* Saturdays and Sundays from 11 a.m. to 5 p.m. *Phone:* 856-768-8585.

**Amwell Valley Vineyard:** Location: 80 Old York Road, Ringoes, Hunterdon County. *Hours:* Saturdays and Sundays from 1 p.m. to 5 p.m. *Phone:* 908-788-5852

**Balic Winery:** *Location:* Route 40, Mays Landing, Cape May County. *Hours:* Mondays through Saturdays from 9:30 a.m. to 5 p.m. *Phone:* 609-625-2166.

**Bellview Winery:** *Location:* 150 Atlantic Street, Landisville, Atlantic County. *Phone:* 856-697-3078. *Hours:* Mondays through Thursdays by appointment, Fridays from 1 P.M. to 7 P.M., Saturdays from 11 A.M. to 5 P.M., and Sundays from 11 A.M. to 3 P.M.

**Cape May Winery & Vineyard:** *Location:* 709 Townbank Road, Cape May, Cape May County. *Hours:* Fridays and Saturdays from 11 A.M. to 5 P.M. *Phone:* 609-884-1169.

**Cream Ridge Winery:** *Location:* 145 Route 539, Cream Ridge, Monmouth County. *Hours:* Mondays through Saturdays from 11 a.m. to 6 p.m. and Sunday from 11 a.m. to 5 p.m. *Phone:* 609-259-9797.

**Four Sisters Winery:** *Location:* 10 Doe Hollow Lane, off route 519, Belvidere, Warren County. *Hours:* March through December, daily 9 a.m. to 6 p.m., closed Wednesdays during January and February. *Phone:* 908-475-3671.

**King's Road Vineyard:** *Location:* 360 Route 579, Asbury, Warren County. *Hours:* Wednesdays through Sundays from 12 p.m. to 5 p.m., tours on weekends, April through October. *Phone:* 800-479-6479.

**Marimac Vineyards:** *Location:* 65 Marimac Road, Bridgeton, Cumberland County. *Hours:* Saturdays from 10 a.m. to 3 p.m. *Phone:* 856-459-1111.

**Poor Richard's Winery:** *Location:* 220 Ridge Road, Frenchtown, Hunterdon County. *Hours:* Weekends from 12 p.m. to 5 p.m. *Phone:* 908-996-6480.

**Renault Winery:** *Location:* 72 north Bremen Avenue, Egg Harbor City, Atlantic County. *Hours:* Tours and tasting daily from 11a.m. to 4 p.m., restaurant open Fridays and Saturdays from 5 p.m. to 8:30 p.m. and Sundays from 4:30 p.m. to 7:30 p.m. *Phone:* 609-965-2111.

**Sylvin Farms:** *Location:* 24 North Vienna Avenue, Germania, Atlantic County. *Hours:* Weekends by appointment. *Phone:* 609-965-1548.

**Tomasello Winery:** *Location:* 225 North White Horse Pike, Hammonton,

Atlantic County. *Hours:* Mondays through Saturdays from 9 a.m. to 6 p.m. and Sundays from 11 a.m. to 6 p.m. *Phone:* 800-666-9463

**Unionville Vineyards:** *Location:* 9 Rocktown Road, Ringoes, Hunterdon County. *Hours:* Thursdays through Sundays from 11 a.m. to 4 p.m. *Phone:* 908-788-0400.

**Valenzano Winery:** *Location:* 340 Forked Neck Road, Shamong, Burlington County. *Hours:* By appointment. *Phone:* 609-268-6731.

# Microbreweries

**Blue Collar Brewing Company:** *Location:* Boulevard Business Park, 1200 South West Boulevard, Building 2, Suit B, Vineland, Cumberland County. *Hours:* Tours every Saturday from 1 A.M. to 5 P.M. *Phone:* 856-690-1950.

**Flying Fish Brewing Company:** *Location:* 18 Olney Avenue, Cherry Hill, Camden County. *Hours:* Free tours tasting every Saturday from 1 P.M. to 4 P.M. *Phone:* 856-489-0061.

**Heavyweight Brewing Company:** *Location:* 1701 Valley Road, Ocean Township, Monmouth County. *Hours:* Tours by appointment. *Phone:* 732-493-5009.

**High Point Wheat Beer Company:** *Location:* 22 Park Place, Butler, Morris County. *Hours:* Free brewery tours on the 2nd Saturday of each month from 2 P.M. to 4 P.M. *Phone:* 973-838-7400.

**River Horse Brewing Company:** *Location:* 80 Lambert Lane, Lambertville, Hunterdon County. *Hours:* Daily from 12 p.m. to 4 p.m. *Phone:* 609-397-7776.

**Triumph Brewing Company:** *Location:* 138 Nassau Street, Princeton, Mercer County. *Hours:* Brewery tours every Saturday at 1 P.M. and 3 P.M. *Phone:* 609-924-7855.

---

**Microbreweries:** produce small batches of beer for sale to wholesalers and retailers in and out of New Jersey.

**Brewpubs:** restaurants that produce small batches of craft brewed beer on site, may sell in their own restaurant and for carry out.

# Brewpubs

**Basil T's Brew Pub & Italian Grill:** *Location:* 183 Riverside Avenue, Red Bank, Monmouth County. *Hours:* Daily from 11:30 A.M. to 1:30 P.M. *Phone:* 732-842-5990.

**Basil T's Brew Pub & Italian Grill:** *Location:* 1171 Hooper Avenue, Toms River, Ocean County. *Hours:* Daily from 11:30 A.M. to 1:30 P.M. *Phone:* 732-244-7566.

**Harvest Moon Brewery and Café:** *Location:* 392 George Street, New Brunswick, Middlesex County. *Hours:* Sundays through Wednesdays from 11 A.M. to 11 P.M. and Thursdays through Saturdays 11 A.M. to 12:30 P.M. *Phone:* 732-249-6666.

**J.J. Bitting Brewing Company:** *Location:* 33 Main Street, Woodbridge, Middlesex County. *Hours:* Mondays through Thursdays from 11:30 A.M. to 1 A.M. Fridays 11:30 A.M. to 2 A.M., Saturdays Noon to 2 A.M., and Sundays 3 P.M. to Midnight. *Phone:* 732-634-2929.

**Krogh's Restaurant & Brew Pub:** *Location:* 23 White Deer Plaza, Sparta, Sussex County. *Hours:* Restaurant open from 11:30 P.M. to 10 P.M., bar is open daily until 2 A.M. *Phone:* 973-729-8428.

**Ship Inn Restaurant & Brewery:** *Location:* 61 Bridge Street, Milford, Hunterdon County. *Hours:* Mondays through Saturdays from 11:30 P.M. to 10 P.M. and Sundays from 12 P.M. to 4 P.M., bar open until 11:30 P.M. on weekends. *Phone:* 908-995-0188.

**Trap Rock Restaurant & Brewery:** *Location:* 279 Springfield Avenue, Berkeley Heights, Union County. *Hours:* Mondays through Fridays 11:30 P.M. to 10 P.M. and Sundays from 4:30 P.M. to 9 P.M. *Phone:* 908-665-1755.

# Stadiums and Race Tracks

*Sand Castle*

# Minor League Baseball Stadiums

**Bears & Eagles Riverfront Stadium:** This stadium is part of the growing revitalization of downtown Newark and is home to the Newark Bears baseball team of the independent Atlantic League. At a cost of 30 million dollars, this stadium is a shining diamond for the City of Newark and the state of baseball in New Jersey. Riverfront Stadium opened in 1999 with a seating capacity of 6,200 and featuring 20 luxury boxes. *Location:* Riverfront Stadium, Bridge Street, Newark, Essex County. *Phone:* 973-483-6900. *Tickets:* $8 box seats, $6 reserve seats.

**Commerce Bank Ballpark:** This state-of-the-art facility is home for the Somerset Patriots of the Atlantic League. With 6,100 seats and 20 luxury suites outfitted with the finest amenities, this is a premiere place to enjoy a game and have some fun. Visitors may also choose to bring a blanket or towel and pick their own seating location in the designated lawn seating areas. The stadium also features a picnic area that is great for company functions and family get-togethers. *Location:* 1 Patriots Park, off East Main Street, Bridgewater, Somerset County. *Phone:* 908-252-0700. *Tickets:* $12 executive field boxes, $9 field boxes, $8 upper boxes, $5 turf club.

**GPU Energy Park:** This recently completed stadium opened just in time for the Lakewood Blue Claws' inaugural, 2001 season. The Blue Claws are another in a growing list of minor league teams sprouting up in New Jersey and are a Class A affiliate of the Philadelphia Phillies. GPU Energy Park has a seating capacity for 6,588-fans with additional grass seating available for up to 3,000 people. The stadium also includes three picnic areas that are perfect for company picnics or family outings. *Location:* 2 Stadium Way at the corner of New Hampshire Avenue and Cedar Bridge Avenue, Lakewood, Ocean County. *Phone:* 732-901-7000. *Tickets:* $8 adults, $6 seniors and children, $5 general admission.

**Sand Castle:** This recently constructed, 14.5 million dollar stadium is home to the Atlantic City Surf of the Atlantic League. The Surf are an independent, professional baseball league. The stadium has a 5,900-seat capacity and features 20-luxury skyboxes on the third level. *Location:* The Sand Castle, Route 40 East, Atlantic City, Atlantic County. *Phone:* 609-344-7873. *Tickets:* $12 club seats, $9 premium seats, $6 reserved seats adults, $4 reserved seats seniors, $3 reserved seat children, and $7 upper-level box seat.

**Skylands Park:** Home to the New Jersey Cardinals, a Class A affiliate of the St. Louis Cardinals, Skylands Park is a bright, open-air venue for baseball fans, young and old, to enjoy a game and get a glimpse of some of tomorrow's superstars. *Location:* Skylands Park, 94 Championship Place, Augusta, Sussex County. *Phone:* 973-579-7500. *Tickets:* $9 box seats, $6 reserve seats, $5 general admission, $3 standing room.

**Waterfront Park:** Located on the banks of the Delaware River in Mercer County, Waterfront Park is home to the Trenton Thunder, the Double-A affiliate of the Boston Red Sox. Built in 1994, this gem of a stadium features a riverfront view and an old-fashioned, close-to-the-action perspective of the game. Waterfront Park has a seating capacity for 6,440 people. *Location:* 1 Thunder Road, Trenton, Mercer County. *Phone:* 609-394-TEAM. *Tickets:* $8 adults, $7 seniors and children for pavilion seats, $5 adults, $4 seniors and children for terrace seats, and $4 for standing room only.

**Yogi Berra Stadium:** Located on the campus of Montclair State University, Yogi Berra Stadium is home to the New Jersey Jackals baseball team of the independent Northern League. It has a seating capacity of 3,784 permanent seats and additional lawn seating that can add another 4,000 spectators. Tickets for lawn seats are only on sale during game days. *Location:* Yogi Berra Stadium, One Hall Drive, Little Falls, Montclair State University, Essex County. *Phone:* 973-746-7434. *Tickets:* $8 box seats, $6 reserve seats.

# Professional Sports Stadiums

**Continental Airlines Arena:** In July of 1981, Bruce Springsteen opened Continental Airlines Arena, originally known as Brendan Byrne Arena, with six sold out concerts. Since that auspicious opening, the arena has played host to a number of shows and events. In addition, this arena is home to the New Jersey Nets of the National Basketball Association and the New Jersey Devils of the National Hockey League. The arena is also the venue of many ice-skating shows and traveling circuses. Continental Airlines Arena, along with Giants Stadium and the Meadowlands Racetrack, make up the Meadowlands Sports Complex in East Rutherford. This complex, situated on 750 acres of land, cost 450 million dollars and is considered one of the greatest sports and entertainment complexes in the world. Continental Airlines Arena has a seating capacity for almost 20,000 people for most events. Its 200 annual events attract over two million people per year. *Location:* Meadowlands Sports Complex, East Rutherford, Bergen County. *Phone:* 201-843-2446.

**Giants Stadium:** Giants Stadium has a seating capacity for 79,670-people. The stadium is home to both the New York Giants and the New York Jets, of the National Football league. This makes Giants Stadium the only facility in the country to host two professional football teams. In 1996, the NY/NJ MetroStars of Major League Soccer began to play in Giants Stadium. Giants Stadium also hosts concerts and large trade shows. Some of the featured artists who have performed at the stadium include Bruce Springsteen and U2. In October of 1995, Pope John Paul II celebrated mass with a record crowd at Giants Stadium. In 1986, this stadium played host to the closing ceremonies of the Statue of Liberty Celebration. Giants Stadium is just one of the facilities that collectively make up the Meadowlands Sports Complex. *Location:* Meadowlands Sports Complex, East Rutherford, Bergen County *Phone:* 201-843-2446.

# Horse Racing Tracks

**Freehold Raceway:** Established in 1853, Freehold Raceway features live, standard bred, harness races for trotters and pacers from August through May. The track is a half-mile long. In addition, there are various fairs and flea markets held throughout the year. *Location:* Park Avenue, Freehold, Monmouth County. *Phone:* 732-462-3800.

**Meadowlands Race Track:** Meadowlands Race Track features both harness and thoroughbred racing on its one-mile oval track. In addition to the racing, there are family games, rides, and entertainment during races. This creates a carnival like atmosphere that is fun for the whole family. There are also a variety of restaurants and lounges located in the main section of the grandstand, which cater to all tastes. *Location:* Meadowlands Sports Complex, East Rutherford, Bergen County. *Phone:* 201-843-2446.

**Monmouth Park:** Monmouth Park is the oldest horseracing track in the State of New Jersey. Its rich history is captured in the period architecture and displays that dot the open walkways. The park features thoroughbred racing at its finest. The season begins on Memorial Day and lasts through September. The signature event at Monmouth Park is the $1,000,000 Haskell Invitational, held at the beginning of every August, which is the richest thoroughbred race in North America. The park features two racing tracks, the main one-mile dirt oval track and the secondary a seven eighths of a mile oval turf track. Monmouth Park also has a few restaurants and a picnic area with gills located near the track. *Location:* Route 36, Oceanport, Monmouth County. *Phone:* 732-222-5100.

# Excursion Travel

*Pine Creek Railroad at Allaire State Park*

# Excursion Railroads

**Black River & Western Railroad:** The Black River & Western Railroad began operating steam powered, passenger trains for excursions in 1965, on track leased from the Pennsylvania Railroad. A few years later they started offering freight service on the line and now serve six freight customers. Today, they are the only regularly scheduled, steam-powered, passenger rail-transport in the State of New Jersey. The train begins each excursion in the town of Flemington, at Liberty Village, which features name brand outlets, specialty shops, and restaurants. The line ends in the town of Ringoes, which offers a small museum and gift shop to browse through and features many old, restored train-cars. *Location:* Liberty Village, Flemington, Hunterdon County. *Schedule:* Trains operate Saturdays and Sundays, March 31 through December 9. During the months of July and August, additional trains run on Thursdays and Fridays. Certain holidays also have additional trains, including Good Friday, Memorial Day, Fourth of July, Labor Day, Columbus Day, and November 23. Trains usually depart from Flemington, starting at 11:30 A.M. with the last train at 5:30 P.M. *Phone:* 908-782-6622. *Ticket Fee:* Round trip tickets: $8 adults, $4 children ages 3 to 12, free for children under 3.

**Pine Creek Railroad:** Founded in 1952, the Pine Creek Railroad is the oldest operating, steam-powered railroad in the United States and the first railroad to utilize volunteers to run its operation. Many excursion lines and railroad museums of today owe their existence to the experiences gained from working on Pine Creek in the early days. Most of the founders of these lines either worked at or were witnesses to the early days of Pine Creek. In 1963, Pine Creek operations moved to Allaire State Park on two and a half acres of land. Today, a steam-powered locomotive entertains visitors by pulling them around a short oval track. *Location:* Allaire State Park, Route 524, Wall Township, Monmouth County. *Phone:* 732-938-5524. *Schedule:* Saturdays, Sundays, and Holidays, trains depart every half hour from 12 P.M. to 4:30 P.M. from April through October. There are additional trains on weekdays in July and August, though the trains are diesel powered, not steam. *Ticket Fee:* $2 per person. Parking: $3 per car.

**Whippany Railway:** Operations on this rail line date back to 1895, when track was laid to haul freight. Today it is home to the Whippany Railroad Museum, which opened in 1985. The museum features one of the largest O-Gauge model train layouts that can be found in New Jersey. There are many artifacts and exhibits that depict different aspects of railroads in New Jersey with an emphasis on Morris County. There are also displays detailing the history of the railroad, photographs, tools, and on-board gadgets such as bells and whistles. Outside the museum is a 180-foot long "Garden Gauge" layout that is designed to operate in all kinds of weather.

Full-size, steam-powered trains run only on special occasions, usually around Easter, Fathers Day, Halloween, and Christmas. Call for exact hours and fees. *Location:* 1 Railroad Plaza, Route 10 West and Whippany Road, Whippany, Morris County. *Phone:* 973-887-8177. *Hours:* Museum is open April through October, on Sundays from 12 P.M. to 4 P.M. *Admission Fee for Museum:* $1 adults, $0.75 children over 12, and $0.50 for children under 12.

# Boat Rides and Dinner Cruises

**Atlantic City Cruises:** Leaving from Gardener's Basin, Atlantic City Cruises offers morning skyline cruises and dinner cruises at sunset. This double-decked ship has a capacity for 150-people and features a bar and restaurant. *Location:* New Hampshire Avenue, Atlantic City, Atlantic County. *Phone:* 609-347-7600.

**Barnegat Bay Sail Charters:** This company features both day and sunset cruises around beautiful Barnegat Bay. Sailing classes are also offered. *Location:* Cedar Creek Marina, 100 Harbor Inn Road, Bayville, Ocean County. *Phone:* 732-269-1351.

**Bay Cruiser Excursions:** Passengers can cruise the waters of the Barnegat Bay on this 35-foot, covered boat. It is also possible to get out of the boat and walk in the bay's shallow waters. *Location:* Wheelhouse Marina, 24th Avenue, Seaside Park, Ocean County. *Phone:* 732-793-3296.

**Captain Sinn's Sightseeing Center:** Captain Sinn's features cruises for whale and dolphin spotting as well as various other sightseeing adventures in the Cape May area. *Location:* Park Boulevard, Wildwood Crest, Cape May County. *Phone:* 609-522-3934.

**Cape May-Lewes Ferry:** This ferry provides a 70-minute commute across the Delaware Bay to the town of Lewes in Delaware. Automobiles may also be transported on the ferry, for an additional fee. *Location:* Sandman Boulevard and Lincoln Drive, North Cape May, Cape May County. *Phone:* 609-889-7200. *Admission Fee:* $4.50 per person from November through April. $6.50 per person from May through October.

**Cape May Whale Watch:** Passengers will love the views of this new 75-foot long vessel that is designed to allow non-obtrusive, up-close viewing of whales and dolphins. The proprietors even offer a guarantee that if no marine mammals are sighted, then the next trip is free of charge. *Location:* 1286 Wilson Drive, Cape May, Cape May County. *Phone:* 609-898-0055.

**Cape May Whale Watcher:** The *Cape May Whale Watcher* is a 100-foot long vessel that offers whale and dolphin watching cruises. This is the largest such boat in all of South Jersey. There is also a special tour of the many lighthouses located off shore on the Delaware Bay. This tour, which lasts approximately five hours, brings the passengers as close to the actual structures of these nineteenth and twentieth century lighthouses as possible. So, be sure to bring your camera for some astounding, up-close shots! A buffet meal is also available on the cruise. *Location:* 2nd Avenue and Wilson Drive, Cape May, Cape May County. *Phone:* 609-884-5445.

**Captain Schumann's Whale and Dolphin Watching Boat Rides:** The captain charters out two and a half hour long, whale and dolphin watching cruises daily. *Location:* 4500 Park Boulevard, Wildwood, Cape May County. *Phone:* 609-522-2912.

***Cornucopia* from the Princess Cruise Line:** This 130-foot long cruise liner features dinner cruises around New York Harbor. A bar and large dance floor are also available on the ship. *Location:* 300 Front Street, Perth Amboy, Middlesex County. *Phone:* 732-697-9500.

***Delta Lady*:** Step back in time while cruising in this authentic, 1850s-style riverboat excursion. Passengers will cruise to the port of Cape May and get a river's eye view of huge mansions, waterfront restaurants, and local bird sanctuaries. Sunset dinner cruises are a favorite trip and feature live entertainment. From late June through Labor Day, a special breakfast cruise is offered with the legendary, seventeenth century, pirate, Captain Kidd, who provides entertainment for the entire family. *Location:* Wildwood Marina, Rio Grande and Susquehanna Avenues, Wildwood, Cape May County. *Phone:* 609-522-1919.

**Horizon Cruises:** This brand new, eight million dollar yacht can accommodate up to 600 people and features three enclosed decks and a promenade that wraps around the vessel. This luxurious ship sails around New York harbor, giving passengers a terrific view of the skyline. *Location:* 1500 Harbor Boulevard, Weehawken, Hudson County. *Phone:* 201-319-0008.

**Riverboat Services:** Cruises along the Shrewsbury and Navesink Rivers are offered on this spacious, 48-passenger vessel. *Location:* Weston's Marina, Park Road, Monmouth Beach, Monmouth County. *Phone:* 732-780-4217.

**River Belle:** The *River Belle* is a replica of an authentic Mississippi Riverboat that offers sightseeing and dinner cruises along the Manasquan and Metedeconck Rivers. *Location:* Broadway Basin, 47 Broadway, Point Pleasant Beach, Ocean County. *Phone:* 732-528-6620.

**River Lady:** This 85-foot, Mississippi-style riverboat, is paddlewheel powered and offers dinner and sightseeing cruises along the Toms River and Barnegat Bay. Passengers will be given detailed information on the rich history of the area. *Location:* 1 Robbins Parkway, Toms River, Ocean County. *Phone:* 732-349-8664.

**River Queen:** Similar to the *River Belle,* the *River Queen* is another replica of a Mississippi Riverboat. Sailing from Brielle, this ship travels along the Manasquan River and into Barnegat Bay. Additionally, Dixieland Band cruises are offered on Wednesdays during the summer. *Location:* Bogan's Basin, 800 Ashley Avenue, Brielle, Monmouth County. *Phone:* 732-528-6620.

**Salt Marsh Safari:** Passengers taking this cruise will explore the coastal wetlands and salt marshes of the Cape May area onboard the 40-foot long *Skimmer.* The *Skimmer* can navigate in waters that are only two feet deep and delivers the best view of the local marine life. This is one of the best areas in New Jersey to view Osprey. *Location:* Miss Chris Marina, 2nd Avenue and Wilson Drive, Cape May, Cape May County. *Phone:* 609-884-3100.

**Silver Bullet Speedboat Rides:** The *Silver Bullet* is one of the world's largest and fastest sailboats. This 70-foot long vessel features a powerful V2 turbo charged engine and can power its way along the coastline. *Location:* Wildwood Marina, Rio Grande and Susquehanna Avenues, Wildwood, Cape May. *Phone:* 609-522-6060.

**Spirit of New Jersey:** The *Spirit of New Jersey* can accommodate up to 300 people and sails into the Hudson River and the New York Harbor. Lunch and dinner dancing cruises are offered. *Location:* 80 Audrey Zap Drive, Liberty Landing Marina, Liberty State Park, Jersey City, Hudson County. *Phone:* 201-333-0603.

**The Lady:** The *Lady* is an elegant, 85-foot long, authentic paddlewheel riverboat, which features impressive views of the New York skyline on its cruises. It has a dance floor on its upper deck and two levels of viewing platforms. *Location:* Liberty Landing Marina, Liberty State Park, Jersey City, Hudson County. *Phone:* 732-291-4354.

**Venture Cruises:** This company operates a 52-foot long vessel that includes two spacious decks, a bar, and a dance floor. It sails along the New York Harbor. *Location:* Perth Amboy Harborside, Perth Amboy, Middlesex County. *Phone:* 877-209-2628.

# County Index

# General Index

# Software License Agreement

You should carefully read these terms and conditions before opening the software packet included with this book ("Book"). This is a license agreement ("Agreement") between you and Skudera Creations Corporation ("Skudera"). By opening the sealed disk package, you are agreeing to be bound by the terms of this Agreement. If you do not agree with the terms of this Agreement, promptly return the Book and the unopened software packet to the place where you obtained them for a full refund.

## Software License

1. Skudera Creations Corporation grants you (either an individual or entity) a nonexclusive license to use one copy of the enclosed software programs ("Software") on a single computer (whether a standard computer or a workstation component of a multi-user network).
2. The Software and the copyright in the entire work is owned by Skudera and is therefore protected under the copyright laws of the United States and other nations, under international treaties. You may make only one copy of the CD-ROM ("Software Media") containing the programs exclusively for backup or archival purposes, or you may transfer the programs to one hard disk drive, using the original for backup or archival purposes. You may make no other copies of the programs.
3. You may not rent or lease the programs, but you may transfer ownership of the program and related written material if you keep no other copies either, and if you make sure the transferee agrees to the terms of this license.
4. You may not decompile, reverse engineer, disassemble, copy, create a derivative work, or otherwise use the program except as stated in this Agreement.
5. This Agreement is governed by the laws of the State of New Jersey.

## Limited Warranty

6. The following warranties shall be effective for sixty (60) days from the date of purchase: (i) Skudera warrants the Software Media to be free of defects in materials and workmanship under normal use; and (ii) Skud-

era warrants that the Software will work when operated on the designed hardware and operating system. If Skudera receives notification within the warranty period of defects in materials or workmanship, Skudera will replace the defective Software Media. Skudera does not warrant that the operation of the Software will be uninterrupted or error free. Skudera is not responsible for problems caused by changes in the operating characteristics of computer hardware or computer operating systems that are made after the release of the programs, or for problems in the interaction of the Software with other installed applications.

# Limitation of Liability

7.   The liability for damages of Skudera and the author under this agreement shall in no event exceed the purchase price paid.

# Remedies

8 (a).   Skudera's entire liability and your exclusive remedy for defects in materials and workmanship shall be limited to replacement of the Software Media, which may be returned to Skudera with a copy of your receipt at the following address: *Skudera Creations Corporation, P.O. Box 940, Eatontown, New Jersey 07724.* Please allow three to four weeks for delivery. This Limited Warranty is void if failure of the Software Media has resulted from accident, abuse, or misapplication. Any replacement Software Media will be warranted for the remainder of the original warranty period or thirty (30) days, whichever is longer.

8 (b).   In no event shall Skudera or the author be liable for any damages whatsoever (including without limitation, damages for loss of business profits, business interruption, loss of business information, or any other pecuniary loss) arising form the use of or inability to use Software.

# Complete Agreement

9.   This Agreement constitutes the complete agreement between Skudera and you, the purchaser.

# Look for these titles coming soon!

**Connecticut**

**Massachusetts**

**New York**

**Pennsylvania**

Visit us on the web at
www.Skudera.com!

# CD-ROM Information

# Minimum System Requirements

Pentium 90Mhz or faster processor
Microsoft Windows 95, 98, 2000, or XP
32 MB RAM
50 MB free hard disk space
SVGA video card
4x CD-ROM drive

# Optional

Printer
14.4 Kpbs modem and Internet access
16-bit sound card and speakers

# Installation Instructions

If the CD-ROM does not automatically load up, from the 'Start' menu, click 'Run' and type "D:\Setup.exe" ("D:\" is usually the CD-ROM drive for most computers, if yours is different, enter in the appropriate drive letter). Then click the 'OK' button.

# Important Notice

By breaking the seal on this disk pack, you accept the terms of the license agreement included in this book.